A Corpus-based Investigation of the Production of
Formulaic Language and Pausing in EAP Speech Fluency

基于学术英语口语语料库的
语块流利产出与停顿研究

王丽芳　著

ZHEJIANG UNIVERSITY PRESS
浙江大学出版社
· 杭州 ·

图书在版编目（CIP）数据

基于学术英语口语语料库的语块流利产出与停顿研究 /
王丽芳著. -- 杭州 ： 浙江大学出版社，2024. 9.
ISBN 978-7-308-25380-2

Ⅰ. H319.9

中国国家版本馆CIP数据核字第2024AJ3841号

基于学术英语口语语料库的语块流利产出与停顿研究

A Corpus-based Investigation of the Production of Formulaic Language and Pausing in EAP
Speech Fluency

王丽芳　著

责任编辑　包灵灵
文字编辑　黄　墨
责任校对　黄静芬
封面设计　项梦怡
出版发行　浙江大学出版社
　　　　　　（杭州市天目山路148号　　邮政编码　310007）
　　　　　　（网址：http://www.zjupress.com）
排　　版　杭州林智广告有限公司
印　　刷　广东虎彩云印刷有限公司绍兴分公司
开　　本　710mm×1000mm　1/16
印　　张　17
字　　数　375千
版 印 次　2024年9月第1版　2024年9月第1次印刷
书　　号　ISBN 978-7-308-25380-2
定　　价　88.00元

Preface

Speech fluency and knowledge of formulaic language are interrelated. The relationship between these two aspects is described in this book by the Holistic Hypothesis, that is, formulaic sequences are believed to be produced as holistic units, without internal pauses, in naturally occurring discourse. However, this hypothesis is mainly based on impressionistic evidence from adult speech. Very few empirical studies have been conducted to examine and compare the production of formulaic language and the presence of internal pauses in large-scale, authentic adult learner and native speaker data. To fill the gap, reported here is an in-depth, mixed-methods, contrastive investigation of the Holistic Hypothesis in two corpora of academic spoken English, one contributed by Chinese learners of English for Academic Purposes and the other by native speakers of American English. The book addresses three main questions. First, it asks whether the learners and the native speakers place pauses in academic formulaic sequences, and if they do, in which sequences they tend to pause. Second, it asks what the patterns and the causes of internal pausing are, and whether there are individual and group-based differences in pausing in the production of the sequences investigated. Building on the first and second questions, the book then examines high frequency two-word formulaic sequences and their patterns of pausing in both corpora. Overall, the Holistic Hypothesis seems to have found more solid and empirical evidence in native speech than in learner speech.

1

The findings can offer useful insights into adult learners' process of automatizing formulaic language and facilitate the design of a speech fluency syllabus, such as including pausing as an explicit teaching agenda, or teaching formulaic sequences as holistic units rather than in a word-by-word manner.

CONTENTS

1

Appendices

3

List of Tables

List of Figures

List of Abbreviations and Acronyms

CIA	contrastive interlanguage analysis
DSS	the Discussion and Seminar Skills corpus
DSSPIgd	clusters in DSS, pauses ignored
DSSPInd	clusters in DSS, pauses included
EAP	English for Academic Purposes
FOD	frequency of occurrence in DSS
FOM	frequency of occurrence in MiniM
FRD	frequency ranking in DSS
FRM	frequency ranking in MiniM
Frq	frequency
HoInBo	clusters holistically produced in both corpora
IELTS	the International English Language Testing System
LCR	learner corpus research
MICASE	the Michigan Corpus of Academic Spoken English
MiniM	the Mini MICASE corpus
MiniMPIgd	clusters in MiniM, pauses ignored
MiniMPInd	clusters in MiniM, pauses included
NFrq	normalized frequency
nHoInBo	clusters produced with pauses in both corpora
OHoInD	clusters holistically produced in DSS only
OHoInM	clusters holistically produced in MiniM only
RFrq	refined frequency
RIg	refined frequency, with pauses ignored
RIn	refined frequency, with pauses included
SLA	second language acquisition
SP	speakers
TEM	the Test for English Majors
TOEFL	the Test of English as a Foreign Language
Txts	dispersion
WS6.0	WordSmith Tools Version 6.0

Chapter 1

Introduction

1.1   Research background

English is the leading language for the transmission of academic knowledge (Hyland & Hamp-Lyons, 2002). When English is taught with the aim of facilitating learners' study or research at undergraduate or postgraduate level in academic settings, it is defined as English for Academic Purposes, or EAP for short (Hyland & Hamp-Lyons, 2002; Coxhead, 2010). EAP learners need to have spoken English fluency, because they need to communicate in academic discourses, to understand their courses, and to conduct their learning (Hyland & Hamp-Lyons, 2002; Li, 2009). Indeed, spoken fluency has played a crucial role in learners' academic, professional, and personal lives (McCarthy, 2009; Segalowitz, 2010; Bolton & Graddol, 2012). It has been frequently employed as an important component of speaking proficiency and assessed in tests such as TOEFL (the Test of English as a Foreign Language) and IELTS (the International English Language Testing System), which aim to diagnose speakers' level of language proficiency, or as a determining factor for a higher level of school education or employment opportunities (Chambers, 1997; Kormos & Dénes, 2004; McCarthy, 2010). Additionally, it is crucial for learners who plan to migrate to or study in English-speaking countries and become involved in the local academic, occupational, and social contexts (Rossiter et al., 2010; Segalowitz, 2010).

However, Chinese EAP learners have encountered difficulties in achieving fluency in spoken English (Yang, 2006; Li, 2009). Various factors, including large class sizes, lack of sufficient authentic language exposure, examination-oriented teaching methods, learners believing in teachers' authority instead of learning by trial and error, and lack of opportunities or motivations to speak in English outside the classroom, may account for why many Chinese learners of English who have been studying this language for over ten years cannot speak it fluently (Hu, 2003; Rublik, 2006; Yang, 2006; Graddol & Mesthrie, 2012; McPherron, 2017). As an English learner myself for more than twenty years and a teacher for over ten years, I have seen and experienced the importance of fluency in spoken English in my academic and professional life. I understand that quite a number of my students or friends, equipped with explicit details of grammar and a high level of reading or writing proficiency, exhibit different kinds of problems with speech fluency. Therefore, the initial motivation for this study stems from my personal interest in understanding what spoken English fluency is and finding ways to enhance efficiency in its learning and teaching.

1.2　Rationale and aims of the study

From a dynamic systems perspetive, speech fluency in this book is defined as one component of spoken language proficiency; it refers to the automaticity and naturalness that speakers manifest in executing the processes of planning and producing interactive speech, with speed, smoothness, accuracy, and pragmatic appropriateness as the overt core features, and is adaptively affected by cognitive and contextual variables (Segalowitz, 2010; De Jong et al., 2013; De Jong et al., 2015). Previous studies of speech fluency have not only consistently testified that fluent speech runs are mainly constructed by formulaic language, but also emphasized that knowledge of formulaic language is the key to native-like fluency (Pawley & Syder, 2000; Hüttner, 2009; Wood, 2015). It has been established that use of formulaic language can indeed facilitate the production of automatic and accurate speech with phonological naturalness and pragmatic appropriateness (Oppenheim, 2000; McCarthy, 2010; Hyland, 2012; Myles & Cordier, 2017).

Formulaic language in this book is defined as continuous or discontinuous recurrent word combination that has phonological, syntactic, semantic, or pragmatic integrity in a particular register, with its individual items described as formulaic sequences (Wray, 2002, 2008; Ellis, 2008; Gries, 2008; Schmitt, 2010; Myles & Cordier, 2017). The term *formulaic sequences* is also used interchangeably with *clusters*, the designated term of the corpus analysis toolkit WordSmith Tools Version 6.0 (WS6.0) (Scott, 2015), two programs of which were applied to processing the corpora particularly compiled for the study reported on in this book. Being one essential constituent of vocabulary, formulaic sequences are ubiquitous in daily conversations and come in many different types, they are conventional and automatic expressions featuring various functional uses, and they have processing advantages in linguistic comprehension and production (Jiang & Nekrasova, 2007; Conklin & Schmitt, 2008, 2012; Ellis et al., 2008; Siyanova-Chanturia et al., 2011a). Not only can they be automatically retrieved, partly automatizing the controlled processes in speech production and facilitating natural language use, they can also free up attentional resources for the construction of novel utterances during controlled processing (Pawley & Syder, 1983; Towell et al., 1996; Derwing et al., 2004; McCarthy, 2009, 2010).

The generally accepted explanation for the processing advantages enjoyed by formulaic sequences together with their crucial importance in speech fluency is known as the Holistic Hypothesis, which posits that formulaic sequences are produced as holistic units, that is, without disruption from internal pauses (Aijmer, 1996; Jiang & Nekrasova, 2007; Lin, 2010). Pauses in this book include silent pauses which are longer than 200 milliseconds (ms), nonlexical fillers, drawls, repetitions, false starts, and repairs (Zellner, 1994; Pawley & Syder, 2000; De Jong, 2016), and internal pauses here solely refer to those occurring in formulaic sequences. Pauses are generally considered as a reflection of cognitive effort in speech production, and they are least expected in the production of formulaic sequences (Bygate, 1998; Pawley & Syder, 2000; Erman, 2007).

The Holistic Hypothesis is formulated based on the following three aspects. First, as conventionalized and shared linguistic choices in a speech community, formulaic sequences perform functional uses in discourse construction and everyday conversational exchanges. Thus, their forms and phonological patterns are likely to have been entrenched in individuals' long-term memory as unanalyzed units and reproduced just as they are regularly and frequently encountered by speakers, with some of them even fused as one word (Ellis, 1996; Erman & Warren, 2000; Foster, 2001; Strik et al., 2010). Second, formulaic sequences are believed to be automatically processed as wholes, although they can be further analyzed into individual components (Sinclair, 1991; Wray, 2002, 2008; Bybee, 2006; Ellis, 2008). In effect, holistic production has been extensively considered as overt psycholinguistic evidence that formulaic language is automatically retrieved as an intact unit (Bybee, 2006; Erman, 2007; Lin, 2010; Myles & Cordier, 2017). Third, as holistic production has already been treated as an indicator of ease in speech processing and a marker of native-like pronunciation, phonological coherence, or an absence of internal pauses, including phonological reduction, it has long been employed as one identifying feature of formulaic language in speech (Peters, 1983; Raupach, 1984; Weinert, 1995; Wood, 2006, 2015; Dahlmann & Adolphs, 2007, 2009; Erman, 2007; Lin & Adolphs, 2009; Myles & Cordier, 2017). Clusters that manifest phonological coherence have been considered more formulaic than those produced with pauses (Lin, 2010; Myles & Cordier, 2017).

However, the Holistic Hypothesis has rarely been empirically tested in authentic speech produced by adult learners of English. In the rather limited amount of previous research into this topic, the data used for investigation are generally clinically or experimentally elicited, the number of participants or of the formulaic sequences investigated is quite small, and the findings observed so far in both learners' and native speakers' speeches are not consistent (Schmitt et al., 2004; Dahlmann & Adolphs, 2007, 2009; Erman, 2007; Lin & Adolphs, 2009; Gao & Fan, 2011; Wu, 2012). The present study aims to redress this balance. It intends to compare the validity of the Holistic Hypothesis by investigating pausing and the production of formulaic sequences in two large-scale corpora of authentic academic speech collected from cohorts of EAP learners and native speakers. As the observable prosodic feature of holistic production is phonological coherence, no pauses, filled or unfilled, repetitions or repairs, are supposed to occur in formulaic language (Erman, 2007; Lin & Adolphs, 2009; Myles & Cordier, 2017). Accordingly, pausing and the production of formulaic sequences need to be investigated in both corpora qualitatively and quantitatively, in order to establish whether formulaic sequences are produced with or without pauses occurring in them. An examination of pausing behavior in its co-text and context is also needed to understand the patterns of pausing and the possible causes of occurrence. Considering the dynamics of language acquisition (Barlow, 2005; Hasko, 2013; De Knop & Meunier, 2015) and to further compare the Holistic Hypothesis in learner and native speaker spoken English, what pausing patterns emerge in learners' production of high frequency formulaic sequences and how they differ from those in native speech are also investigated.

Three questions are therefore addressed:

Do learners and native speakers place pauses in formulaic language in academic speech? If so, in which clusters are pauses more likely to occur?

What are the general patterns and the causes of the internal pausing in learner speech and in native speech?

What are the patterns of pausing in high frequency formulaic sequences in learner speech and in native speech?

Studying the occurrence of pauses in relation to the production of formulaic language follows the guidelines suggested for investigating speech fluency from a complex dynamic systems perspective, as pausing and the use of formulaic language not only are crucial and principal components of the system, but also interact with one another over time in a dynamic, supportive, and adaptive manner (Pawley & Syder, 2000; Larsen-Freeman & Cameron, 2008a; Segalowitz, 2010; Myles & Cordier, 2017). This study has profound significance. Apart from empirically testing the Holistic Hypothesis, it can provide insights into the internal processing in producing formulaic language, further the understanding of the process of learning formulaic sequences and how learners develop formulaicity, validate the use of phonological coherence in identifying formulaic language in speech, and reveal pausing patterns in and around formulaic language in learner and native speech. The study can also inform us about how learners use pauses and formulaic language to construct fluent connected speech and help with establishing a syllabus for the explicit teaching of these two aspects, as learners can enhance their level of fluency if explicitly taught how to place pauses and how to take advantage of formulaic language in speech production (Guillot, 1999; Morales-López, 2000; Derwing et al., 2004; Watanabe & Rose, 2013; De Jong, 2016).

The study also has implications for the assessment, speech therapy, natural language processing, and learners' socio-economic achievements. Raising learners' awareness about holistic production and the placing of pauses at grammatical boundaries may also improve learners' performance in assessment of their oral fluency (Guillot, 1999; Cucchiarini et al., 2000; Bosker et al., 2013). This investigation could also contribute to speech language therapy as training in appropriate pausing and using formulaic language may help with stutters (Marshall, 2000). Moreover, modeling the placement of pauses and the production of formulaic language can not only reduce errors but also improve the naturalness of speech synthesis, which can further the development of automatic speech recognition devices (Zellner, 1994; Strik et al., 2010). In everyday life, improved spoken English fluency can help learners to secure socio-economic benefits (McCarthy, 2009; Segalowitz, 2010).

1.3   Study design

Since speech fluency is conceptualized as a dynamic complex system in this book, this requires the methodology to be mixed-methods (Dörnyei, 2007; Larsen-Freeman & Cameron, 2008b; Richards et al., 2012). In fact, this study is mixed-methods in design at two different levels. First, to provide epistemologically valid answers to the research questions, an extensive investigation of the occurrence of pauses in and around formulaic language in learners' and native speakers' authentic spoken English is conducted from both quantitative and qualitative perspectives. Learner corpus research (LCR), a branch of corpus linguistics, is adopted as the methodology; it explores second language acquisition (SLA) matters by utilizing corpus linguistic methods and tools, and investigating quantitatively and qualitatively different levels of linguistic features for the evidence required by the research questions (Granger, 2002, 2009, 2015; Barlow, 2005; Callies & Paquot, 2015). Second, to explore which formulaic sequences are produced as wholes and which are used with pauses, LCR allows for an integration of a corpus-based approach and a psycholinguistic approach to identify formulaic sequences. The corpus-based approach provides the convenience of screening the clusters based on structures, frequencies, and dispersion values (Biber, 2009; Granger, 2009; Simpson-Vlach & Ellis, 2010; Hyland, 2012; Martinez & Schmitt, 2012), and the psycholinguistic approach explores the presence of internal pauses in the production of the concerned clusters (Schmitt, 2010; Durrant & Mathews-Aydınlı, 2011; Myles & Cordier, 2017).

Corpus-based and *corpus-driven* are two general methodological directions in the study of lexico-grammar in corpus linguistics (Tognini Bonelli, 2001; Biber, 2009; McEnery & Hardie, 2012; Gray & Biber, 2013). This study is corpus-based, out of the following considerations. On the one hand, a corpus-based approach is deductive and hypothesis-testing (Tognini Bonelli, 2001; McEnery et al., 2006; Flowerdew, 2009). Corpus-based analysis generally selects the clusters that are concerned with the research questions and analyzes the corpus, investigating their patterns of uses for the validation of a linguistic theory (Biber, 2009; Gries, 2010). On the other hand, corpus-driven research is inductive and hypothesis-formulating (Tognini Bonelli, 2001; McEnery et al., 2006; Flowerdew, 2009). Without any pre-determined restrictions regarding what is to be examined, corpus-driven analysis makes few theoretical assumptions. It takes full advantage of automatic corpus analytical techniques to explore the potential of a corpus, investigating all the possible structures that may not be identified otherwise. Patterns of use that emerge while the corpus is being analyzed are used to formulate a hypothesis about its language use or development (Tognini Bonelli, 2001; Biber, 2009; Gries, 2010; Gray & Biber, 2013). Another crucial distinction between corpus-based and corpus-driven research originates from the perception of what corpus linguistics is: the former basically treats corpus linguistics as a method, whereas the latter takes the corpus-as-theory stance (Gries, 2010, 2011; McEnery & Hardie, 2012). According to McEnery and Hardie (2012), researchers who choose a corpus-based approach generally consider corpus linguistics as a method. When corpus linguistics is a methodological paradigm, it is about using corpus techniques to study either the properties of a corpus or the linguistic features based on corpus data (Gries, 2011; McEnery & Hardie, 2012). However, analyses of formulaic language often incorporate both approaches (Biber, 2009). Researchers may start with some clusters that are theoretically interesting and explore the corpus, investigating how these clusters behave in their co-texts and contexts, or the other way around (Flowerdew, 2009). According to Xiao (2009) and Gries (2010, 2012), there is no pure corpus-driven analysis. They pointed out that human intuition and already-acquired theory will unconsciously interfere in the analysis, and furthermore, even research that claimed to be corpus-driven is in effect corpus-based.

Contrastive interlanguage analysis (CIA) is the method chosen for data analysis. Accordingly, the Discussion and Seminar Skills (DSS) corpus, a corpus of Chinese learners' academic spoken English, is compiled; this is contrasted with MiniM, a reference corpus of American English native speakers' academic speech selected from the Michigan Corpus of Academic Spoken English (MICASE) (Simpson et al., 2002). DSS is made up of 89,633 words of Chinese first-year university students' classroom EAP speech. MiniM has 63,845 words, produced by junior undergraduates of an American university when they were conducting discussions or oral presentations. In addition to following the common design criteria and procedures of constructing speech corpora (Thompson, 2004; Adolphs & Knight, 2010), pauses in both corpora are annotated so that WS6.0 can automatically process the data separately either with pauses included or excluded. Contrastive analysis of the production of formulaic sequences and of pausing in or around them in DSS and MiniM are conducted consecutively, and mainly utilize the two fundamental corpus-handling techniques of frequency analysis and concordance analysis (McEnery et al., 2006; Evison, 2010). Two programs of WS6.0, WordList and Concord, are applied to the analysis (Scott, 2015). With WordList, two-to-six-word continuous formulaic sequences that occur with the required frequency and dispersion values in both corpora are extracted twice, first with pauses ignored and the second time with pauses included; they are then examined qualitatively in the concordance lines generated using Concord. In so doing, the three research questions posed in this book are resolved.

1.4 Book overview

Following this introductory chapter, Chapters 2 and 3 show how the literature has helped to refine the rationale for the investigation on which the book reports. Chapter 2 proposes the working definition of speech fluency based on an overview of previous research into this area, which is organized according to whether speech fluency is approached from a speaker- or listener-based perspective, whether the speech samples investigated in previous studies are monologic or dialogic, and whether the underlying ontology and epistemology of the studies is reductionism or anti-reductionism. It concludes with the belief that knowledge of formulaic language is the key to speech fluency.

It is the aim of Chapter 3 to explore formulaic language in great depth. It starts with a review of the features formulaic language manifests, where it can be seen that its ubiquity, conventionality, automaticity, and functional uses are the main reasons behind the widespread assumption that formulaic language contributes positively to speech fluency. The most direct correlation between the use of formulaic language and fluency is that formulaic language is believed to be produced as wholes or free from internal pauses, echoing the Holistic Hypothesis formulated previously in this chapter. As the ultimate aim of this study is to facilitate learning and teaching of spoken English fluency, the processes of learning formulaic language are also reviewed. Moreover, to link this chapter to Chapters 4 and 5, common approaches and procedures that have been used to investigate formulaic sequences are reviewed here.

Research design is the focus of Chapters 4 and 5. To justify that LCR is the right research methodology for achieving the aims of the study, Chapter 4 starts with the theoretical justification and a discussion of the strengths and weaknesses of LCR. It then elaborates the rationale behind the choice of CIA as the analytical method, along with the explanations regarding why a corpus of American academic spoken

English is chosen as the benchmark. Chapter 5 reports on the details of compiling and annotating an adult learner corpus of academic spoken English, namely, DSS, and a reference native corpus of academic speech, MiniM. DSS is built from scratch, so considerations at the design stage, including the context of data collection, data types, participants, the size of the corpus, and ethics, are elucidated, and the rationale behind the decisions of data recording, data transcription and annotation is discussed. MiniM is edited based on the already existent MICASE, so the comparability, the selecting criteria, and the building procedures are clarified.

Chapter 6 is primarily intended to present the quantitative findings regarding which formulaic sequences are produced as wholes by the learners and the native speakers, and in which formulaic sequences pauses may occur. It first elaborates the variables and the criteria used to identify formulaic sequences in DSS and in MiniM, and then introduces the two programs on WS6.0 used for the subsequent analysis. The rest of this chapter demonstrates the detailed analytical procedures, which are an integration of group- and individual-based scrutiny using both qualitative and quantitative methods. Adopting a structural taxonomy and basically based on their frequencies of occurrence, formulaic sequences are categorized as prepositional clusters, subject verb clusters, verb phrases clusters, noun phrases clusters, those consisting of conjunctions followed by pronouns, part of noun phrases, or adverbs, and of *that*, repetitions, and other linguistic elements.

Qualitative investigation is the focus of Chapters 7 and 8, which aim to answer the second and third questions. Chapter 7 examines the patterns, the causes, and the individual and group-based differences of internal pausing concerning the five main types of formulaic sequences. Internal pauses are analyzed based on their behavior, such as occurring alone in formulaic language or being accompanied by other pausing phenomena that immediately precede or follow the clusters investigated. To resolve the remaining issues from Chapter 7 and to investigate the Holistic Hypothesis thoroughly, Chapter 8 probes the patterns of pausing in relation to the production of high frequency two-word formulaic sequences, comparing and contrasting them for individual- as well as group-based differences and similarities. The inquiry is first conducted based on whether the clusters are produced with or without pauses, and then, the holistic production is inspected with reference to whether they have pauses on both sides or on either side and whether they involve repetitions or are embedded in longer fluent units. Some of the clusters may have been contracted as one word. If they were to be observed in the analysis, they would be examined separately.

Chapter 9 concludes the study. It first summarizes the findings of the analysis and discusses their relevance and pedagogical implications. The limitations of the study are identified and the way as to how they might be overcome in further research is also considered. Lastly, directions for future studies are provided, largely based on the findings of the study reported in this book.

Chapter 2

Speech Fluency

2.1 Introduction

Speech fluency, spoken fluency, or speaking fluency, is an important and frequently used notion in almost every language-related discipline, but it is under-researched and considered notoriously complex to understand, evaluate, and teach (Chambers, 1997; Guillot, 1999; Koponen & Riggenbach, 2000; Segalowitz, 2010; Brown & Muller, 2014). It is originally applied to native speaker speech and identified as abilities to talk with few pauses using meaningful expressions with situational appropriateness, novelty, and imagination, but now it almost exclusively refers to learner speech produced by speakers of a second or foreign language, and has multiple interpretations (Chambers, 1997; Guillot, 1999; Fillmore, 2000; Koponen & Riggenbach, 2000). Not only do applied linguists and laypersons outside the field of linguistics conceptualize differently what fluency is, but even among applied linguists themselves, there are controversial understandings of what it means (Sajavaara, 1987; Riggenbach, 1991; Chambers, 1997; Guillot, 1999; Koponen & Riggenbach, 2000; Segalowitz, 2010; Brown & Muller, 2014). In non-academic settings such as job markets and casual conversations, the concept of fluency simply refers to overall oral proficiency (Guillot, 1999; Koponen & Riggenbach, 2000), and fluency of a second language is mainly viewed as a component of language proficiency and reflected in speedy and smooth linguistic production (Chambers, 1997; Bosker et al., 2013). In psycholinguistic studies, fluency is generally conceptualized as an automatic procedural skill in speech processing (Schmidt, 1992, 2000; Kormos, 2006). In English language learning and teaching, the notion of fluency appears to be a degreed concept, spanning a continuum that ranges from ease of speech production, in contrast to accuracy and complexity in linguistic choice, to communicative competence, and to overall oral proficiency (Brumfit, 2000; Tavakoli & Skehan, 2005; Brown & Muller, 2014).

Speech fluency has been approached from different perspectives, some of which appear somewhat overlapping. It has been distinguished into *performance fluency* and *perceived fluency* based on whether the study takes a speaker- or a listener-oriented standpoint (Ejzenberg, 2000; Lennon, 2000; Derwing et al., 2004; Götz, 2013). Performance fluency is mainly concerned with the impact of individual differences and contextual factors exerted on fluency performance from a speaker-based standpoint; from a listener-based standpoint, perceived fluency is concerned with the construct of fluency itself, with speed and smoothness as its core identifiable features (Chambers, 1997; Ejzenberg, 2000; Derwing et al., 2004). Moreover, most of the previous studies are monologue-based, but in some of them, fluency is perceived as an interactive and negotiated achievement and known as *conversational fluency*, where apart from the speed and accurate use of lexico-grammar, the ability of co-constructing the conversational flow is included (Sajavaara, 1987; Guillot, 1999; Morales-López, 2000; McCarthy, 2005). Given its increasingly important role in language education, the term *pedagogical fluency* is adopted to indicate the study of speech fluency in educational settings (Brumfit, 2000; Ellis, 2003; Skehan, 2009). However, studies regarding performance fluency, perceived fluency, and pedagogical fluency generally take a reductionist approach, that is to say, fluent features and the factors influencing them are investigated independently, resulting in an overlooking of their interactions and changes over time.

It is not until recently that the underlying ontology and epistemology of speech fluency is shifted to the anti-reductionism, and the dynamic interconnectedness of different aspects of speech fluency, the many factors that contribute to it and their interactions with the context receive attention. Consequently, a broader conceptual framework has been adopted to understand and investigate the field. Adopting a dynamic systems persepective, Segalowitz (2010) distinguished three senses of speech fluency: cognitive fluency, utterance fluency, and perceived fluency, corresponding respectively to the efficiency of speech processing, the fluidity of utterances, and the communicative acceptability of utterances. It is this perspective that the working definition of fluency in this book is drawn on. In what follows, Sections 2.2–2.6 review respectively performance fluency, perceived fluency, conversational fluency, pedagogical fluency, and a dynamic systems approach to fluency, with the ultimate aim of establishing the belief that the key to speech fluency is knowledge of formulaic language.

2.2   Performance fluency

Performance fluency refers to a speaker's efficiency in translating thoughts into linguistic expressions under time and context constraints (Cucchiarini et al., 2000; Ejzenberg, 2000; Lennon, 2000). Previous studies of this area have generally focused on individual differences, factors related to the target language, and contextual variables that affect performance fluency. In terms of individual differences, the extensively investigated ones include speakers' first language (Derwing et al., 2009; Segalowitz, 2010; Foster, 2013), their initial level of language proficiency (Derwing et al., 2004), vocabulary knowledge (Hilton, 2008; Skehan, 2009), working memory (Towell & Dewaele, 2005; Mizera, 2006), affective variables such as stress, anxiety, attitudes, willingness to communicate and self-confidence, and motivations (Dewaele, 2002; Derwing et al., 2007; Segalowitz et al., 2009). Notable factors related to the target language include knowledge of the related cultural norms (Doutrich, 2000; Rublik, 2006), practice of repetitions (Bygate, 1996, 2005), speakers' knowledge of fluency features (Gatbonton & Segalowitz, 2005; Derwing et al., 2006; Wood, 2009; Rossiter et al., 2010), and exposure to the target language (Schmidt, 1983; Freed, 2000; Derwing et al., 2007), and the rigorously studied contextual variables include context (Fillmore, 2000; Morales-López, 2000; Ellis, 2009; Segalowitz, 2010), task types (Foster & Skehan, 1996; Ejzenberg, 2000; Derwing et al., 2004; Skehan, 2009) and planning (Mehnert, 1998; Ellis, 2009). In most of these studies, the factors are investigated one by one, although some of them, such as task types, planning and repetitions, willingness to communicate, levels of proficiency, and motivations supportively interact with each other (Bygate, 2009; Segalowitz, 2010).

To elaborate on the effects of the above-mentioned variables, first, it needs to be noted that spoken fluency has been shown as a language-specific phenomenon. Speakers may on the one hand achieve a high level of fluency in one language but remain non-fluent in another, on the other hand, those who fail to speak fluently their native language seem unlikely to become fluent second language users (Derwing et al., 2009; Segalowitz, 2010; Foster, 2013). Studies have also pointed out that speakers' initial language proficiency seems to affect their willingness to communicate and lead to passive exposure to authentic language use, which may reduce the efficiency in the attainment of fluency (Segalowitz & Freed, 2004; Derwing et al., 2007). Moreover, both Lennon (2000) and Skehan (2009) suggested that lexical knowledge is a crucial factor to distinguish fluent speakers from nonfluent ones. Fluency is in effect lexically based, and a skillful mastery of lexical diversity, especially formulaic language, is considered contributing a great deal to performance fluency (Oppenheim, 2000; Hilton, 2008). Derwing et al. (2004) indicated that among speakers of low-proficiency, lack of required linguistic knowledge is the cause of the production of nonfluent speech. As to working memory, a high capacity is generally believed to be facilitative to the fast production of long fluent and creative speech runs while a low capacity can cause processing problems; however, for learners at advanced levels of language proficiency, there seems to be no strong correlation between the capacity of working memory and performance fluency (Mizera, 2006; Skehan, 2009). Motivations and affective factors such as positive attitudes or anxiety also have an impact on speech production. Speakers who are motivated and think positively about themselves or the target language are more likely to achieve rapid progress in speech fluency, and in a low-anxiety context, speakers have been reported to produce English with greater ease, and their speech seems less scattered with pauses (Dewaele, 2002; Derwing et al., 2007; Ellis, 2009; Segalowitz, 2010).

Fluency is also considered culturally specific and context-bound. Fluent features may be perceived differently in different cultures (Doutrich, 2000; Rublik, 2006). For instance, repetitions are accepted as either a fluency-enhancing strategy or a disturbing factor that impairs discoursal fluency, depending on in which social cultural context they occur (Ejzenberg, 2000). As for Chinese learners of English, cultural factors such as the concept of face, respecting authority, and maintaining group harmony seem to prevent them from actively participating in classroom interactions, which may have a negative impact on the speakers' oral fluency, even when they are advanced learners of English (Rublik, 2006). Knowledge of the differences between first language fluency and second language fluency also seems to affect learners' performance fluency. Learners who received specific instruction of fluency features in the target culture are found to be more fluent in speech production than those who did not (Rossiter et al., 2010). Regarding language learners who study abroad and have an opportunity for exposure to authentic target language, their speech is generally more fluent than that produced by their peers who learn the language in a classroom-based setting (Freed, 2000). Context here refers to the physical setting, with the notable variables including time, place, and the presence of the interlocutor. A speaker can be more fluent in speech production in a familiar and intimate context than when he or she faces a change to a strange location or is in the presence of unfamiliar interlocutors (Guillot, 1999; Segalowitz, 2010). In terms of task types, second language speakers are more fluent if they are familiar with the formality of the on-going topic or when performing structured tasks (Bygate, 1998; Ejzenberg, 2000; Skehan, 2009). Moreover, planning is believed to have a positive effect on speech fluency. If given enough planning time, speakers can increase the fluency of speech flow (Mehnert, 1998; Ellis, 2009).

As affected by these various factors, speakers' fluency may change in different situations and every speaker may be fluent in a different way (Lennon, 2000; Segalowitz, 2010; Foster, 2013). In addition to being approached from a speaker-based perspective, fluency studies also adopt a listener-based perspective and investigate the construct of fluency itself (Ejzenberg, 2000; Derwing et al., 2004). In this line of research, fluency is generally known as perceived fluency, specifically discussed in the next section.

2.3   Perceived fluency

Perceived fluency is about the listener's impressionistic or instrumental judgment about a speaker's ease with oral production (Lennon, 1990; Ejzenberg, 2000; Freed, 2000; Kormos & Dénes, 2004; Rossiter, 2009; Götz, 2013). Relying on trained raters (Lennon, 1990; Riggenbach, 1991; Ejzenberg, 2000; Wennerstrom, 2000) or untrained raters (Freed, 2000; Derwing et al., 2004; Rossiter, 2009), four different approaches have been adopted to establish what aspects and measures are the reliable indicators for different levels of fluency. First, listeners or raters are asked to categorize speech samples into different fluency levels based on their subjective perceptions of what features they believe fluent speech is supposed to display (Lennon, 1990; Riggenbach, 1991; Freed, 1995, 2000; Segalowitz & Freed, 2004). Alternatively, raters are offered a list of fluent features and asked to use them to evaluate the fluency level of a number of selected speech samples (Derwing et al., 2004; Kormos & Dénes, 2004; Derwing et al., 2007; Derwing et al., 2009; Rossiter et al., 2010). The third approach is a matter of between-group comparison: some researchers may use the first language (L1) speech samples as the baseline measures and contrast them with their second language (L2) speech output (Rossiter, 2009; De Jong et al., 2015), while some may compare the speech collected from fluent and nonfluent language users (Kormos & Dénes, 2004). The fourth approach tracks the development of fluency features longitudinally. For instance, using the speech samples collected from the same group of speakers over a period of time, Lennon (1990) and Towell et al. (1996) investigated the factors that play a crucial role in fluency development. However, as individual raters or researchers may have their own interpretation or focuses regarding what matters for speech fluency, perceived fluency is generally subjective and cannot be considered as an exact mirror of performance fluency (Lennon, 2000).

Nevertheless, perceived fluency has been evaluated by many acoustic, temporal, and phonetic measures (Koponen & Riggenbach, 2000; Tavakoli & Skehan, 2005; Bosker et al., 2013). They mainly fall into three categories based on Skehan and his colleagues' categorization (Skehan, 2003; Skehan & Foster, 2005; Tavakoli & Skehan, 2005). The first category is about silence and subtitled as *breakdown fluency*, where measures including frequency, duration, and location of pauses in speech are used. The second is known as *speed fluency*, including measures such as the rate of speech, articulation rate, amount of speech, phonation time ratio, and mean length of run. The third is concerned with repairs; also known as *repair fluency*, it is measured by false starts, repetitions, and corrections. Additionally, phonological properties, including distributions of stress (Kormos & Dénes, 2004), intonation (Wennerstrom, 2000), weak forms and contracted forms (Brown, 2003; Strik et al., 2010), vowel duration (Derwing et al., 2009), and accent (Freed, 2000; Derwing et al., 2004; Derwing et al., 2006) affect the impression listeners have about speakers' linguistic production. Freed (2000) claimed that fluency is like beauty, the perception of which is in the ears of listeners, so the same fluent measures may be perceived differently by raters. For instances, pauses, repairs, and repetitions are generally treated as markers of disfluent speech, but they can also be used as fluency-enhancing devices or time-gaining strategies, allowing speakers to hold the conversational floor or buy time for online speech planning (Lennon, 1990; Riggenbach, 1991; Guillot, 1999; Pawley & Syder, 2000). Moreover, some features are more difficult to evaluate than others, as they are unspecific and subjective. For instance, it is challenging to decide on what measures are most appropriate to evaluate phonological naturalness, but pauses and speed of delivery can be identified and quantified objectively (Lennon, 1990, 2000; Guillot, 1999; Cucchiarini et al., 2000; Ushigusa, 2008).

Although perceived fluency has drawn on various component measures, it is the temporal properties of speech that have been focused on in previous studies, the measures that are used to indicate speedy and smooth speech delivery being the most widely employed (Chambers, 1997; Koponen & Riggenbach, 2000; Lennon, 2000; Segalowitz, 2010). Among the measures mentioned above, speech rate, pauses, and length of speech runs have been consistently considered most influential in perceptions of fluency and taken as the core measures, and fluent speakers are thus believed to speak at a faster rate, pause less frequently and with shorter durations, and produce longer speech runs between pauses (Towell et al., 1996; Chambers, 1997; Wood, 2001, 2006, 2015; Rossiter et al., 2010; Bosker et al., 2013).

2.3.1 Speech rate

As one of the most commonly used indexes of speech fluency, speech rate, or rate of delivery, generally refers to the number of syllables or words produced per second or per minute (Nation, 1989; Lennon, 1990; Riggenbach, 1991; Chambers, 1997; Kormos & Dénes, 2004). It marks the speed and density of the speech sample in terms of the time units. A fluent speaker is supposed to manage his or her oral production with an appropriate rate of speech, neither so fast as to cause difficulty in having himself or herself understood nor so slow as not to be able to hold the listener's attention (Guillot, 1999). High rate of speech production does not necessarily mean that a speaker has a high level of speech fluency (Koponen & Riggenbach, 2000; Lennon, 2000). Speech rate is context-dependent, varying with the change of the discourse mode, the subject topic, and speaker-hearer relationship (Lennon, 2000; McCarthy, 2009). It is also influenced by individual speaking styles, as some speakers may just utter at a relatively slow or fast speed (Segalowitz, 2010; Foster, 2013). Although arguably it reveals little information about speech processing, speech rate has always been an important descriptor of perceived fluency because of its interrelation with the occurrence of pauses and the length of speech runs (Wood, 2006). Different speech rates can reflect the differences in the number, duration, and location of pauses (Lennon, 1990; Nation, 1991; Zellner, 1994), which also lead to the production of longer or shorter fluent speech runs (Towell et al., 1996).

2.3.2 Pauses

Pauses refer to any break, whether natural, involuntary, or disruptive, in the syntactic or semantic continuity of an utterance, which are fundamentally a natural phenomenon and expected in fluent speech (Griffiths, 1991; Riggenbach, 1991; Zellner, 1994; Guillot, 1999; Pawley & Syder, 2000; Segalowitz, 2010). There are physiological, interactional, and cognitive explanations for their occurrence in daily speech (Zellner, 1994; Guillot, 1999; Pawley & Syder, 2000). First, normal physical reactions such as breathing and swallowing may cause speakers to stop talking; if for these reasons pauses occur, they are called physiological pauses (Zellner, 1994; Pawley & Syder, 2000). Second, in interactive speech, speakers may pause intentionally to start a new topic or indicate a shift of topic, to draw attention from the listener, to achieve a rhetorical effect, to give the listener time to digest what he or she has just heard, or to provide contextual cues. Pauses that happen for these reasons are also known as planned pauses (Chambers, 1997; Guillot, 1999). On the other hand, unplanned pauses refer to those that are produced unintentionally, whose occurrence is mainly due to human biological limits and time limits in spontaneous conversations (Zellner, 1994; Pawley & Syder, 2000). Both planned and unplanned pauses are called cognitive pauses, and they are overt manifestations of the time needed for cognitive processes in speech production (Pawley & Syder, 2000; Erman, 2007).

Pauses are generally categorized into unfilled and filled pauses (Griffiths, 1991; Riggenbach, 1991; Pawley & Syder, 2000). Unfilled pauses, also known as silent pauses, are silent gaps in the course of an utterance (Zellner, 1994; Freed, 2000). In fluency studies, there seems a lack of agreement regarding the cut-off points for silent pauses. With regard to the lower cut-off points, these generally range from 200 ms to 400 ms. The minimum duration of silent pauses in some fluency studies is set at 200 ms because this is considered the lowest perceptible length (Raupach, 1984; Lennon, 1990; Zellner, 1994; Pawley & Syder, 2000). It is also because pauses shorter than 200 ms show little processing difficulty and are seldom observed within a word (Hilton, 2009; Myles & Cordier, 2017). Kormos and Dénes (2004), De Jong et al. (2013, 2015), and De Jong (2016) adopted 250 ms as the lower boundary, pointing out that shorter micro pauses are irrelevant to fluency studies. In Riggenbach (1991), Freed (2000), Tavakoli and Skehan (2005), and Tavakoli (2011), the lower threshold is 400 ms, as pauses under this length are believed to be common features in native speech. The higher cut-off points range from one to three seconds (Griffiths, 1991; Riggenbach, 1991; Foster, 2013; De Jong, 2016). It is believed that if unfilled pauses in English conversation last for one second or more, they may either indicate topic shifts or cause the listeners to believe that it is their turn to step in (Carter & McCarthy, 2006; Segalowitz, 2010; Foster, 2013). Moreover, if speakers pause longer than three seconds, they may have ended the ongoing topic (Griffiths, 1991; Riggenbach, 1991).

Also known as fillers, filled pauses refer to any place-holding sound during a break, used as a cover term in this book for lexical and nonlexical filled pauses, drawls, repetitions, false starts, and repairs (Griffiths, 1991; Riggenbach, 1991; Zellner, 1994; Guillot, 1999; Freed, 2000; Pawley & Syder, 2000). Lexical filled pauses are realized by words but contain little semantic information in the context, such as *you know*, *I mean* and *sort of*, whereas nonlexical fillers such as *ah* and *um* are neither recognized as words nor carrying meaning (Chambers, 1997; Pawley & Syder, 2000; Carter & McCarthy, 2006). In fact, filled pauses were categorized differently in previous studies. In Riggenbach (1991) and Freed (2000), apart from lexical and nonlexical fillers, filled pauses included drawls, which refer to the lengthening of one or more segments in or after a word, and are generally indicated in the transcribed speech by the colon symbol (:), such as *a:nd*, *we:ll*, *i:s*, *do:*, and *so:*. Repetitions include repeating syllables, part or exact words, phrases, or utterances, and false starts or reformulations are about rephrasing part of the original utterance (Riggenbach, 1991; Freed, 2000). Riggenbach (1991: 427) and Freed (2000: 248-249) both categorized repetitions and false starts as repairs, but Zellner (1994: 44) considered them as filled pauses. However, repairs may also include corrections and using lexical fillers (Sacks et al., 1974: Freed, 2000; Skehan, 2003; Segalowitz, 2010).

Based on whether pauses are used to positively deal with time pressure and contribute to speech fluency, Segalowitz (2010) categorized them into three types, namely, repetitions, lexicalized pauses, and nonlexicalized pauses. Repetitions are about repeating what the speakers themselves or other interlocutors have said. They can be a strategy used by high-fluency speakers to deal with potential breakdowns and to maintain fluent speech flow. When occurring at the beginning of an utterance or a clause, they are claimed to have a positive impact on both performance and perceived fluency (Ejzenberg, 2000; Carter & McCarthy, 2006). Lexicalized pauses are actual words, which are the same as the lexical filled pauses defined in the last paragraph, whereas nonlexicalized pauses consist of silent pauses, nonlexical fillers, and drawls. As lexicalized pauses are generally realized by formulaic language and frequently located outside of a clause structure, they are considered effective time-gainers for online speech planning (Skehan, 1998; Carter & McCarthy, 2006). Non-lexicalized pauses are normally treated as indicators of a lack of fluency (Carter &

McCarthy, 2006; Segalowitz, 2010). The occurrence of silence and nonlexical fillers such as *ah* or *um* generally reflect that speakers are having difficulty in topic-shifting or online speech formulation (Lennon, 2000; Skehan & Foster, 2005). Segalowitz (2010) also considered repairs as lexicalized pauses. However, repairs do not always involve complete words or phrases, because they may be repetitions or corrections of part of a word or an utterance (Riggenbach, 1991; Freed, 2000). Thus, repairs may be lexicalized or nonlexicalized pauses. It was pointed out that the occurrence of repairs, including false starts, may indicate topic-shifting or self-monitoring in speech processing and be evidence of a clash between fluent and accurate language use (Skehan, 1996; Ellis, 2003; Carter & McCarthy, 2006; Bygate, 2009).

In the studies of perceived fluency in learner speech, pauses are commonly investigated in terms of their frequency, length, location, and the influence on the pausing patterns from learners' first language, and they are generally compared with those in native speech (Chambers, 1997; Guillot, 1999; Riazantseva, 2001; Tavakoli, 2011; De Jong, 2016). It has been established that native speakers can easily deliver speech without pausing frequently or for a noticeable period of time (Zellner, 1994; Foster, 2013), although they may also pause relatively long when experiencing difficulty in lexical retrieval or planning for the following content (Chambers, 1997; Erman, 2007). With regard to durations, Pawley and Syder (1983) suggested that native speakers hardly pause longer than 500 ms in the middle of a clause, and when they place pauses at clause junctures, the duration would not last more than two seconds. However, when native speakers communicate with learners, they may deliberately pause more often than they normally do and with a slightly longer duration, to leave time for the learners to process the conveyed information and to prepare for their speech production (Chambers, 1997; Guillot, 1999). Moreover, they may use pauses as boundary markers to separate one meaning unit from another, so they generally pause between phrases or at clause boundaries (Zellner, 1994; Pawley & Syder, 2000; Carter & McCarthy, 2006; De Jong, 2016). Learners in general pause more frequently and with longer durations than native speakers, but the main difference lies in where pauses are placed in the utterance (Riggenbach, 1991; Freed, 2000; Pawley & Syder, 2000; Segalowitz, 2010). Different from native speakers who often pause at syntactic boundaries, learners tend to pause at non-grammatical junctures such as within a phrase or in the middle of a clause (Chafe, 1980; Deschamps, 1980; Pawley & Syder, 1983; Lennon, 2000; Wood, 2006; Tavakoli, 2011; De Jong, 2016). In fact, based on the location of pauses, Chambers (1997) differentiated natural pauses from unnatural pauses. Natural pauses refer to those that appear at nonintegral boundaries, whereas unnatural pauses are those occurring within a phrase or a meaning unit. Studies have pointed out that learners produce more and longer unnatural pauses than native speakers (Pawley & Syder, 2000; Hilton, 2009; Bosker et al., 2013; De Jong, 2016).

The reason for native speakers' producing few unnatural pauses is believed to be that they construct utterances by making use of formulaic language that may have been retrieved automatically as holistic units from their memory (Ejzenberg, 2000; Fillmore, 2000; Oppenheim, 2000; Pawley & Syder, 2000; Erman, 2007). Most learners, however, do not have this kind of linguistic knowledge in store, so they may build utterances on a word-by-word basis, thus pausing unnaturally (Pawley & Syder, 2000; De Jong, 2016). The occurrence of unnatural pauses in learner speech could be an indicator of difficulties in lexical retrieval (Chambers, 1997; Hilton, 2009; De Jong, 2016), but there is also a possibility that learners have personalized their own pausing styles because of their physiological constraints, including respiratory capacity, articulatory rate, and muscular tone (Zellner, 1994). Like native speakers, learners may also show agency in deciding where to pause and how long they would like to pause, either for dramatic effects, for emphasis, or to show they are being thoughtful, in which case pauses are also the indicators of individual speakers' speaking styles or preferred pausing schemes (Guillot, 1999; Segalowitz, 2010; Foster, 2013). Furthermore, learners' pausing patterns may be influenced by some of the factors discussed in Section 2.2, including their working memory, pausing in native language, the level of language proficiency, task types, planning, and context (Zellner, 1994; Foster & Skehan, 1996; Chambers, 1997; Ejzenberg, 2000; Ellis, 2009; Wu, 2012; Foster, 2013).

2.3.3 Length of speech runs

Length of a speech run generally refers to the number of the syllables or words between two pause boundaries (Lennon, 1990; Towell et al., 1996; Freed, 2000).

This measure is indicated in two similar ways: mean length of speech runs and fluent speech units. The mean length of runs is typically calculated as an average number of syllables or words produced in utterances between two pauses (Lennon, 1990; Towell et al., 1996; Mehnert, 1998), and the measure of fluent speech units widely refers to stretches of connected speech free from any disruption, including silent pauses, fillers, drawling, repetitions, and repairs (Pawley & Syder, 1983; Freed, 2000; Myles & Cordier, 2017). Most relevant to the study reported on in this book are fluent speech units, which are also known as tone units, thought groups, and fluent pronunciation units (Underhill, 1994; Grant, 2001; Chung, 2005; Gilbert, 2005; Levis & Wichmann, 2015). Nonfluent learners may produce shorter fluent speech runs between pauses than native or fluent speakers, but they can increase the length if they are able to utilize formulaic language (Towell et al., 1996; Ejzenberg, 2000; Oppenheim, 2000; Wood, 2006), the reason for which is that formulaic sequences have been widely known to be the main constituent elements of fluent units (Towell et al., 1996; Ejzenberg, 2000; Fillmore, 2000; Lennon, 2000; Oppenheim, 2000; Pawley & Syder, 2000; Myles & Cordier, 2017).

Two aspects regarding length of fluent speech runs should be noted. First, the lengths between silent pauses are measured differently using different standards. As discussed above, the cut-off points for silent pauses have not yet been standardized, and accordingly, the exclusive criterion for their duration used as the boundary marker for fluent speech runs is not consistent in previous studies. For instance, it is 200 ms in Myles and Cordier (2017), 280 ms in Towell et al. (1996), and one second in Mehnert (1998). Because of this, the common length of fluent speech runs has been different. Pawley and Syder (1983) observed that fluent speech units generally had four to ten words, which was also supported by Ellis (1996); Pawley and Syder (2000) further pointed out that the length of a fluent unit is six words on average, but Grant (2001) suggested that the average length is about three words. Second, the boundaries of fluent speech units do not necessarily coincide with those of phrases, although it has been pointed out in previous studies that pauses generally occur at the end of grammatical constituents such as prepositional phrases, verb phrases, and noun phrases (Pawley & Syder, 1983, 2000; Grant, 2001; Chung, 2005, 2012; Gilbert, 2005).

The length of fluent speech runs is interrelated with speech rate and pausing. An increase in the length of fluent units is dependent on speech rate and the location of pauses, and conversely, placing natural pauses facilitates the production of longer fluent speech runs and enhances the rate of delivery (Nation, 1991; Chambers, 1997; Pawley & Syder, 2000; Wood, 2009; Bosker et al., 2013; De Jong et al., 2013). Studying these three quantifiable variables can not only offer a platform for the objective interpretation of a speaker's oral proficiency, but also provide indirect but empirical evidence for studies of the psycholinguistic processes underlying speech production (Chambers, 1997; Lennon, 2000). However, these temporal characteristics are indeed the tip of the iceberg in understanding fluency. Fluency is in effect a negotiated enterprise (Riggenbach, 1991; Guillot, 1999; Morales-López, 2000; McCarthy, 2005). Apart from the above-mentioned factors, perceptions of fluency should consider the interactive dimension and coherence of discourse (Sajavaara, 1987; Riggenbach, 1991; Ejzenberg, 1992, 2000; Guillot, 1999; Bavelas, 2000; Doutrich, 2000; Morales-López, 2000; McCarthy, 2005, 2009, 2010). The next section is thus dedicated to conversational fluency.

2.4 Conversational fluency

Conversational fluency is not only concerned with individual speakers' linguistic qualities, but also includes their ability to cooperate with each other and talk appropriately in conversations (Guillot, 1999; Morales-López, 2000; McCarthy, 2005, 2009, 2010). Despite the fact that the conversation may be influenced by different contextual and cultural factors, it appears to be a fairly well-organized activity and follows almost the same conversational pattern: after the opening utterances, the rest generally acts as a response to the preceding turn in the co-construction of the conversational flow (Dörnyei & Thurrell, 1994). Accordingly, conversational fluency is considered as an interactive phenomenon, where speakers scaffold each other's performance (Guillot, 1999; Morales-López, 2000; McCarthy, 2005). Fluent speakers are expected to break smoothly into a conversation, to adapt their speech planning and production efficiently to the demands imposed by contextual factors, to change the subject, and to react quickly if it is their turn to initiate or to close a turn. They are also obliged to hold listeners' interest, direct listeners' attention to the information conveyed, or to respond to what has been said by other interlocutors. On the other hand, fluent listeners are expected to have the ability to use communicative strategies and to give responsive signals, such as using fillers to support the continuity of the conversational flow, to acknowledge, to agree or disagree, to predict, or to complete the speaker's turns when needed (Sajavaara, 1987; Morales-López, 2000; McCarthy, 2005, 2009, 2010; Kirk & Carter, 2010).

The messages conveyed by this interactive view of speech fluency are that first, speakers are capable of accurate and effortless delivery of natural language use; second, speakers have the ability to scaffold each other's performance, conducting smooth turn-taking in the conversation (Guillot, 1999; McCarthy, 2005). Accordingly, it can be seen that conversational fluency involves two layers of meaning: one is about individual speakers' speech performance in the presence of the listeners, and the other is about their communicative competence in creating the flow of talk cooperatively. When conversational fluency is evaluated, apart from the linguistic qualities manifested in the aspects of phonology, lexico-grammar, meaning, and situational appropriateness, other factors that need taking into consideration include speakers' turn-taking skills, the ability to use speech management strategies such as discourse marking, repairs, or repetitions to organize communicative resources, as well as the ability to manage listening comprehension skills and to negotiate meaning to be communicated in the context (Guillot, 1999; Morales-López, 2000; McCarthy, 2005).

Crucially, to achieve a smooth conversational flow, the transition at turn boundaries should be brief, in other words, pauses across speaker turns are supposed to be short (Sacks et al., 1974; McCarthy, 2009, 2010). McCarthy (2009, 2010) suggested that pauses between turns for English are around 250 ms. Kirk and Carter (2010) reported that if a between-turn pause lasted longer than expected, whatever cultural background the learner came from, the interlocutors noticed the awkwardness. A limited number of studies have investigated the pauses at turn-taking, where the observed short, between-turn pauses suggest that speakers feel it imperative to take a quick turn so as to avoid unease or confusion (McCarthy, 2009,

2010). This indicates that automatic retrieval of ready-made linguistic chunks at turn-taking is a preferable choice, so knowledge of formulaic language is crucial for smooth transitions. Additionally, nonverbal factors such as speakers' ability to use body language and show confidence in speaking should be considered, as they also contribute to the perception of conversational fluency (Bavelas, 2000; Brown, 2003).

2.5 Pedagogical fluency

Fluency has been interpreted variously in pedagogic contexts (Chambers, 1997; Guillot, 1999; Koponen & Riggenbach, 2000; Foster, 2013). Lennon (2000) distinguished a lower-order fluency from a higher-order fluency. The lower-order fluency is fluency in a narrow sense, which basically corresponds to natural language use with speed and smoothness, practically having been the most widely accepted notion in classroom contexts and paralleling accuracy and complexity as one major language developmental index (Skehan, 1996, 1998; Ellis, 2003; Ellis & Barkhuizen, 2005; Housen & Kuiken, 2009; Larsen-Freeman, 2009). Brumfit (2000) is considered the first to distinguish fluency from accuracy in organizing classroom-based activities, with fluency focusing on speedy linguistic production and accuracy on correct and appropriate use of lexico-grammatical patterns. Complexity as the third dimension of linguistic performance was added in the 1990s, referring to the creative and flexible use of lexico-grammar (Skehan, 1996; Housen & Kuiken, 2009). Since then, in contrast to accuracy and complexity, fluency in a narrow sense has been dominant among language educators (Lennon, 2000; Ellis, 2003; Skehan, 2009). The high-order fluency is fluency in a broad sense. It refers to overall spoken language competence, including a learner's linguistic knowledge, processing skills, interactive skills, and pragmatic appropriateness. This notion of spoken fluency appears partly similar to conversational fluency discussed in the last section, the main difference of which lies in that Lennon (2000) focused more on individuals' psycholinguistic performance. However, conversational fluency is not only about speakers' automaticity in retrieving lexico-grammar but also their ability to co-construct conversational flow at a discourse level (Guillot, 1999; Morales-López,

2000; McCarthy, 2005).

It used to be believed that there was no need to teach fluency in classrooms and that fluency would emerge naturally out of practice in verbal activities such as role plays, group discussions, or communicating with native speakers of English (Chambers, 1997; Guillot, 1999; Ellis, 2003), but it was also pointed out that a lack of explicit instruction in fluency features is one underlying cause of difficulty in fluency development (Derwing et al., 2007; Derwing et al., 2009; Rossiter et al., 2010). Recent theoretical insights and teaching practice in speaking have suggested that, apart from providing planning time, using task repetition and offering opportunities to practicing the production of spontaneous speech in a limited time, fluency can be explicitly taught, and learners should be made aware of fluency-relevant features, including natural pronunciation, pausing patterns, lexico-grammatical accuracy and appropriateness, and communicative strategies (Bygate, 1998, 2009; Gatbonton & Segalowitz, 2005; Wood, 2009; Rossiter et al., 2010; Goh, 2012; Watanabe & Rose, 2013).

2.6 A dynamic systems approach to speech fluency

The adoption of a dynamic systems approach to speech fluency is mainly due to a change in the conceptual framework (Segalowitz, 2010). The term *dynamic systems* is also known as complex systems or complex adaptive systems, depending on which dimension of the nature of the system is emphasized (Larsen-Freeman and Cameron, 2008a). If the aspect focused on is that of being dynamic, complex systems are then known as dynamic or dynamical systems, but alternatively, when the adaptive feature is the focus, they are known as complex adaptive systems (Becker et al., 2009; Segalowitz, 2010; Larsen-Freeman, 2012; Richards et al., 2012). As can be seen in the review above, although the narrow sense of fluency seems to be predominant in previous studies, research in the area should be expanded beyond speedy and smooth speech production (Chambers, 1997; Guillot, 1999; Lennon, 2000; McCarthy, 2005; Segalowitz, 2010; Brand & Götz, 2011; Bosker et al., 2013). It is a typical, piecemeal, reductionist approach to examine individual speakers' performance, specific fluency features or their affecting factors one by one; from a broader wholesale anti-reductionist perspective, a dynamic systems approach investigates speech fluency comprehensively and explores the development of its component elements in dynamic interaction with one another over time (Larsen-Freeman, 2009; Segalowitz, 2010).

Segalowitz (2010) appears to be the first to introduce a dynamic systems perspective on speech fluency. As any dynamic system, speech fluency comprises a wide range of elements and agents, and manifests the features of being interactive, dynamic, nonlinear, open, and adaptive (Larsen-Freeman & Cameron, 2008a; Beckner et al., 2009; Segalowitz, 2010; Larsen-Freeman, 2012; Richards et al., 2012). According to Segalowitz (2010), the four primary system components are cognitive processes of speech production, the communicative context speakers' experience, speakers' motivation to learn or use the target language, and their exposure to and experience of using the language in authentic settings, each of them further consisting of their own subsystems. These main components and subcomponents interact with each other, not only changing over time, but also creating different layers of dynamic, complex, and adaptive systems. For instance, with increased lexico-grammatical knowledge, learners may become quite efficient in speech planning, but if they stopped using the language for a long time, they would have difficulty in retrieving the needed lexico-grammar. Fluency development is nonlinear: a change in one element may not necessarily bring about a proportionate change in the system (Dörnyei, 2009; Ellis, 2009; Larsen-Freeman, 2009). For example, when speech rate goes up, fluency may not be necessarily enhanced (Segalowitz, 2010). The openness of speech fluency suggests that it is subject to external influences, and that context and external factors such as task types and planning interact with fluency performance and perception. Fluency is also adaptive in that speakers negotiate meaning in conversation, co-adapting to each other's performance to maintain conversational dynamism (Guillot, 1999; McCarthy, 2005). To fully understand fluency as a dynamic system and to avoid overestimating its flexibilities or overlooking the regularities in the system, the guidelines include identifying comprehensively the system components and describing their mutual interaction, system dynamics and co-adaption (Larsen-Freeman & Cameron, 2008a;

Segalowitz, 2010). Only by following them can we offer new insights into the study of speech processing, dynamics of fluent features and of the interaction between fluency, accuracy, and complexity, the influence of the social context, and the role of speakers' agency and individual differences in monitoring and managing the speech flow (Larsen-Freeman & Cameron, 2008a; Larsen-Freeman, 2009, 2012; Segalowitz, 2010).

In terms of the underlying production processes, speaking is widely acknowledged as an activity involving conceptualization, formulation, articulation, and monitoring (Hulstijn, 2007; Bygate, 2009; Segalowitz, 2010). These four phases of processing appear sequential but occur mostly simultaneously in native speakers' production (Bygate, 1998; Kormos, 2006). Usually, conceptualization is the phase where speakers resort to their encyclopedic knowledge and contextual knowledge to plan what to say, but the planning would be constrained by the factors including the formality of the conversation, the interpersonal relation with the interlocutors, speaker's confidence, and level of language proficiency. This is where knowledge of the discourse structure is required. The stage of formulation is retrieving lexico-grammatical patterns from the mental lexicon, mainly affected by individual speakers' preferred linguistic choices. Articulation is where the processing of segmental and suprasegmental phonology happens. At this stage, prosodic features such as pausing, pace, and stress reflect not only individual speakers' preferred phonological representations but also the influence of biological and time limits at the time of speaking. The process of monitoring basically takes place throughout all phases of the speaking act, and it is overtly and covertly affected by psycholinguistic or interpersonal contextual factors (Bygate, 2009). Covert monitoring in general occurs at the stage of formulation and before articulation, while overt monitoring mostly takes place after articulation (Bygate, 1998; Kormos, 2006).

Corresponding to the four underlying processes of speech production, learners may stumble upon at least four critical fluency vulnerability points in communication (Kormos, 2006; Bygate, 2009; McCarthy, 2009, 2010; Segalowitz, 2010). They may have the first one at the conceptualizing stage, especially when there involves a change of the conversational topic, where linguistic choice is constrained by the speaker's common knowledge about the world and the context, the contextual

30

pressure from the interlocutor, and the communicative goals. In this process, automatic access to long-term memory and tracking of contextual variables such as knowledge about the interlocutor, his or her expectations, and communicative purposes are crucial. When a topic shifts, learners tend to encounter processing difficulties because their initial planning and preparations have to be changed for the new topic (Segalowitz, 2010). The second and third fluency vulnerability points involve the morpho-syntactic and phonological encoding processes, which may respectively occur in the phase of formulation and in that of articulation (Kormos, 2006; Segalowitz, 2010). When speakers transform a concept into words, they need to decide what lexical items or syntactic structures are used to express the concept; however, they may not be able to efficiently retrieve the required lexico-grammar (Bygate, 2009). For learners, dysfluencies are most likely to occur at formulation, as there is a possibility that both L1 and L2 lexico-grammar compete for selection (Lennon, 2000). In the phonological encoding process, learners may hesitate when they find it challenging to formulate overt speech with appropriate pronunciation and intonation, with self-corrections being the evidence of overt monitoring (Lennon, 2000). Furthermore, turn-taking would be the fourth vulnerable point if learners lacked a store of pragmatically appropriate expressions for turn-opening, closing, or transition (McCarthy, 2009, 2010).

A dynamic systems approach emphasizes context as an intrinsic part of the system, further categorized as biological and contextual constraints, although it can be detailed, including the intrinsic dynamics of the speaker such as the cognitive context or the biological constraints involved in speech processing, the socio-cultural context, the pedagogical context, and even the physical and socio-political environment (Larsen-Freeman & Cameron, 2008a, 2008b). Speaking is intended to achieve communicative purposes under these conditions (Pawley & Syder, 2000; Bygate, 2009; Segalowitz, 2010). As with any other type of human activity, speech production involves complex socio-cognitive processes. It is inevitably affected by speakers' biological limits, including attentional capacity and working memory, beliefs, attitudes, motivation, or other psycholinguistic or cognitive conditions (Bygate, 1998, 2009; Skehan, 1998, 2009; Pawley & Syder, 2000; Hughes, 2002, 2010; Segalowitz, 2010; Goh, 2012). When speech production is carried out in the presence of the interlocutor under reciprocity and time pressure conditions, this means that, on the one hand, speakers should be able to adjust their production according to listeners' knowledge, interests, expectations, and reactions, and on the other hand, they are expected to produce the speech within time limits and facilitate the listeners' understanding of and participation in the talk. Apart from the presence of the interlocutor, Segalowitz (2010) explicitly pointed out that speech production is also affected by the contextual variables such as the complexity of the tasks used to elicit speech samples, time available for planning, and when and where the speaking activity takes place. Additionally, the interaction of other socio-contextual factors like task demand, arousal, and feedback may impact either positively or negatively on processing and production (Bygate, 1998).

With also a focus on human agency and individual differences in a dynamic systems approach, different levels of speech fluency are found within individuals and between individuals, and accordingly, they are classified as within-individual fluency gaps and between-individual fluency gaps (Segalowitz, 2010). The former addresses the phenomena where learners are undoubtedly fluent in their native languages but somehow find it challenging to achieve the same level of proficiency in their L2 as in their L1, or where learners show different fluency levels in performing the same task in different contexts. According to Segalowitz (2010), explanations for within-person fluency gaps are mainly psycholinguistically based, that is, the degree of automaticity with which L1 and L2 speech is produced is different. In L1 speech production, attention is usually applied to produce semantically dense utterances, while in L2 production, attentional resources are not only required for the transformation of thought into language but also for the search of right lexico-grammar and natural pronunciation, considering that learners' lexico-grammatical and phonological encoding may not be fully automatized. A lack of automaticity in processing lexico-grammatical and phonological knowledge may lead to learners' slow and nonfluent oral production (Chambers ,1997; Kormos, 2006). However, in some situations, learners may rush the speed because they are nervous or falsely believe that a speedy performance can create a fluent impression (Lennon, 2000). With regard to the latter, the between-individual fluency gap, it is suggested that there exist remarkable individual differences in fluency development and that some learners seem more capable of achieving native-like fluency than others. The possible causes include differences in learning aptitude, learning motivations and strategies, personality traits such as being more introvert or extrovert, the amount of input learners are exposed to, the output they practice, the feedback they receive, the amount of time they devote to the L2, the learning settings, and the wide socio-cultural contexts learners are immersed in.

Segalowitz (2010) identified three types of speech fluency: cognitive fluency, utterance fluency, and perceived fluency, which interact dynamically with the social context and individual speakers' agency. Cognitive fluency refers to the efficiency of speech processing and is a property of individual speakers' cognitive system. Processing speed, processing stability, and processing flexibility are the three suggested measures for cognitive fluency; they differ from the common temporal measures such as speech rate and pauses. Processing speed and stability are considered as two convincing indices of cognitive fluency in lexical access, and processing flexibility is treated as a reliable indicator of grammatical processing. However, with the changing viewpoint that lexis and grammar are in effect built into each other (Altenberg, 1998; Carter & McCarthy, 2006; Goldberg, 2006; Römer, 2009; Leech, 2011; Gries, 2012; De Knop & Meunier, 2015), the validity of separating lexis from grammar or vice versa in processing experiments and the reliability of the correspondent results need to be reconsidered. When language learners efficiently operate cognitive processing mechanisms, manifested in utterance fluency are the features such as few unnatural pauses, long fluent speech runs, negotiated interaction, smooth turn-taking, and accurate and appropriate lexico-grammar. Thus, utterance fluency is treated as the overt manifestation of speakers' underlying speech processing efficiency as well as their emotional state at the time of speaking. Learners who have utterance fluency can generally speak as quickly as they do in their L1, without noticeable pauses or nonnative errors. Perceived fluency is about listeners' judgment about speakers' processing efficiency based on the fluidity and communicative acceptability that speech samples manifest in terms of utterance fluency. Speakers' perceived fluency would also indicate their relationships with the community they experience, and whether they observe a series of social norms in communication. If speakers failed to produce situationally acceptable expressions, the judgment of cognitive fluency, i.e., efficiency of their speech processing, would be impaired, and correspondingly, the impression of utterance fluency of the speech samples would be compromised (Segalowitz, 2010).

A dynamic systems approach to fluency comprises three interconnected levels of hierarchy: the micro level deals with the interaction between fluent features such as speech rate and pausing, the mezzo level is about the correlation of the three dimensions of speech performance, namely, accuracy, fluency, and complexity, and at the macro level, it consists of four main system components, namely, the processes of speech production, the motivations to communicate, the social context, and the communication opportunities that are focused on; they are again interacting with each other in a variety of ways (Segalowitz, 2010). At the micro level, the notable fluency features are smoothness of delivery, absence of hesitation, length of speech run, pausing, and other temporal and pronunciation characteristics, as already discussed in Section 2.3, but their complexity is reflected in their dynamic interconnectedness and in the nonlinear correlations with the variables at the mezzo and macro levels (Larsen-Freeman & Cameron, 2008b; Segalowitz, 2010). As to the interconnectedness at the mezzo level, fluency is more than being interdependent with lexico-grammatical accuracy and complexity—the mutual dependence among these three dimensions develops over time; there is also a trade-off relation between them. As we have limited attentional capacity, if we focus on fluency, with a possible lack of attention, our complexity and accuracy at the level of lexico-grammar may be impaired; if accuracy and complexity are carefully handled, fluency is inevitably compromised (Skehan, 1996, 1998; Ellis, 2003). In these cases, human agency plays a crucial role in deciding which dimension to prioritize, that is, speakers can choose to prioritize fluency, accuracy, or complexity (Skehan, 2009). Previous studies have established that incorrect use or a limited knowledge of lexico-grammar indeed affects perceived fluency. In Riggenbach (1991), one participant was labeled as non-fluent for her many grammatical errors, although she seemed to be identical to fluent speakers in the aspects of pausing and speed of delivery. Accurate use of linguistic expressions has been suggested to be able to improve the inefficient impression caused by the slow speed of delivery (Kormos & Dénes, 2004), but if learners pay too much attention to the production of accurate speech, they may speak exceedingly slowly and fail to hold listeners' attention (Morales-López, 2000; Ellis, 2003). It is believed that fluency judgment is more affected by slow speed than by minor linguistic errors, and thus, it seems more acceptable to keep a natural flow of speech with a couple of grammatical mistakes than to simply speak slow (Koponen & Riggenbach, 2000; Lennon, 2000; Mizera, 2006).

At the macro level, the notable affecting components of fluency are speakers' willingness to communicate, motivations for, attitudes towards, and opportunities of learning and using the target language. Apart from interacting with each other, they interact with the subsystem components at the micro and the mezzo levels. For instance, willingness to communicate may be influenced by speakers' familiarity with the task topics: when speakers conduct familiar tasks, they tend to produce contextually acceptable utterances, and may even mindfully choose the expressions that are readily accepted by the interlocutors (Sajavaara, 1987). Communicative acceptability of the speech output in a given context has been in effect taken as a positive indicator of perceived fluency (Segalowitz, 2010). In Koponen and Riggenbach (2000), some language learners were considered nonfluent for lack of pragmatic appropriateness in their language use, although they made no grammatical mistakes or spoke at an acceptable speed. Learners are suggested to adopt socio-culturally expected language. If they fail to do so, they themselves may feel anxious or self-conscious at a certain point of speech production, resulting in the slow speech delivery or the placement of unnatural pauses; they may also impact the listeners' efficiency in speech processing, so the dynamics between the interlocutors may be influenced. Moreover, learners' motivations to use or learn the target language are partly affected by ease or difficulty in speech production. Segalowitz (2010) held that speakers are more motivated to engage in communicative activities if they encounter little difficulty or anxiety in speech production. Learners' beliefs about and attitudes towards the target language speakers and their community may also have an impact on their fluency development. Learners tend to become interested in learning the target language if they are intrinsically motivated and believe the language would help them to be accepted by the speech community. Additionally, according to the dynamic systems theory, to improve speakers' cognitive fluency, it is essential for them to practice using the linguistic resources in a context where they need to fulfill genuine communicative goals (Segalowitz 2010). Thus, learning activities in instructional settings are supposed to provide learners with an opportunity for consistent and authentic repetition, where the whole set of the processes that involve planning, assembling, and articulating can be repeatedly practiced.

Segalowitz's (2010) dynamic systems approach to speech fluency is not entirely new, but is certainly multidimensional and panoramic, emphasizing the dynamic and adaptive interactions between its system components and subcomponents as well as their longitudinal development. Putting its emphasis on system dynamics and mutual interactions aside, it seems equivalent to Lennon's (2000) higher-order fluency: perceived fluency in Segalowitz (2010) is similar to the notion of *perceived fluency* in Lennon (2000), referring to listeners' impression about speakers' ease in speech processing and production; although Lennon (2000) did not separate cognitive fluency from utterance fluency, he did emphasize the efficiency in the psycholinguistic processing of speech production. Moreover, cognitive fluency in Segalowitz (2010) appears close to McCarthy's (2009, 2010) perception of fluency, only with the latter concerning more with the use of formulaic language and smooth transition at turn-taking. As to utterance fluency, apart from the commonly used measures for speed and smoothness (Chambers, 1997; Guillot, 1999; Freed, 2000; Bosker et al., 2013), Segalowitz (2010) also included the component of accurate use of linguistic expressions. According to Segalowitz (2000), speed, smoothness, and accuracy are all related to the automatization of controlled processes in speech production. As automaticity is about the ability to retrieve linguistic patterns without any effort, its effortlessness would naturally bring in accuracy in language use (Schmidt, 1992; McCarthy, 2009, 2010; Segalowitz, 2010). Furthermore, when learner speech is in question, accuracy in language use should be considered as part of fluency, as errors in speech production may have a negative impact on perceptions of fluency (Freed, 2000; Kormos & Dénes, 2004; Brand & Götz, 2011).

A dynamic systems framework for thinking about speech fluency is overarching and complex, but what lies at the center is cognitive fluency, the efficiency of operating underlying cognitive processes in speech production (Segalowitz, 2010).

The reasons are as follows. First, all processes of speech production are affected either by choice or automation, also known as controlled and automatic processing (Bygate, 1998, 2009; Hulstijn, 2007; Segalowitz, 2010). Automatic processing is fast and effortless, requiring little attention in speech production, and is directly linked to fluency, whereas controlled processing needs attentional resources to evaluate and verify production processes (Segalowitz, 2000). Automatic and controlled processing work independently but can be coordinated based on speakers' choice. For instance, although it is the automated processing that is dominant at the articulation stage for native speakers, it can be consciously controlled (Bygate, 2009). Controlled processing is generally at work at the stage of conceptualization, which, however, may be partly automated when the discourse contexts are familiar to the speakers. At the stage of formulation, especially when involving the selecting and structuring of lexico-grammar, automation is needed to accelerate the speed of processing whereas choices are made for its accuracy, complexity, and situational appropriateness. For native or fluent speakers, controlled processing generally takes place at conceptualization and monitoring stages, and occasionally at formulation, but this is not the case for the nonfluent learners who may resort to controlled processing to operate all four phases of speech production, with the specific actions including selecting context-bound discoursal routines, acceptable lexico-grammar, pausing patterns or stressing, and monitoring before or after production (Bygate, 2009, Segalowitz, 2010). Since controlled processes are inherently slow and act against speedy and smooth production, they are the underlying reasons why fluency vulnerability points or breakdowns in learner speech occur especially when there is topic-shifting or turn-taking, or when learners retrieve or articulate lexico-grammatical patterns, which are also affected by socio-psychological conditions (Lennon, 2000; Bygate, 2009; Segalowitz, 2010). Thus, one decisive step to improve cognitive fluency is to automatize controlled processing in the above-mentioned actions, most of which are essentially about automatizing the process of retrieving lexico-grammar in speech production (Lennon, 2000; Ellis, 2003; Kormos, 2006; Segalowitz, 2010).

To automatize controlled processing, or to improve automaticity in speech processing, one way is to create opportunities for consistent repetition in identical task types, and the other is to accumulate automatized linguistic knowledge, both of which are fundamentally related to the use of formulaic language (Bygate, 1998, 2009; Lennon, 2000; Segalowitz, 2000, 2010; Ellis, 2003; McCarthy, 2005, 2010). Ultimately, the improvement of automaticity in speech production is a matter of acquiring and using formulaic language (Ellis, 1996, 2012; Towell et al., 1996; McCarthy, 2009, 2010; Segalowitz, 2010). Previous studies have established that using formulaic language can achieve this by not only helping retrieve effortlessly the required linguistic expressions, but also freeing up time and attentional resources for other uses such as formulating grammatically complex expressions and predicting when to take speaking turn (Bygate, 1998; Wray, 2002; Ellis, 2003; McCarthy, 2009, 2010; Schmitt, 2010). Moreover, automatic use of formulaic language can bring with it correctness and naturalness in speech production (Pawley & Syder, 1983; Schmidt, 1992; Segalowitz, 2010). To ensure the speed, smoothness, and accuracy of the conversational flow with natural pronunciation and pragmatic appropriateness, it is crucial for speakers to take the best advantage of formulaic language (McCarthy, 2005, 2009, 2010; Schmitt, 2010; Segalowitz, 2010). Therefore, studying the use of formulaic language can be the starting point of investigating speech fluency with a dynamic systems approach.

2.7 Chapter summary

This chapter reviews previous research into speech fluency and categorization based on whether it is approached from the standpoint of the speaker or from the perspective of the listener, interpreted as speakers' successful linguistic production in monologic performance or in conversation, and investigated with a reductionist approach or an overarching, comprehensive dynamic systems approach. Speech fluency is now conceptualized as automaticity and naturalness in speech production in the context of complex dynamic systems theory, reflected in the speed, smoothness, accuracy and appropriateness of speech output and influenced by different cognitive and socio-cultural contexts, including subject matter and interlocutors, individual differences in terms of speakers' language proficiency, biological limits, affective filters such as anxiety or feeling accepted by the speech community, attitudes towards, motivations for and experiences of using the language for daily communication. One fundamental step to understand speech fluency is to investigate the use of formulaic language, which can facilitate automatic and accurate production of lexico-grammatical patterns with communicative acceptability. The reasons will be discussed in the following chapter.

Chapter 3

Formulaic Language

3.1 Introduction

Formulaic language has been defined differently in SLA, applied linguistics, psycholinguistics, corpus linguistics, cognitive linguistics, and other areas (Wray, 2002; Simpson, 2004; Goldberg, 2006; Pawley, 2007; Myles & Cordier, 2017). Along with the term *formulaic language* (Wray, 2002; Schmitt & Carter, 2004; Biber, 2009; Erman, 2009; Myles & Cordier, 2017), other commonly used labels include *lexical phrases* (Nattinger & DeCarrico, 1992), *lexical bundles* (Biber et al., 1999; Biber et al., 2004; Biber, 2006; Biber & Barbieri, 2007; Hyland, 2012), *prefabs* (Erman & Warren, 2000; Erman, 2007), *chunks* (Foster, 2001; Carter, 2012), *clusters* (McCarthy & Carter, 2002; Carter & McCarthy, 2006), *constructions* (Goldberg, 2006; Gries, 2012), *phraseology* (Gries, 2008), and *multiword units* or *multiword expressions* (Adolphs, 2006; Dahlmann & Adolphs, 2007). The use of these miscellaneous terms is due to the researchers coming from different backgrounds or having their own research interests or agendas (Wray, 2009; Schmitt, 2010; Myles & Cordier, 2017). However, these terms refer to more or less the same linguistic construct, the commonly accepted defining feature of which seems to be that an example of such language has a unitary status either in its pronunciation, lexico-grammar, meaning, or pragmatics (Pawley & Syder, 1983; Altenberg, 1998; Foster, 2001; McCarthy & Carter, 2002; Wray, 2002; Schmitt, 2010; Leech, 2011; Gries, 2012; Wood, 2015; Myles & Cordier, 2017). Formulaic language has nevertheless been the term most extensively accepted in applied linguistics, language pedagogy, and SLA (Wray, 2002; Schmitt & Carter, 2004; Ellis et al., 2008; Corrigan et al., 2009; Schmitt, 2010; Simpson-Vlach & Ellis, 2010; Ellis, 2012; Wood, 2015; Myles & Cordier, 2017).

Being conventional expressions in a speech community, and because of their automatic and pragmatic uses, formulaic sequences are believed to reduce processing efforts for language comprehension and production; they display multi-layered features in phonology, meaning, and functional uses, and their lexico-grammatical structures vary on a continuum of compositionality, ranging from being fixed to highly productive (Pawley & Syder, 1983; Wray, 2002; Schmitt & Carter, 2004; Ellis et al., 2008; Biber, 2009; Corrigan et al., 2009; Schmitt, 2010; Wood, 2015). Provided in the following sections first is an overview of the main features formulaic language manifests and then its role in speech fluency. To better understand the occurrence of pauses and the production of formulaic language in learner speech, then briefly reviewed are previous studies concerned with learning and acquisition of formulaic language. Four common approaches to identifying formulaic language are also discussed, followed by a chronological overview of the three different procedures that have been widely implemented in former investigations.

3.2 Features of formulaic language

Formulaic sequences in academic spoken English share almost the same features as those in everyday natural language use (Simpson, 2004; Biber, 2006, 2009; Simpson-Vlach & Ellis, 2010; Hyland, 2012). This section attempts to review the salient features of formulaic language and how they have been studied. The ubiquity of formulaic language is first discussed, followed by an exploration of its conventionality, automaticity, and pragmatic uses as well as other features in phonology, structure, and meaning. As can be seen, most of these features are interrelated.

3.2.1　Ubiquity

Formulaic language is widespread in academic spoken English (Leech, 2000; Simpson, 2004; Biber, 2009; Hyland, 2012). Three methods have been adopted to evaluate the pervasiveness of formulaic language in spoken discourse, namely, counting manually based on native speakers' intuition, automatic extraction using computer analysis, and computerized selection combined with native speakers' judgment (Altenberg, 1998; Erman & Warren, 2000; Foster, 2001; McCarthy & Carter, 2002; Simpson-Vlach & Ellis, 2010; Wood, 2015). The results have rigorously indicated that formulaic language is ubiquitous in everyday English discourse, although the calculated percentages presented in previous studies differ (Altenberg, 1998; Erman & Warren, 2000; Foster, 2001). According to Lin (2010) and Schmitt (2010), the causes of the different results are due to using different spoken English corpora, various defining criteria, and different identification procedures.

Given its ubiquity in language use, formulaic sequences may in fact co-exist with single words as the basic unit of linguistic description in some areas of linguistic inquiries (Sinclair, 1991; McCarthy & Carter, 2002; Goldberg, 2006; Gries, 2012; Schmitt, 2023). Single words, strings of letters normally separated by space in writing, used to be treated as the sole basic unit in meaning construction and also the focus of traditional linguistic theory and language pedagogy (Freeborn, 1995; McCarthy & Carter, 2002), but this has been challenged by recent studies in corpus linguistics and cognitive linguistics, for the reason that formulaic language has now also been considered as one basic unit of linguistic description (Sinclair, 1991; McCarthy & Carter, 2002). The reasons are as follows. First, many formulaic sequences have higher frequencies of occurrence than those of single words (McCarthy & Carter, 2002). Second, the meaning of a single word is affected by its neighboring words in contexts (Schmitt & Carter, 2004). Moreover, although language can be constructed based on both an open-choice principle and an idiom principle, it is the idiom principle that has played a dominant role in linguistic constructions (Sinclair, 1991). Despite the fact that formulaic sequences can be analyzed into smaller components, their holistic use has been preferably adopted, which has been consistently identified to be the case in recent studies (Altenberg, 1998; Biber et al., 1999; Erman & Warren, 2000; McCarthy & Carter, 2002; Ellis, 2008; Biber, 2009; Römer, 2009). Therefore, along with single words, formulaic language could be viewed as the basic meaning unit in language representation (Goldberg, 2006; Ellis, 2008).

Apart from being ubiquitous in spoken discourse, formulaic language has also been widely considered as the main constituent of fluent speech (Pawley & Syder, 1983; Foster, 2001; Schmitt, 2010; Hyland, 2012). The primary reason is that formulaic language can provide processing advantages in language use: first, it traditionally expresses common meanings using regular forms; second, it contributes to automaticity in retrieving units of speech from the mental lexicon; and third, it is connected to specialized functional uses, performing a wide range of discoursal and communicative functions (Pawley & Syder, 1983; Wray, 2002; Schmitt & Carter, 2004; McCarthy, 2010; Schmitt, 2010; Segalowitz, 2010; Hyland, 2012; Martinez & Schmitt, 2012; Wood, 2015; Myles & Cordier, 2017). These aspects are interconnected, which will be respectively discussed in the following subsections.

3.2.2 Conventionality

Originally created as novel expressions and then repeatedly used by language users in a speech community, formulaic sequences become conventionalized over time, and they are then habitually spoken and constantly heard with little creativity (Pawley & Syder, 1983; Schmitt & Carter, 2004; Biber & Barbieri, 2007; Schmitt, 2010; Segalowitz, 2010; Hyland, 2012). Within a complex dynamic systems framework, conventionalized use of certain linguistic patterns is a result of the self-organization and co-adaptation in a system (Dörnyei, 2009). Moreover, being conventionalized expressions in a speech community, formulaic sequences distinguish linguistic modes, genres, disciplines and authors (Schmitt & Carter, 2004; Hyland, 2012). They carry context marking, that is, common socio-cultural knowledge shared by the members of a given speech community, so they are recognized and preferred by almost everyone within the same speech community

(Pawley & Syder, 1983; Swales, 1990; Erman & Warren, 2000; Hyland, 2012). Although native speakers are capable of producing numerous utterances to express the same idea based on the syntactic rules of the language, they tend to select the most frequently used formulaic expressions in real-time communication (Pawley & Syder, 1983). Formulaic sequences are also easy to use and easy to understand; using them not only helps language users to conform to widely accepted ways of passing messages but also improve listeners' speech comprehension, thus promoting communicative efficiency (Pawley & Syder, 1983; Biber et al., 1999; Schmitt & Carter, 2004; Segalowitz, 2010; Hyland, 2012).

The conventionality of formulaic language in a speech community can be measured by frequency (Pawley & Syder, 1983; McCarthy & Carter, 2002; Biber & Barbieri, 2007) and dispersion (Gries, 2015; Gries & Ellis, 2015), the two interrelated indicators of occurrence in corpus linguistics. Both of them have two layers of meaning. Frequency of a formulaic sequence provides information about its typicality, by which it indicates the times a formulaic sequence occurs in a corpus or how often it is used by a speech community, whereas dispersion is either concerned with its distributional information in an individual corpus or its breadth of use across corpora (Stubbs, 2002; Gries, 2010, 2015; Gries & Ellis, 2015; Scott, 2015). Frequency used to be considered as a more salient indicator of conventionality than dispersion, as the latter is generally neglected or taken for granted (Gries, 2015). It should be noted, however, that a recurrent formulaic sequence in one corpus may not necessarily have a high frequency of occurrence in another (Biber & Barbieri, 2007; Leech, 2011; Gries & Ellis, 2015), so dispersion should be a complementary measure, to guard against idiosyncratic use in one particular text (Gries, 2015).

High frequency of occurrence in multiple texts is a necessary indicator of formulaicity in most studies (Biber et al., 1999; Biber et al., 2004; Biber, 2006, 2009; Biber & Barbieri, 2007; Ellis, 2008; Gries, 2008; Leech, 2011). Conventionalized expressions have high frequencies of occurrence and the recurrence reinforces the conventionality in actual language use (Pawley & Syder, 1983; Fillmore, 2000; Wray, 2002; Alali & Schmitt, 2012; Hyland, 2012). Moreover, if a formulaic sequence is distributed across texts in corpora or used by different speakers, it means the sequence has broad conventionality (Gries & Ellis, 2015; Myles &

Cordier, 2017). Four caveats need to be noted when frequency is taken as a measure of formulaicity. First, the frequency cut-off points have generally been arbitrarily decided in previous studies (Altenberg, 1998; Leech, 2011). Second, raw frequencies are confined by the size of the corpus, so a sequence with a high frequency in one corpus may occur rarely in another corpus (Leech, 2011; Myles & Cordier, 2017). Third, some formulaic sequences such as idioms may have low frequencies in use but are still considered formulaic because of the close associations between their component words; if calculated by computer software, they may have a high mutual information (MI) value, a measure of attraction or repulsion between two component words (Schmitt, 2010; Simpson-Vlach & Ellis, 2010; Leech, 2011; Gries, 2015). Furthermore, not all recurrent word-combinations have been considered formulaic (Altenberg, 1998; Gries, 2008; Simpson-Vlach & Ellis, 2010). For instance, even though clusters such as *in the* and *of the* are very frequently used in discourse, they are not viewed as formulaic language in some sudies for being syntactically incomplete or for not having semantic integrity (Nattinger & DeCarrico, 1992; Altenberg, 1998; Gries, 2008; Simpson-Vlach & Ellis, 2010). However, these fragmentary strings can have either pragmatic integrity or discourse value when they are associated with semantic, pragmatic, or discoursal functions (Biber et al., 1999; McCarthy & Carter, 2002; Hyland, 2012). They may also be treated as single units phonologically if they are free from any internal disruption in speech production (Myles & Cordier, 2017).

Despite the considerations listed above, it seems certain that if a sequence is used recurrently in the same form within a speech community, it must be the conventionalized choice and contribute to natural language use (Pawley & Syder, 1983; Ellis, 1996; Wray, 2002; McCarthy, 2010; Hyland, 2012). Because of this, formulaic language is believed to be entrenched in memory and automatically retrieved in language production and perception (Gatbonton & Segalowitz, 1988; McCarthy, 2010; Schmitt, 2010; Leech, 2011; Siyanova-Chanturia et al., 2011b). In this sense, the conventionality of a formulaic sequence improves its automaticity in use. But on the other hand, the automatic use of a sequence reinforces its conventionality. The next subsection therefore discusses formulaic language and automaticity.

3.2.3　Automaticity

As indicated earlier, automaticity in speech processing is essentially the ability to retrieve units of speech quickly and effortlessly from the mental lexicon (McCarthy, 2009, 2010). Using formulaic sequences can improve automaticity in speech production, because they are believed to be automatically used as single units of speech (Pawley & Syder, 1983; Oppenheim, 2000; Kormos, 2006; McCarthy, 2009, 2010; Segalowitz, 2010). As formulaic language is highly frequent and wide in use in everyday conversation, it is believed to have perceptual salience, having become automatized linguistic knowledge and stored in long-term memory (Ellis, 1996; Wray, 2002; Hulstijn, 2007; Hyland, 2012). When speakers have biological or time limits on the capacity to create utterances on each occasion of speaking, they can retrieve automatically the already stored formulaic language from the mental lexicon as wholes instead of applying syntactic rules to generate new expressions on a word-by-word basis (Pawley & Syder, 1983, 2000; Wray, 2002; Schmitt, 2010). In fact, from a psycholinguistic perspective, formulaic sequences are defined as strings of words that appear to be stored in and retrieved from the mental lexicon as holistic units each time they are used (Wray, 2002). This can not only help speakers by freeing up their memory and processing resources for speech planning, formulating, and executing oral production, but also leave time for them to monitor pronunciation and grammar, or to compose new utterances from scratch if needed (Pawley & Syder, 1983; Schmitt, 2010; Segalowitz, 2010). Because of these automatic uses, formulaic language may be further used widely and frequently in speech production, resulting in a higher level of conventionality.

Two approaches have generally been adopted to investigate the relations between formulaic language and automaticity. One is to measure the speed of processing formulaic language by using psycholinguistic experiments including eye-tracking (Underwood et al., 2004; Siyanova-Chanturia et al., 2011a), grammatical judgment (Jiang & Nekrasova, 2007; Ellis et al., 2008), and reading activities (Schmitt & Underwood, 2004; Conklin & Schmitt, 2008), while the other is to examine holistic production either based on transcribed speech (Wood, 2006; Dahlmann & Adolphs, 2007, 2009; Erman, 2007; Lin & Adolphs, 2009; De Jong, 2016; Myles & Cordier, 2017) or by combining psycholinguistic and corpus linguistic methodologies

(Schmitt et al., 2004; Ellis et al., 2008). Results from psycholinguistic analyses have demonstrated that formulaic language does enjoy faster processing speed than nonformulaic language (Underwood et al., 2004; Jiang & Nekrasova, 2007; Conklin & Schmitt, 2008; Siyanova-Chanturia et al., 2011a); the limited results derived from the speech-related studies suggest that formulaic language does not always seem to be produced with coherent intonational contour as it is expected to, and in some sequences, pause may occur, which may indicate some difficulties in their retrieval, or in other words, the formulaic sequences involved are not considered to be automatically retrieved (Schmitt et al., 2004; Dahlmann & Adolphs, 2007; De Jong, 2016). Apart from phonology, automaticity and conventionality also affect the manifested features in structures, meaning, and pragmatic uses.

3.2.4 Phonological properties

Formulaic language has its own specific pronunciation properties, which, however, have often been largely neglected in previous studies (Wood, 2006; Wray, 2008; Dahlmann, 2009). Compared to the prosody of the same string of words in other contexts, formulaic use may have a different pronunciation pattern, including phonological coherence, reduced pronunciation, fast speech rhythms, and restricted stress placement (Foster, 2001; Wray, 2008; Lin, 2010; Strik et al., 2010; Wood, 2015). As pointed out in Subsection 3.2.3, holistic production can directly reflect automaticity in production studies, and it exhibits phonological coherence, with contracted or reduced pronunciation included. The former means that formulaic language is produced without pauses, or as an intact whole (Peters, 1983; Hickey, 1993; Weinert, 1995; Wray, 2004; Lin, 2010; Myles & Cordier, 2017). The latter refers to the fact that formulaic language may have reductions in pronunciation (Bybee, 2002, 2003; Wood, 2004; Strik et al., 2010). For instance, the two-word sequence *give me* is reduced as *gimme* and the four-word chunk *I am going to* is contracted as *I'm gonna*. Phonological coherence has been mostly used as a term including reduced pronunciation in previous studies. Allied to the aspects of phonological coherence and reduction is fast speech rate in producing speech; it has been found that formulaic sequences are uttered at a faster rate than novel combinations in conversational speech (Bybee, 2006; Lin, 2010; Wood, 2015).

Moreover, the placement of stress in a formulaic sequence may differ from that in the same sequence of words that are not used formulaically (Ashby, 2006; Lin, 2010).

Phonological coherence, including phonological reduction, has been most extensively investigated among the above-mentioned prosodic features (Bybee, 2002, 2003, 2006; Lin, 2010; Strik et al., 2010; Wood, 2015). It is not only the overt support for easy processing (Lennon, 2000; Segalowitz, 2010), but also suggests the level of conventionality and the degree of automaticity (Bybee, 2002, 2006; Wood, 2015; Myles & Cordier, 2017). High frequency of occurrence is the main reason why formulaic language manifests phonological coherence and phonetic reduction (Bybee, 2002, 2006; Wood, 2015). This is because recurrent formulaic sequences are so often uttered and heard in communication that their phonological features have been entrenched in language users' memory; accordingly, when they are reproduced, they are naturally uttered as intact intonation units (Pawley & Syder, 1983; Peters, 1983; Ellis, 1996; Foster, 2001; Wray, 2008; Wood, 2015). High frequency formulaic language is found to be more likely to be phonetically reduced than mid- or low-frequency formulaic sequences and nonformulaic language (Bybee, 2002, 2006; Strik et al., 2010; Leech, 2011). On the other hand, as reduced pronunciation is mainly a consequence of a formulaic sequence being highly frequent in use, it barely causes difficulties in speech comprehension in communication; instead, it is what makes one's speech sound natural and native-like (Bybee, 2006; Strik et al., 2010; Leech, 2011).

3.2.5　Structural length, flexibility, and completeness

As indicated above, formulaic language can be treated as the basic unit in meaning-making, and some recent linguistic studies seem to have rejected the grammar-lexicon dichotomy. It has been pointed out to be inappropriate to treat lexis and grammar as two distinct components in linguistic description and language education (Sinclair, 1991; Altenberg, 1998; Carter & McCarthy, 2006; Gries, 2008, 2012; Römer, 2009; De Knop & Meunier, 2015). The results of recent corpus linguistic and cognitive linguistic investigations have revealed that lexis and grammar are inseparable and that the boundaries between them are blurred. Formulaic language may best represent the interdependence between lexis and grammar, as it straddles the lexis-grammar boundaries (Altenberg, 1998; Carter & McCarthy, 2006; Goldberg, 2006; Pawley, 2007; Gries, 2008,2012; Römer, 2009).

The length of a formulaic sequence refers to the number of words that constitute it (Moon, 1998; Wray, 2002; Gries, 2008). Since formulaic language can be single words, lexico-grammatical patterns, and even entire clauses, the length can be as short as one word, as long as an utterance such as 'you can lead a horse to water, but you can't make him drink', or anything in between (Schmitt & Carter, 2004: 3). One-word formulaic language includes hyphenated word formations and contracted words such as *it's* and *they're* (Erman & Warren, 2000; Hasselgren, 2002; McCarthy & Carter, 2002; Wray, 2002). The most recurrent sequences generally consist of two-to-four words, but it is three-to-five-word clusters that have been extensively investigated in previous research (Biber et al., 1999; McCarthy & Carter, 2002; Simpson, 2004; Biber, 2009; McCarthy, 2010; Götz & Schilk, 2011). Four words seems to be the preferred length because four-word sequences are considered more phrasal in nature than the rest, and they are neither as common as two- or three-word clusters, nor as rare as five- or six-word bundles (Simpson, 2004; Biber, 2009; Simpson-Vlach & Ellis, 2010; Hyland, 2012).

Formulaic sequences have positional flexibility, as they are either continuous or discontinuous word groupings (Wray, 2002; Schmitt & Carter, 2004; Hyland, 2012). The components of continuous sequences are generally fixed, without any interruption from other words. They are also nearly non-compositional, allowing for little scope for the substitution of any element, such as in *by and large*. However, if a sequence is discontinuous, its constitution would allow for variation. In addition, some formulaic sequences are semi-fixed and some can be abstracted patterns such as *verb indirect object direct object*. These can be filled with a wide range of words under grammatical or semantic constraints, the structure of which is hence usually compositional (Schmitt & Carter, 2004; Gries, 2008; Schmitt, 2010). Moreover, structural fixedness or compositionality is mostly a result of conventionalized selection (Pawley & Syder, 1983; Foster, 2001; Sinclair, 2004; Schmitt, 2010). Out of many possible expressions that can be constructed using syntactic rules, Pawley and Syder (1983) pointed out that formulaic sequences are just the preferred choice over their equivalents, because they are more frequently used in their community and have established their conventionality. Moreover, despite the margin for variation, that is, being fixed or flexible to varying degrees, high frequency word combinations not only indicate that the component elements of the sequence habitually co-occur and thus function as a single unit, but they are also pragmatically appropriate in the speech community (Foster, 2001; McCarthy, 2010; Schmitt, 2010).

With regard to structural unity, formulaic language can be syntactically complete or incomplete (Biber et al., 1999; McCarthy & Carter, 2002; Schmitt & Carter, 2004; Simpson, 2004; Carter & McCarthy, 2006; Schmitt, 2010; Myles & Cordier, 2017). Typically represented by different kinds of phrases, complete syntactic structures are grammatical units such as noun phrases, prepositional phrases, verb phrases, and clauses (Nattinger & DeCarrico, 1992; Simpson, 2004). Incomplete structures are the fragmentary strings such as *in the*, *of the*, and *have the*; a large number of corpus-driven clusters are of this type (Altenberg, 1998; Biber et al., 1999; McCarthy & Carter, 2002). It is acknowledged that a structural complete unit such as *I think*, *you know*, or *on the other hand* has more psycholinguistic salience than an incomplete structure such as *in the* and *one of the* (Hyland, 2012). Some researchers have structural requirements for formulaic sequences: word combinations have to be complete in structures to have a formulaic status (Nattinger & DeCarrico, 1992; Altenberg, 1998; Gries, 2008; Simpson-Vlach & Ellis, 2010). By contrast, some researchers choose to overlook the structurally incomplete feature; instead, they focus more on the integrity in phonology, semantics, or pragmatics (McCarthy & Carter, 2002; Carter & McCarthy, 2006; Hyland, 2012; Myles & Cordier, 2017). Even though some incomplete structures may not have semantic value (Gries, 2008), they can still serve important discoursal functions such as bridging two structural units, or play pragmatic roles (Biber et al., 1999; McCarthy & Carter, 2002; Carter & McCarthy, 2006; Biber & Barbieri, 2007). For instance, according to Carter and McCarthy (2006), the two-word chunk *on the* may indicate the relation of place, a three-word cluster *it was a* may have syntactic uses, and the four-word string *a lot of the* may express the quantity whereas *a bit of a* can be used as a modifier or a downtoner in speech. Moreover, if these structures are free from internal pauses in speech production, they are considered to have phonological integrity (Myles & Cordier, 2017). Therefore, complete or incomplete, a sequence is considered formulaic if it frequently appears in corpora, having phonological, syntactic, semantic, or pragmatic unity (McCarthy & Carter, 2002; Stubbs, 2002; Carter & McCarthy, 2006; Hyland, 2012; Myles & Cordier, 2017).

The inseparability of lexis and grammar can now be detected by computer software (McCarthy & Carter, 2002; Carter & McCarthy, 2006; Gries, 2008, 2012; Römer, 2009). A corpus analytical tool kit such as WS6.0 (Scott, 2015) can not only automatically extract formulaic sequences with a designated length and frequency, but also provide the convenience of investigating their structural variability. Along with WSConcGram on WS6.0, another type of corpus linguistics software named ConcGram (Greaves, 2009) can handle the positional variation regarding formulaic sequences. An introduction to the main functions of WS6.0 is provided in Chapter 6. In the case of evaluating whether a lexico-grammatical pattern has structural coherence, aside from frequency and native speaker intuition, the calculated MI can be another indicator (Simpson-Vlach & Ellis, 2010; Leech, 2011; Wood, 2015). It has been pointed out that formulaic language with high MI tended to have greater structural coherence; however, the MI value was originally designed to measure the association between two-word clusters; it may not be a reliable measure for those consisting of more than two words (Hyland, 2012; Gries, 2015).

3.2.6 Semantic transparency, unity, and prosody

The meaning of formulaic language can be illustrated in four dimensions, namely, semantic transparency, unity, preference, and prosody (Sinclair, 1991, 2004; Schmitt & Carter, 2004; Schmitt, 2010). First, formulaic sequences can have semantic transparency or opaqueness (Schmitt & Carter, 2004; Simpson, 2004; Schmitt, 2010; Myles & Cordier, 2017). Thus, the meaning of some formulaic language is a combination of its components and can be predicted from its surface structure. However, for some formulaic sequences, especially idioms, their meanings are difficult to tell from their surface constituents. Second, formulaic sequences can be complete or incomplete meaning units (Biber et al., 1999; McCarthy & Carter, 2002; Carter & McCarthy, 2006; Gries, 2008). For instance, word groupings such as *I think* and *you know* represent complete meaning units; however, clusters such as *of the* and *the end of the* do not have semantic integrity. Semantic preference means that the co-occurrence of lexical items is semantically constrained, which controls the habitual lexico-grammatical patterning (Sinclair, 2004). For instance, *strong tea* and *powerful car* are habitual collocations, and it seems relatively uncommon to use the word *strong* to collocate with *car*, or vice versa (McCarthy & Carter, 2002). Moreover, formulaic language carries semantic prosody, expressing attitudinal and pragmatic meaning (Schmitt & Carter, 2004; Schmitt, 2010). According to Sinclair (1991), semantic prosody is mainly about why certain lexico-grammatical choices are made to express the meaning in one way rather than another, and it is mostly associated with either positive or negative evaluative meaning.

The judgment of whether a formulaic sequence has semantic transparency or integrity is generally subjective, relying on native speaker or expert user intuition (Simpson, 2004). With regard to semantic preference and prosody, large corpora can reveal language users' intention of why certain sequences were chosen over other structures (Sinclair, 2004; Hyland, 2012). Ultimately, the meaning conveyed is encoded in the prosody, which conversely influences semantic choice and decides the use of regular lexico-grammatical patterns that can be automatically generated by computer software (Sinclair, 2004). Concordance lines extracted by corpus analytical tools can provide a wide context to investigate semantic preference and prosody (Sinclair, 1991, 2004; Schmitt & Carter, 2004).

3.2.7 Pragmatic integrity

Formulaic language is widely used to perform two main aspects of pragmatic function: one is discoursal and the other communicative (McCarthy & Carter, 2002; Biber et al., 2004; Schmitt & Carter, 2004; Biber & Barbieri, 2007; Schmitt, 2010; Segalowitz, 2010; Simpson-Vlach & Ellis, 2010). The discoursal functions that formulaic sequences are used to fulfill generally include topic-initiating, hedging, signposting, and expressing vagueness, or they are used as fillers, structuring devices, turn-openers or closers (Pawley & Syder, 2000; Wray & Perkins, 2000; Hasselgren, 2002; Schmitt & Carter, 2004; Simpson, 2004; Fung & Carter, 2007; McCarthy, 2010). Common communicative functions include phatic communication, speech acts such as acknowledging, apologizing, or declining, or is realized by the expressions used to save face, convey politeness, or to establish mutual solidarity

(McCarthy & Carter, 2002; Carter & McCarthy, 2006; Schmitt, 2010; Segalowitz, 2010). Formulaic sequences also convey precise information in technical and social service discourses, which is an economic way to meet recurrent communicative needs (Schmitt & Carter, 2004; Schmitt, 2010; Segalowitz, 2010). Supported by corpus analytical tools, functions can now be qualitatively categorized based on an analysis of the co-text and context in their concordance lines (McCarthy & Carter, 2002; Biber et al., 2004; Simpson, 2004; Biber & Barbieri, 2007).

As each functional use is usually realized by conventionalized expressions in a speech community, using formulaic language can quickly fulfill communicative purposes (Nattinger & DeCarrico, 1992; Schmitt, 2010; Segalowitz, 2010). Moreover, formulaic language that performs everyday pragmatic function occurs repeatedly in native speakers' or expert users' spontaneous speech, its repeated use would result in it being automatized and stored in the same mental space, and accordingly, it can be effortlessly accessed in speech processing (Pawley & Syder, 1983; Ellis, 2003; McCarthy, 2010; Schmitt, 2010). Because of its conventionality and automaticity, the usual functional use of formulaic language can reduce the processing load of speech production and comprehension (Pawley & Syder, 1983, 2000; Wray, 2002; Kormos, 2006), and these two features may be the reason behind the various functions that formulaic language performs in discourse. Conversely, the miscellaneous functional uses would help to reinforce its conventionality and promote automaticity (McCarthy, 2009, 2010; Segalowitz, 2010). Thus, the interconnection between these three aspects may be the core reason why formulaic language is widespread in everyday language use.

3.2.8 Summary

Formulaic sequences are everywhere in academic spoken discourses, and the three interconnected features, namely, conventionality, automaticity, and functional use, appear to be the reason why they can facilitate fast and efficient processing in both production and perception. They have manageable lengths and observable prosodic features. Their lexico-grammatical structures vary along a cline from fixed to free word combinations, and their meanings form a continuum from the opaquest to the most transparent. Most importantly, all of them appear to have integrity in either phonology, structure, meaning or functional uses. The features that are particularly related to speech fluency and language acquisition are further discussed in the next two sections.

3.3　Formulaic language and speech fluency

Based on the review of the varied features that formulaic language manifests in the last section, both native and nonnative speakers of English may benefit from the efficiency of utilizing formulaic language for comprehension and production, and use of formulaic language can contribute to speech fluency in different dimensions and at different levels (Towell et al., 1996; Myles et al., 1998; Wray, 2002; Derwing et al., 2004; Schmitt, 2010).

First, formulaic language can facilitate speech processing cognitively and socially (Pawley & Syder, 1983; Bygate, 1998, 2009; Kormos, 2006; McCarthy, 2009, 2010; Segalowitz, 2010). Topic-shifting and turn-taking are the places where learners' speech fluency generally decreases, but they are also where formulaic expressions are found most extensively used to transfer from one topic to another or from one turn to another (Dörnyei & Thurrell, 1994; McCarthy, 2010; Segalowitz, 2010). At the stage of lexico-grammatical formulation, learners as speakers may fail to quickly retrieve the required expressions, so they probably formulate their utterances online with controlled processing, resulting in the occurrence of abnormally long pauses or other dysfluent features in conversation (Segalowitz, 2000, 2010). Some learners may only be able to process a small chunk of the utterances at one time, reflected in relatively shorter and choppy output (Oppenheim, 2000; Pawley & Syder, 2000). Moreover, they may choose inappropriate expressions for lack of genre awareness, so their output may sound unnatural or be difficult to understand (Granger, 1998; Hyland, 2012). Because of these problems, learners as listeners may have certain processing pressure to decode speakers' messages, slowing down the process of comprehension or failing to take a natural turn at the transition relevance point, where one speaker stops and another is supposed to take over the speaking turn with minimum overlaps or between-turn pauses (House, 1996; Guillot,

1999; McCarthy, 2010; Segalowitz, 2010). The solutions to these problems can be that learners as speakers learn to use automatically formulaic language to meet the high demand of real-time language production or as problem-solving strategies, and as listeners, treat formulaic sequences as the signposting signals to help them to comprehend the messages or to take over turns (Dörnyei & Thurrell, 1994; Guillot, 1999; McCarthy, 2009). In this way, the time needed for retrieving and processing is reduced, and communication efficiency can be improved for both message producers and receivers (McCarthy, 2010). Apart from the slow controlled processing at the stage of formulation which leads to a correspondent delay in articulation, learners are likely to have a tip-of-the-tongue problem at the articulation stage. They may hesitate or stutter in articulating, although they may be able to formulate the speech in their mind (Bygate, 1998; Segalowitz, 2010; Mirzaei & Heidari, 2013). The possible causes include that learners may use controlled processing in phonological selection, or that they may not be aware of the importance of using appropriate pausing strategies (Watanabe & Rose, 2013; Gan, 2013; Mirzaei & Heidari, 2013). If learners knew that formulaic language can and should be holistically uttered, or they were able to automatically produce them as wholes, they would present phonological coherence or a better pausing profile in articulation.

Using formulaic language can also help improve utterance fluency in terms of speedy and smooth performance with naturalness and accuracy in lexico-grammar as well as in pronunciation, which will also create a positive impact on listeners' perceived fluency (Pawley & Syder, 1983, 2000; Towell et al., 1996; Oppenheim, 2000; Kormos, 2006; Wood, 2006; Erman, 2007; Ushigusa, 2008; Derwing et al., 2009; Rossiter et al., 2010). Specifically, the use of formulaic language not only plays a positive role in improving speech rate and extending the length of fluent runs between pauses (Towell et al., 1996; McCarthy, 2005; Wood, 2006), but also reduces the duration and the frequency of occurrence of pauses and other hesitation phenomena (Raupach, 1984; Pawley & Syder, 2000). After a qualitative analysis of why learners were able to produce longer fluent speech runs over time, Towell et al. (1996) pointed out that the development in the mean length of runs is a result of proceduralizing the use of formulaic language. Moreover, Wood (2006) suggested that an effective use of formulaic language could facilitate the production of longer connected speech without being interrupted by pauses. Raupach (1984) also found that the number of pauses was reduced in learners' speech when they used a wide range of formulaic sequences as time buyers. In addition, using formulaic language to start, to change, to take, to react to, or to close a turn can facilitate smooth cross-turn transition (Dörnyei & Thurrell, 1994; McCarthy, 2009, 2010). However, complex the manifestation of turn-taking may be, it is argued to be governed by subtle rules (Widdowson, 1989; Dörnyei & Thurrell, 1994; McCarthy, 2009, 2010). The transition of speakers' turns should be quick and automatic, and any pauses in-between short, and thus, automaticity is highly required for smooth turn-taking in dyadic or multi-party conversations (McCarthy, 2009, 2010). The short duration of pauses between speakers' turns can be taken as evidence for automaticity in turn-taking (Stivers et al., 2009) and it is mostly an outcome of using formulaic language for turn-taking (McCarthy, 2010).

A dynamic systems approach to fluency also suggests that perceived fluency includes the dimension of natural use of language, that is, speakers' ability to produce contextually appropriate expressions in communication (Segalowitz, 2010). Formulaic language is inherently social in nature and carries register markings, so the knowledge of formulaic language is conventionalized in a speech community's shared lexicon, intimately intertwined with the social dimension of fluency (Coulmas, 1979; Segalowitz, 2010; Hyland, 2012). Thus, using regular formulaic sequences that are familiar to language users is an indicator of natural language use. As indicated in Subsection 3.2.5, among a great number of grammatically possible expressions that can be constructed to express the same meaning, some of the structures are more situationally acceptable than others in certain contexts (Pawley & Syder, 1983; Erman & Warren, 2000). Even advanced learners of English have been found to produce grammatically correct but contextually inappropriate expressions (De Cock, 2000; Granger, 2002). If learners are aware of this conventionality, by resorting to formulaic expressions instead of creating structures from scratch in communication, their output would observe the social norms involved. Moreover, using formulaic sequences can improve communicative competence, as they can be used as discourse markers or time-gaining devices (Fung & Carter, 2007; McCarthy, 2010; Segalowitz, 2010). As discussed in Subsection 3.2.7, formulaic language serves various functional uses such as face-saving, expressing politeness, and performing speech acts. Thus, language users' sociolinguistic communicative competence is reflected in their ability to use formulaic language to fulfill these functions (Pawley & Syder, 1983, 2000; Segalowitz, 2010; Hyland, 2012). In addition, using formulaic language may help learners to establish their social positions and identities, which would have an effect on their perceived fluency (Segalowitz, 2010).

Moreover, using formulaic language can help learners to balance fluency, accuracy, and complexity in performance. Learners may have difficulty in balancing these aspects of linguistic production because of their limited capacity for second language processing, their developing lexico-grammatical knowledge, and also the different strategies used in speech planning (Chambers, 1997; Skehan, 1998; Foster, 2001; Ellis, 2003). Generally, syntactic rules are used to facilitate comprehension and production of novel expressions, whereas fixed or partially fixed word combinations are used to express conventionalized and familiar meanings (Skehan, 1996; Foster, 2001). Attending to both form and meaning by balancing these two ways of language building may cost a considerable amount of cognitive resource, so learners would have to sacrifice either accuracy or complexity of language use to maintain fluent speech flow, or the other way around (Skehan, 1996; Ellis, 2003). That is to say, they may either resort to syntactic rules to construct novel expressions, impairing fluent speech production, or overuse the structures they have already acquired, the simplicity in lexico-grammatical choice thus sabotaging overall fluency (Fillmore, 2000; Foster, 2001). Using formulaic language would help learners to cope with these problems, because not only can formulaic language be automatically retrieved, but its application would also save attentional resources for the construction of relatively complex syntactic structures. Myles and Cordier (2017) reported that L2 learners enjoyed the processing advantages that formulaic language offers in speech formulation. Moreover, using formulaic language can improve grammatical accuracy (Oppenheim, 2000), the reason for which is that there is little possibility that errors might occur when formulaic language is automatically retrieved. In other words, using formulaic language can ensure the correct use of lexico-grammatical forms.

Using formulaic language therefore not only helps to promote the main dimensions of speech fluency, that is, cognitive fluency, utterance fluency, and perceived fluency, but also contributes to the interactions between different levels of fluency development. As can be seen, the belief that knowledge of formulaic sequences is the key to speech fluency is reinforced mainly because they have both cognitive processing and socio-interactional advantages: using formulaic language can help improve automaticity in selecting lexico-grammatically correct and contextually appropriate expressions. Based on the interconnectedness of the three core features, namely conventionality, automaticity, and pragmatic uses, as well as other features manifested in the fronts of phonology, structure, and meaning, one widely acknowledged but mainly impressionistic assumption is that formulaic sequences are processed and produced holistically while speaking, with the overt phonological presentation that they are produced as wholes, that is, being free from the interruption of internal pauses. This is called the Holistic Hypothesis in this book.

Given the predominant role formulaic language plays in speech fluency, it is essential to validate empirically whether formulaic sequences are indeed produced as unitary units and whether holistic production or phonological coherence can be used as an identifying criterion for formulaicity. However, as pointed out in Chapter 1, there is a lack of large-scale empirical research into this hypothesis in adult learner and native speech, and the results of the very limited number of previous studies are controversial, not to mention that the data investigated could have been more authentic (Schmitt et al., 2004; Dahlmann & Adolphs, 2007; Lin & Adolphs, 2009; Gao & Fan, 2011; Wu, 2012). This study is thus aimed to fill this gap, testing the Holistic Hypothesis by comparing the production of formulaic language in corpora of native and learners' speech collected from academic contexts. Considering that the study is ultimately to help learners to enhance speech fluency by learning to use formulaic language, before justifying the choice of the methodology, how formulaic language is acquired or learned and how it is identified are reviewed in the next two sections.

3.4　Formulaic language in language acquisition

Studies of the role of formulaic sequences in first and second language acquisition have been widely undertaken since the 1970s, and those about formulaic language learning processes are mainly concerned with first language children and young second language learners (Wong-Fillmore, 1979; Peters, 1983; Myles et al., 1998; Pawley, 2007; Bannard & Lieven, 2012). In first language acquisition, children who are gestalt learners are found mostly to treat formulaic sequences as the units of acquisition and learn them as memorized wholes; this is in contrast with analytic learners, who use individual words as the starting point for learning and have a tendency to decompose formulaic sequences into small components (Peters, 1983; Corrigan et al., 2009). If initially acquiring formulaic sequences as holistic units, children who use gestalt learning strategies would notice their internal relations, analyzing and segmenting them, and then develop more general categories or schemas until they reach adult-like mastery of formulaicity (Peters, 1983, 2009; Wray, 2002; Schmitt & Carter, 2004; Bannard & Lieven, 2012). At a certain stage, analytical children become consciously aware of the co-occurrence of the individual words that constitute highly frequent formulaic sequences, and then associate them with obvious functions they are exposed to (Peters, 1983; Wray, 2002; Bannard & Lieven, 2012). Second language children have been found to be mostly similar to first language young learners in the process of learning formulaic language. They may also first learn a formulaic sequence as a single whole, and then be able to analyze and segment it into separate constituents when they realize that the sequence admits some lexical variation (Schmitt, 2010). Like first language children, young second language learners can also treat formulaic language both as communication and as learning strategies (Wong-Fillmore, 1979; Weinert, 1995; Myles et al., 1998). For instance, they may use formulaic language as a quick route into a conversation or to adapt their utterances to new contexts, or utilize formulaic sequences as a learning basis for further language development or to generate creative utterances by combining different formulae (Weinert, 1995; Myles et al., 1998; Schmitt & Carter, 2004; Ellis, 2012).

With regard to second language adult learners, few studies have been conducted to investigate their process of learning formulaic language, directly and empirically (Schmitt & Carter, 2004; Ellis, 2008). It can be inferred, though, that their learning processes are complex and dynamic, based on the insights from SLA studies in general, that different variables, including learners' individual differences such as age, working memory, learning aptitude, the input received, motivations, learning strategies, first language background, and social learning environment may have effects on learning (Wray, 2002; Dörnyei, 2009; Ellis, 2012; De Knop & Meunier, 2015). Previous studies of formulaic language in performance data have indicated that adult learners of second languages have difficulties with the use of formulaic language not only at the beginning stage of learning but also when they have achieved a certain level of language proficiency (Pawley & Syder, 1983; Granger, 1998; Pawley, 2007; Myles & Cordier, 2017). Knowledge of formulaic language seems to lag behind other aspects of linguistic knowledge, mainly reflected in the following three problems. First, learners may underuse or avoid using idiomatic expressions due to lack of the relevant lexico-grammatical knowledge or confidence in using it (De Cock, 1998; Howarth, 1998). Absence of regular formulaic sequences used by a speech community has been taken to indicate a lack of pragmatic fluency (Hyland, 2012). Second, they may overuse the type of formulaic language that is familiar to them (De Cock, 1998, 2000, 2004; Foster, 2001; Götz & Schilk, 2011; Ellis, 2012). Overreliance on certain expressions is not only considered as a sign of nonnativeness but also makes learners' speech lack semantic density, and accordingly linguistic expressions may lack creative uses. This leads to fossilized fluency (Lennon, 2000), or impairing the second and fourth levels of speech fluency in Fillmore's (2000) category. Third, they may misuse formulaic language, grammatically or pragmatically (Pawley & Syder, 1983; Granger, 1998; Howarth, 1998; Skehan, 1998; Oppenheim, 2000). Similar to the reasons for underuse or avoidance, an insufficient store of formulaic knowledge is one notable reason, but learners and native speakers may have different storage of formulaic language in their mental lexicon (Ellis et al., 2008; Wray, 2008). Learners may also produce "unnatural" or "foreign" language use because the formulaic sequences they choose to use are different from those generally used by expert and fluent users (Pawley & Syder, 1983; Howarth, 1998; Ellis et al., 2008). There have been recorded cases when learners produced grammatically correct structures that sounded unnatural in the context, so learners may have overlooked the feature that formulaic language is genre-specific and applied it in a wrong context. An idiosyncratic use of formulaic language may be initially caused by an uncertainty in linguistic selection, which is generally incorrect or unidiomatic in the target language; however, learners may have automatized the misuses and store them as holistic units, so they repeatedly use the wrong expressions in communication (Schmidt, 1983; Oppenheim, 2000; Ellis, 2003). This, on the other hand, indicates that adult second language learners are more likely to use formulaic language as a communicative strategy in spontaneous communication rather than as a learning basis to develop linguistic competence.

Linked to the key features of formulaic language and their measures discussed in Section 3.2, these underuse and overuse phenomena seem to be more related to conventionality, as they are generally estimated by the frequency or the dispersion of the formulaic sequences involved, whereas syntactic and pragmatic misuses appear more closely linked to conventionality and functional use, as they are about lexico-grammatical accuracy and situational appropriateness. Based on this, it can be seen that automaticity, another crucial feature of formulaic language and an important element concerned with the promotion of cognitive fluency in particular, has not been probed in previous research. Section 3.2 already pointed out that first, if speakers are frequently exposed to formulaic sequences as unanalyzed units in a speech community, they tend to utter the sequences in just the same way as they are exposed to, and second, formulaic sequences are believed to be represented as independent units in language users' mind, so they can be directly processed as single units instead of being assembled afresh with each use (Pawley & Syder, 1983, 2000; Ellis, 1996; Foster, 2001; Wray, 2002, 2008; Schmitt & Carter, 2004). Based on these premises, formulaic language is presumed to be automatically used as a holistic unit. Despite the fact that processing speed and phonological properties of formulaic language are the two commonly researched aspects regarding automaticity, only the latter is discussed in this study, as speed of processing is mostly evaluated by means of psycholinguistic experiments.

Although previous studies have established that young children tend to use formulaic sequences as wholes, especially when they learn them initially as unanalyzed units and store them as unitary units in their mental lexicon, and that they have also been found to not yet have the grammatical competence for the formulation of creative utterances (Wong-Fillmore, 1979; Peters, 1983; Hickey, 1993; Myles et al., 1998; Bannard & Lieven, 2012; Myles & Cordier, 2017), this is not necessarily the case with second language adult learners, who tend to learn formulaic language explicitly because they already have a mature linguistic system and have developed their grammatical competence in generating grammatically complex expressions (Wray, 2002; Ellis, 2005). Furthermore, formulaic language has different levels of structural flexibility (elaborated in Subsection 3.2.5). Regarding the sequences that are constituted by strings of words with open slots, partially or completely pre-specified, their variability does facilitate the creative and flexible use of language, but in the meantime makes it more challenging for learners to master their use, than in the case of other fixed sequences (Pawley & Syder, 1983; Schmitt, 2010). When learning relatively stable structures, adult learners may pick them up as unanalyzed wholes, or explicitly unpack them into different components but then be able to formulate new utterances using the individual components; regarding formulaic sequences with open slots for structural flexibility, they may first learn the fixed part and then the slots to be filled with semantically constrained words or phrases (Weinert, 1995; Ellis, 2003; Ellis, 2008, 2012; Corrigan et al., 2009; Schmitt, 2013). Given the occurrence of these potential issues in the process of learning formulaic sequences, learners may not always produce them as wholes.

The ability to automatically use formulaic sequences as holistic units will nevertheless develop over time, especially through explicit instruction and consistent practice in context (Oppenheim, 2000; Wood, 2001, 2010; Ellis, 2003; Derwing et al., 2004; Rossiter et al., 2010). Formulaic language is teachable, as explicit instruction of its application can raise learners' awareness of using it holistically and appropriately, while guided and repeated practice would eventually lead to its automaticity in lexical selection (Hasselgren, 2002; Derwing et al., 2004; Rossiter et al., 2010). A lack of input in teaching is suggested to be one reason why certain types of formulaic language are underused, overused, or misused (Howarth, 1998; Ellis, 2012). Howarth (1998) blamed teachers for learners' underuse and lack of flexibility in manipulating formulaic language. He also pointed out that teachers themselves have insufficient knowledge of formulaic language, and simply treat English language at two extreme poles of a continuum of formulaicity, thus overlooking the value of teaching semi-fixed forms. Hyland (2012) emphasized the importance of teaching formulaic language in EAP classrooms. Although he focused on written academic discourse, formulaic language in academic speech should have identical teaching values. Myles and Cordier (2017) stressed the importance of explicitly teaching formulaic sequences as holistic units. They assumed that if one cluster is taught holistically, there is a high probability that learners are made aware of its holistic nature. If learners learn formulaic sequences as wholes, there is a high chance that they use them in the same way, thus improving their fluent linguistic production (Ellis, 1996; Hyland, 2012; Myles & Cordier, 2017). Apart from explicit teaching, learners' exposure to formulaic language and their repeated use in meaningful communication are the primary factors that influence the automatization of formulaic knowledge (Ellis, 1996, 2012; Schmitt, 2010; Segalowitz, 2010; Götz & Schilk, 2011; Leech, 2011). The ability to use formulaic language is acquired through engaging in meaningful social interactions (Segalowitz, 2010; Leech, 2011). As every genre in English has its own formulaic sequences, the highly contextualized nature of formulaic language would be better learned through repeated exposure in natural discourse (Erman & Warren, 2000; Ellis, 2003; Hyland, 2012).

In summary, although young learners of second language and first language seem to share a similar process in learning formulaic language, little research has been directly conducted investigating adult second language learners' process of learning formulaic language (Wray, 2002; Ellis, 2008; Myles & Cordier, 2017). The issues that have been observed in their performance, namely, avoidance, overuses, misuses of formulaic sequences in a wrong context, or not treating formulaic language as wholes, have an impact on their speech fluency at different levels but reflect the developmental features of their lexico-grammatical knowledge in the course of learning the target language (Lennon, 2000; Ellis, 2003; Skehan, 2009). Knowledge of formulaic language, especially its automatic use, can, however, be improved with explicit teaching and repeated exposure in appropriate contexts. As this study explores the use of formulaic language in native speakers' and learners' spoken English taking a mixed-methods approach, to further understand this methodological choice, provided in the following is an overview of the approaches and procedures that have been applied to research of formulaic sequences.

3.5   Approaches to identifying formulaic language

Due to formulaic language having multi-faceted features, the aspects that have been focused on in previous studies are not the same, so the approaches and the criteria used to identify formulaic sequences have been different (Wray, 2009; Schmitt, 2010). The phraseological approach, the corpus-based approach, the functional approach, and the psycholinguistic approach are commonly adopted to identify formulaic language (Schmitt, 2010; Durrant & Mathews-Aydınlı, 2011; Wood, 2015), each focusing on two or more facets of the features discussed in Section 3.2. These approaches are reviewed respectively in the following paragraphs, but as will be seen below, they have been mostly integrated rather than used alone in most previous studies.

The phraseological approach, initially widely used by Russian scholars, focuses on the aspects of lexico-grammatical substitutability and semantic transparency (Cowie, 1998; Erman & Warren, 2000; Erman, 2007, 2009; Pawley, 2007; Schmitt, 2010). The practice of this approach includes an examination of whether or not the elements involved can be substituted or whether the meaning of a word string can be predicted from the combination of its component parts. This approach not only emphasizes the necessity of meaning integrity and structural substitutability, but also includes structurally complete units only (Erman & Warren, 2000; Schmitt, 2010). Thus, structural fragments such as *in the* and *out of the* are not included in the phraseological approach (Altenberg, 1998). With regard to meaning transparency, researchers have different viewpoints: for some, formulaic sequences have to be those whose meaning cannot be told from their surface structures, while for others, they include semantically transparent ones (Erman & Warren, 2000; McCarthy & Carter, 2002). Basically, this approach has been considered problematic for two reasons. First, it is difficult for researchers to operationalize the criteria of transparency and substitutability, because some formulaic structures may have substantial variability, for example, in British English but also in other variants such as American English or Australian English (Schmitt, 2010). Second, this approach depends on subjective judgment, and manual identification can be unreliable or incomplete (Schmitt, 2010; Wood, 2015). Since the beginning of the 1990s, subjective judgment relying on native speakers' or expert users' intuition has been gradually replaced by a more objective method utilizing corpus analytical techniques, so the phraseological approach has lately become known as the corpus-based approach. Starting with a list of pre-selected formulaic sequences that researchers are interested in, the patterns of uses for the clusters concerned are then systematically investigated in a corpus (Biber, 2009; Gray & Biber, 2013).

Taking a corpus-based approach, most previous studies have generally used indicators of conventionality such as frequency and dispersion as screening filters, followed by analyses of grammatical and functional features of the selected formulaic sequences (Altenberg, 1998; McCarthy & Carter, 2002; Biber et al., 2004; De Cock, 2004; Simpson, 2004; Biber, 2009; Cortes, 2013; Gray & Biber, 2013). The corpus-based approach is not only statistically objective but also a mixed-methods approach (Barlow, 2005; Granger, 2009; Gries, 2010; Leech, 2011; McEnery & Hardie, 2012). Using computer programs, it begins with an automatic extraction of formulaic language with statistical requirements on length, frequency, dispersion, or MI, and then generates the co-texts or contexts for a wide qualitative investigation of basically every level of linguistic or paralinguistic feature it presents, or its functional uses (Biber & Barbieri, 2007; Hyland, 2008, 2012; Evison, 2010; Gries, 2011; Myles & Cordier, 2017). However, partly similar to the caveats discussed above in Subsection 3.2.2, when using corpus-derived statistics as formulaicity measures, five issues need to be approached with caution. First, the length, frequency, and dispersion thresholds are arbitrarily decided (Altenberg, 1998; Biber et al., 1999; Hyland, 2008; Chen & Baker, 2014). Second, frequency is not always considered as a necessary criterion in studies of formulaic language (Myles & Cordier, 2017). This is because, on the one hand, although language use seems to be socially constructed, what is most frequent in use may not always be grammatically acceptable in a strict sense, and on the other hand, frequency may vary from time to time and domain to domain, high frequency of occurrence in one corpus does not guarantee similarly high frequency in another. Indeed, Strik et al. (2010) disregarded frequency as a marking feature for formulaicity in their study. Third, despite the fact that frequency of a formulaic sequence is a sufficient indicator of the habitual co-occurring of its constituent elements (McCarthy, 2009, 2010), and that corpus software can retrieve its regular structures used in a speech community, as to the lexico-grammatical structures with variability, except for frequency of use, it is difficult to use current concordancing packages to identify them automatically from corpora (Schmitt, 2010). The fourth problem is that some frequently occurring clusters are not considered to have idiomaticity, whereas some idiomatic expressions are difficult to retrieve due to their low frequency (Wray, 2002). A complementary solution is to measure the strength of association between component words using MI. However, as discussed in Subsection 3.2.5, this measure does not seem to work well with sequences longer than two words (Hyland, 2012; Scott, 2015). Furthermore, researchers have different opinions about incomplete structural units. Considering their high frequency of occurrence, Hyland (2012), along with Biber and his colleagues (for instance, Biber et al., 1999; Biber et al., 2004; Biber, 2006, 2009; Biber & Barbieri, 2007), has identified these as having a formulaic status, whereas Altenberg (1998), Simpson (2004), Gries (2008), and Simpson-Vlach and Ellis (2010) has taken a different stand.

The corpus-based approach as the first step to identify formulaic language is largely a bottom-up approach to phraseological analysis. Conversely, formulaic language can also be identified by a top-down process, with certain linguistic features pre-selected and annotated by researchers (Flowerdew, 2009). Durrant and Mathews-Aydınlı (2011) first annotated the corpus with functions in the text, and then used corpus analytic tools to calculate the different uses of functions. This is called the function-first approach to studying formulaic language. By its name, it can be seen that this approach is most concerned with the functions formulaic language plays in discourse. Durrant and Mathews-Aydınlı (2011) investigated its discoursal functions in student essays and research articles, but the pragmatic uses of formulaic sequences in social interaction can also be explored using this approach. Moreover, this approach is also a corpus-based approach if a corpus constitutes the data resource for the study involved (Flowerdew, 2009). The function-first approach to identifying formulaic language has pedagogical significance and is well-accepted in EAP research, as teachers tend to focus on teaching the functional uses of language in curricula (Nattinger & DeCarrico, 1992; Flowerdew, 2009; Simpson-Vlach & Ellis, 2010). Similar to the phraseological approach, the function-first approach has two salient caveats. First, researchers tend to discard structurally incomplete units (Nattinger & DeCarrico, 1992; Simpson-Vlach & Ellis, 2010). Second, a colossal amount of qualitative work is required, as it involves meticulous manual inferencing of the functions formulaic sequences play in their contexts, and the functions have to be annotated for further computer analysis.

The psycholinguistic approach, or the acquisition approach, generally adopted by psycholinguists and language acquisition specialists, identifies formulaic language based on its processing advantages or phonological properties (Erman, 2007; Schmitt, 2010; Myles & Cordier, 2017). Psycholinguistic experiments have demonstrated that formulaic sequences have processing advantages over creative expressions either in reading (Schmitt & Underwood, 2004; Underwood et al., 2004; Conklin & Schmitt, 2008; Siyanova-Chanturia et al., 2011a) or in grammaticality judgment (Jiang & Nekrasova, 2007; Ellis et al., 2008), which mainly results from their high frequency of occurrence and meaning predictability (Ellis et al., 2008; Siyanova-Chanturia, 2015). On the other hand, the phonological aspect is believed to directly reflect the nature of speech processing (Bybee, 2006; Wray, 2008; Schmitt, 2010; Myles & Cordier, 2017). By investigating phonological features, the psycholinguistic approach appears methodologically valid to study formulaic sequences with structural flexibilities (Schmitt, 2010; Myles & Cordier, 2017), which the phraseological and corpus-based approaches have found difficult to identify. Previous studies have adopted the psycholinguistic approach to identify formulaic language in spoken discourses and so far they have mainly focused on phonological coherence and the nature of pauses (Peters, 1983; Raupach, 1984; Weinert, 1995; Wood, 2004, 2006; Erman, 2007; Schmitt, 2010; Myles & Cordier, 2017). Basically, a sequence is considered formulaic if it presents phonological coherence, but non-formulaic if it contains internal pauses or transformations in its production (Weinert, 1995; Erman, 2007; Lin, 2010; Myles & Cordier, 2017). Alternatively, pauses have been used as a boundary marker for formulaic language (Pawley & Syder, 1983,

2000; Raupach, 1984; Dahlmann & Adolphs, 2007, 2009; Myles & Cordier, 2017). In fact, brief pauses before formulaic language or no internal pauses have been used as an indicator of automaticity in retrieving formulaic language (Chambers, 1997; Erman, 2007; McCarthy, 2010). In spontaneous speech, pauses are believed to rarely occur in formulaic sequences in native speaker speech; if they do occur, their durations before formulaic language have been found to be shorter than those before nonformulaic language (Wray, 2004; Erman, 2007; Myles & Cordier, 2017). However, this may not be the case in learner speech, especially regarding adult learners, who seem to have complex processes of learning formulaic sequences with structural flexibility (Weinert, 1995; Wray, 2002; Granger, 2009; Schmitt, 2010).

These four approaches can be re-categorized as speaker-internal and speaker-external approaches (Myles & Cordier, 2017). Speaker-external approaches investigate the linguistic features such as lexico-grammatical structure, frequency of occurrence and functional uses, whereas speaker-internal approaches are concerned with language users' mental linguistic representations by examining how formulaic sequences are stored and retrieved (Wray, 2008; Myles & Cordier, 2017). Myles and Cordier (2017) considered the phraseological approach, the corpus-based approach, and the function-based approach as speaker-external approaches, and the psycholinguistic approach as a speaker-internal approach to formulaicity. However, this classification seems over-simplified. First, behavioral psycholinguistic experiments currently only offer indirect evidence of how formulaic language is mentally processed, unless advanced neuro-imaging techniques such as Functional Magnetic Resonance Imaging (fMRI) are used to have relatively direct access to the linguistic processing in the human brain (Huth et al., 2016; Jeong et al., 2016). Second, the criterion used to distinguish whether an approach is speaker-external or -internal should consider the involvement of the language users. For instance, if a corpus-based approach is adopted to identify formulaic language in a corpus, the contributors to which are well annotated with detailed information of their language learning background or known by the researcher, a study of the manifested lexico-grammatical features based on such a corpus can shed light on the storage and retrieval of formulaic language in these contributors' mental lexicon. That is to say, although the study involves a corpus-based approach, it is also a speaker-internal approach, since it explores the mental processing of formulaic language using corpus analysis.

Based on the discussion above, it can be seen that each of the four approaches tends to focus on different aspects of formulaic language, with some of them overlapping while some weighing more than others. In actual practice, some aspects appear more difficult to measure than others. For instance, the length of formulaic sequences can be directly measured by looking at how many words constitute them, but the structures with flexible lexical choices are not easy to identify or automatically extract using current corpus analytical tools. There is no such thing as universally acknowledged benchmarks that can be applied to defining and identifying all formulaicity in a language. According to Weinert (1995), even the two earliest and most extensively cited studies by Wong-Fillmore (1979) and Peters (1983) failed to do so. Most researchers have adopted their own criteria for the studies and adjusted them in the process, and they have usually integrated two or more of these approaches to achieve their research agendas. The next section is thus focused on the common blending of the approaches used in previous studies.

3.6 Procedures for investigating formulaic language

Each of the four approaches discussed above has been used as one crucial step in investigating formulaic language, and in previous studies they have been cross-matched in different ways, commonly with native speakers' or expert users' judgment integrated. The different combinations of these approaches primarily fall into three categories, namely, the diagnostic approach, the mixed-methods approach, and the hierarchical approach, which are presented below.

3.6.1 The diagnostic approach

With a diagnostic approach, researchers have generally made intuitive judgments about what formulaic language is, based on a checklist of criteria for formulaicity (Foster, 2001; Pawley, 2007; Wray, 2008; Wood, 2015). The previously discussed phraseological approach and the function-first approach are generally used as part of the diagnostic procedure. The common practice is that a group of native speakers or expert users are first asked to familiarize themselves with a list of diagnostics, and then to go through a data set to mark formulaic sequences based on their independent judgment (Foster, 2001; Wood, 2006; Wray, 2008). The most recent and inclusively applied criteria are found in Wray (2008), covering the aspects of structural irregularity, meaning transparency, speech acts, regular or idiosyncratic use of language, phonological unity, idiolect, preferred expressions, creative use of the original expressions, situational appropriateness or pragmatic inappropriateness, and using language beyond or under the users' proficiency level. Except for the last criterion, which is specially targeted at language learners (Wray, 2008), the rest can be linked to the features discussed in Section 3.2. For instance, speech acts are connected with the functions the formulaic language performs, and situational appropriateness is related to conventionalized use of formulaic language (Wray, 2002; Pawley, 2007; Wood, 2015).

Being diagnostic, not all criteria are expected to be met for speech output to be counted as a formulaic sequence (Myles & Cordier, 2017). The first notable study following this procedure was Foster (2001), in which seven native speakers of English were asked to identify what part of the speech output was constructed by a formulaic sequence and what was formulated on a word-by-word basis. Foster did not offer specific criteria to these native speaker informants, who were also experienced university teachers of applied linguistics. Only those parts chosen by more than five native speakers were considered formulaic. If we look at the results, we can see that the judges identified formulaic sequences mostly based on the functions they played in the transcribed speech. Moreover, all the listed formulaic sequences are structurally complete and transparent in meaning. Furthermore, a series of studies conducted by Wood (2001, 2004, 2006, 2007, 2010) undertook a similar procedure. For instance, Wood (2006: 21-22) asked three judges using five criteria for phonology, structure and meaning to identify formulaic language; the items accepted had to be positively evaluated by two or all three of the native speakers of English.

Wray (2002) listed five weaknesses of this approach. First, it mostly works with small data sets; when a large quantity of data is processed, native speakers' judgment would be inefficient and effort-consuming. Second, inconsistent results may be generated by different judges because of their fatigue or use of different judgment thresholds. Third, individual perception of formulaicity between judges may vary. Additionally, the boundaries of formulaic language may vary in different contexts. Lastly, formulaicity itself is difficult to intuit, as some formulaic sequences may be counter-intuitive and treated as noise based on subjective judgment. Selecting judges who have similar backgrounds can minimize the individual differences in perceiving what is formulaic (Foster, 2001; Wray, 2002), and a different approach can be adopted to tackle other weaknesses. For instance, the corpus-based approach can be used to process a large amount of data and automatically extract counter-intuitive formulaic sequences (Hunston, 2002; Leech, 2011; McEnery & Hardie, 2012). Regarding the difficulty in marking the boundaries of the formulaic structures with variability, the psycholinguistic approach can be used to examine their prosodic features (Bybee, 2006; Schmitt, 2010; Myles & Cordier, 2017). Nevertheless, research by its very nature needs human interpretation and is virtually impossible not to be influenced by intuitive judgment. Native speakers' intuition and instructor insights are valuable input for the evaluation of the usefulness of a formulaic sequence in learning and teaching (Ellis et al., 2008; Simpson-Vlach & Ellis, 2010; Hyland, 2012; Wood, 2015). As a matter of fact, for small-sized corpora, native speaker or expert user intuition seems a better choice than computer analysis (Foster, 2001; Wood, 2015).

3.6.2 The mixed-methods approach

A mixed-methods procedure for investigating formulaic language combines two or more of the approaches discussed above. Early research in formulaic language tends to be a combination of the phraseological approach and the functional approach (Nattinger & DeCarrico, 1992; Erman & Warren, 2000). Since corpus-based analysis started to be used in the early 1990s (Gray & Biber, 2013), it has been integrated with one or two other approaches in most studies (Flowerdew, 2009). The corpus-based approach is usually the initial step for data analysis because it offers automatic extraction of formulaic sequences in a data set, large or small. The next step is either incorporating the phraseological approach to investigate the lexico-grammatical patterns, or the functional approach, analyzing the functions formulaic sequences perform in the discourse (Biber & Barbieri, 2007; Flowerdew, 2009; Götz & Schilk,

71

2011). Quite a number of studies of formulaic language have utilized all these three approaches (Altenberg, 1998; McCarthy & Carter, 2002; Biber et al., 2004; Hyland, 2008; Cortes, 2013). However, Simpson-Vlach and Ellis (2010) added one more step, including language practitioners' intuitive judgment. On the other hand, the corpus-based approach has been combined with the psycholinguistic approach to test the formulaicity of lexico-grammatical patterns: one way is using a list of corpus-extracted strings of words as the prompts for psycholinguistic experiments (Schmitt et al., 2004; Jiang & Nekrasova, 2007), and the other is investigating the phonology of formulaic language in a corpus of transcribed speech (Dahlmann & Adolphs, 2007, 2009; Erman, 2007; Lin & Adolphs, 2009; Strik et al., 2010). These two approaches have been further integrated with intuitive research. For instance, Ellis et al. (2008) triangulated the formulaicity of 108 clusters by using a corpus-based approach, a psycholinguistic approach, and expert users' judgment. They first selected a representative number of formulaic sequences from five corpora, asking expert users to judge these formulae in terms of structural fixedness, meaning or functional unity, and pedagogical value, and then the same list of formulae was designed as prompts for three different psycholinguistic experiments.

The mixed-methods procedure for the study of formulaic language is considered a preferred choice because it pragmatically combines quantitative automated analysis and qualitative manual work (Larsen-Freeman & Cameron, 2008b; Martinez & Schmitt, 2012; Richards et al., 2012). Pure statistical information would be meaningless without qualitative interpretation, whereas qualitative analysis depends on large amounts of corpus data for quantitative support. However, in empirical research, what approaches are decided to be integrated very much depends on the nature of the query and the composition of the data. It is also worthy of note that corpus-based research itself is mixed-methods by nature (Carter & McCarthy, 2006; Granger, 2009; Evison, 2010; Richards et al., 2012), which is to be elaborated in Chapter 4. With a mixed-methods procedure, the relation between the chosen approaches is complementary. There have also been studies involving the integration of two or more approaches to explore formulaic language, but the relation between the approaches is hierarchical. The next subsection is thus dedicated to the hierarchical procedure used to investigate formulaic sequences.

3.6.3 The hierarchical approach

Following a hierarchical procedure, some features of the formulaic sequences are taken as the core necessary features, while some others as referencing criteria (Hickey, 1993; Martinez & Schmitt, 2012; Myles & Cordier, 2017). The reason for certain criteria being treated as core is that they appear more applicable to the particular data resource, or are more closely related to the researchers' agenda (Martinez & Schmitt, 2012; Myles & Cordier, 2017). Regarding the features that are considered as core, they have to be present in the identification (Myles & Cordier, 2017). In Hickey (1993: 32), which appears to be the first to follow this procedure to investigate formulaic language, among the nine criteria listed, length and phonological coherence were the two necessary conditions. Martinez and Schmitt (2012) treated high frequency, meaningfulness, and relative non-compositionality as three core criteria. They integrated the corpus-based with the phraseological approach by first extracting clusters with the designated statistical threshold by computer software, and then selecting the clusters that met these three criteria. Highlighting pedagogical value, they only chose the sequences which were complete meaning units or had pragmatic integrity. Moreover, any sequence that could be easily analyzed for meaning was discarded, as it was considered of little pedagogic value. Myles and Cordier (2017) treated phonological coherence as the primarily necessary criterion. To be counted as a formulaic sequence, they indicated that the criterion of coherent pronunciation had to be satisfied; even when the sequence fulfilled all the other requirements, if it had any internal disruption in its pronunciation, it was not taken as a formulaic sequence. For instance, the idiom *it's raining cats and dogs* seems undoubtedly formulaic in a general sense, but if a speaker placed a pause in this string of words when uttering it, it was not considered a formulaic sequence for this speaker. Moreover, in Myles and Cordier (2017), the necessary additional criterion was that a sequence should have structural, semantic, or pragmatic unity, and frequency was the reinforcing criterion.

This approach, being hierarchical, means that some features are more important than others in defining formulaic language. This is especially so when there is a clash when applying different criteria (Hickey, 1993). As formulaicity is a degreed concept (Pawley, 2007; Biber, 2009; Myles & Cordier, 2017), a hierarchical approach seems able to differentiate the word sequences that are more formulaic from those that are less formulaic. However, the relations between the use of more and less formulaic sequences in speech production are dynamic and nonlinear (Larsen-Freeman & Cameron, 2008a; Larsen-Freeman, 2009; Richards et al., 2012). For instance, learners may place pauses when they start to use certain formulaic sequences, but when they arrive at a higher level of linguistic proficiency, they become capable of using the sequences as wholes. The occurrence of pauses in formulaic language is an indicator that learners have not yet automatized the relevant formulaic knowledge, but it may also be caused by contextual factors. Especially for learners, a sequence can only be considered nonformulaic in one particular situation or at one particular stage, because it may have formulaic status in other contexts or over time. Therefore, it seems important to keep in mind that learners' knowledge of formulaic language is dynamic and accumulative, and that simply using one or two criteria to rule out a certain sequence as a formulaic sequence in learner speech may not be applicable.

As speech fluency has been perceived as a dynamic, complex system (Segalowitz, 2010), and a mixed-methods methodology has recently been considered as a better fit for the study of complex systems (Dörnyei, 2007; Larsen-Freeman & Cameron, 2008b; Richards et al., 2012; Hasko, 2013; Gray, 2014), the next chapter thus attempts to justify the choice of LCR as the methodology for the study and then to introduce the practical aspects of the research design.

3.7   Chapter summary

This chapter has reviewed the varied features that formulaic language presents in terms of its ubiquity, conventionality, automaticity, phonology, structure, meaning, and pragmatic uses. The reasons why formulaic language is considered the key to speech fluency have also been made apparent. Since the present study has an SLA backdrop, also discussed is how formulaic language is commonly acquired and learned in first and second language learning. Furthermore, an overview of four approaches and three procedures widely used to investigate formulaic language in previous studies is provided, in order to lay the foundations for the construction of Chapters 4 and 5, where a justification regarding why LCR as a mixed-methods methodology is considered a best suit for the theme of this study and the research design are provided.

Chapter 4

Learner Corpus Research (LCR)

4.1　Introduction

To expound why LCR is taken as the research methodology, this chapter is structured as follows. Section 4.2 explains the rationale behind the choice of LCR. Section 4.3 not only highlights the advantages but also addresses the weaknesses of applying LCR in current SLA studies. Section 4.4 discusses the decision to use CIA as the analytical method and justifies the inclusion of a native speaker corpus.

4.2　LCR and its theoretical support

Adopting LCR for this study is out of the following considerations. First, the choice of methodology is decided by researchers' epistemological assumptions, which are further influenced by their ontological stances (Dörnyei, 2007; Larsen-Freeman & Cameron, 2008b; Richards et al., 2012; Gray, 2014). Recent studies of speech fluency are suggested to be informed by the complex dynamic systems theory (Segalowitz, 2010). With the application of this broad conceptual framework for the conceptualization of what speech fluency is, correspondent change is required in the choice of the methodology (Dörnyei, 2007; Larsen-Freeman & Cameron, 2008b; Richards et al., 2012; Gray, 2014). Taking a pragmatic stance, quantitative and qualitative research methods are proposed to contribute to the study of complex linguistic phenomena with their individual strengths (Dörnyei, 2007; Larsen-Freeman & Cameron, 2008b; Larsen-Freeman, 2012; Richards et al., 2012; Gray, 2014), so mixed-methods research methodology would appear to be particularly suitable for the study of speech fluency from a dynamic systems approach. Defined as the type of research where elements of both quantitative and qualitative research methods are combined in a single study so as to discover different facets of the research topic (Dörnyei, 2007; Richards et al., 2012; Gray, 2014), mixed-methods approaches have now increasingly become the third major research paradigm following quantitative and qualitative research approaches (Johnson et al., 2007; Gray, 2014). The elements that can be blended include qualitative and quantitative perspectives, data collection, analysis, and inference techniques (Dörnyei, 2007; Richards et al., 2012; Gray, 2014). As pointed out in Chapter 1, and as will be elaborated in Chapters 6, 7, and 8, this study is mixed-methods at two levels: one is that a corpus-based approach and a psycholinguistic approach are combined to identify formulaic sequences, and the other is that both corpora compiled for this study are analyzed quantitatively and qualitatively.

LCR has been well acknowledged as a mixed-methods methodology used to study SLA matters. As an innovation within SLA and derived from English corpus linguistics, LCR combines quantitative and qualitative approaches to investigate the research target; it utilizes corpus analytical tools and procedures to process large-scale systematic collections of computerized authentic spoken or written language produced by foreign or second language learners in a variety of language settings (Granger, 2002, 2015; Barlow, 2005; McCarthy & O'Keeffe, 2010; Mackey & Gass, 2012; Callies & Paquot, 2015; De Knop & Meunier, 2015; Gilquin & Granger, 2015). These principled collections of contextualized learner language data are compiled into learner corpora, having become one legitimate type of research data in SLA studies (Granger, 2002, 2009, 2012; Barlow, 2005; Hasselgård & Johansson, 2011; Callies & Paquot, 2015; Gries, 2015). Learner corpora can be approached from both a positivist and an interpretative epistemology, considering that the same method of data collection can be studied both quantitatively and qualitatively (Oliver, 2014). Indeed, O'Keeffe et al. (2007) explicated that both qualitative and quantitative analysis can be carried out using corpus data. In fact, the two basic corpus-handling techniques, frequency analysis and concordance analysis, correspond respectively to a positivist epistemology and an interpretative epistemology. The former category of analysis mostly involves in automatically generating frequency-based wordlists or cluster lists, which is quantitative and independent of human interference. The latter is an interpretative process and mainly about observing patterns, relying on researchers' identification of similarities and differences to group them based on their informed applied linguistic theories (Evison, 2010; Hunston, 2010; McCarthy & O'Keeffe, 2010). As one of the main aims of this study is to calculate how many formulaic sequences are produced as wholes in learner and native speaker speech, this is positivistic and requires quantitative information. However, exploring what may cause the occurrence of the internal pauses and what causes the differences in learners' and native speakers' pausing patterns needs to be qualitatively investigated in the co-text and context provided by the two corpora compiled specifically for this study.

LCR contributes to SLA both theoretically and pedagogically. The main theoretical contribution is that by offering rich usage learner data, LCR provides empirical evidence to test SLA theories and furthers understanding of learning processes and outcomes (Granger, 2002, 2009, 2012; Altenberg, 2011; Hasko, 2013; Callies & Paquot, 2015; De Knop & Meunier, 2015; Gries, 2015). Samples of learners' language are considered as the primary basis for exploring language processing and learners' dynamic development of linguistic knowledge (Ellis & Barkhuizen, 2005; Hasko, 2013). Apart from raising learners' awareness of the potential challenges that they may encounter, which may facilitate self-study (Tognini Bonelli, 2010; Walsh, 2010; Mauranen, 2011), learner corpora are also useful sources for the study of the differences and similarities between their spoken and written English, the occurrence or non-occurrence of certain linguistic elements in the language varieties produced by those from different first language backgrounds, and deviant and developmental features at different stages of language acquisition (Granger, 2002; Lu, 2010; De Knop & Meunier, 2015). They have provided continuous contextualized discourses for the study of over-, under- and misuses based on a comparison of linguistic types and frequencies (Altenberg, 2011; Gilquin & Granger, 2015). Moreover, learner corpora have direct pedagogical relevance (Leech, 2011). LCR also provides insights for foreign and second language teaching, learning, and assessment (Granger, 2002, 2009, 2012; Hasko, 2013; Callies & Paquot, 2015). On the one hand, LCR-based results can lead to improved design of teaching materials, teaching methods, and compilation of learner dictionaries, thus meeting the learners' needs (McCarthy & O'Keeffe, 2010; Hasselgård & Johansson, 2011; Granger, 2012, 2015; De Knop & Meunier, 2015; Gilquin & Granger, 2015). On the other hand, they contribute to the assessment of learners' language proficiency and help to design natural language processing tasks such as automatic scoring, error detection, and part-of-speech tagging (Callies & Paquot, 2015; Gilquin & Granger, 2015).

LCR can be adopted to study the production of formulaic language in EAP learners' spoken English, although it was primarily restricted to studying English as a foreign language (EFL) learners in the late 1980s, and still has a focus on them (Granger, 2002, 2012; McCarthy & O'Keeffe, 2010; Callies & Paquot, 2015). LCR in EAP stepped in initially in the early 1990s when language educators and applied linguistic researchers realized the importance of using learner corpora to teach and describe language use (Flowerdew, 2014; Callies & Paquot, 2015). Different from common SLA studies that generally focus on morphology and grammar, in LCR there has been an increasing interest in the study of lexis, formulaic language, and discourse (Granger, 2009; Gilquin & Granger, 2015). The study of lexis would inevitably involve its grammatical behavior, and thus, it is lexico-grammatical patterns or formulaic sequences that are in effect under investigation. Recent corpus-based findings have consistently supported that lexis is phrasal in nature and that linguistic structures are not separately constituted by lexis and grammar as used to be argued (Goldberg, 2006; Römer, 2009; Leech, 2011; Granger, 2015). In fact, the study of formulaic language has been expanded to spoken discourse, despite the fact that it is still mostly concerned with learners' written English (Hasselgård & Johansson, 2011; Flowerdew, 2014; Granger, 2015). Furthermore, learner corpora have been taken as an empirical basis for the study of fluency or dysfluency features in learner language (Gilquin & De Cock, 2011; Götz, 2013). In order to further justify why LCR is the right methodology to investigate holistic production of formulaic language in spoken English, its strengths and weaknesses are discussed in the next section.

4.3　Strengths and weaknesses of LCR

LCR is considered advantageous over other methodologies that have been used to study learner language, because it is a meeting place for corpus linguists and SLA practitioners, where corpus linguistics offers methodological convenience for the investigation of large volumes of learner language, and SLA provides theories of language learning and development to explain the results of corpus analysis (Aijmer, 2009; Granger, 2009, 2012, 2015; Hasselgård & Johansson, 2011; Hasko, 2013). It also involves a wider range of research topics than other SLA studies and has more interest in observable linguistic features (Hasko, 2013; De Knop & Meunier, 2015). The following paragraphs elaborate the strengths and weaknesses of LCR by comparing and contrasting it with other SLA research and common corpus linguistic studies.

The main advantages of LCR over other non-corpus-based SLA studies lie in the methods of analysis and the nature of the data. First, LCR enjoys the same technical benefits in analyzing learner language data as corpus linguistics contributes to the study of language overall. By using the same corpus analytical software as corpus linguistics, LCR automatizes or semi-automatizes the process of analysis, generating quantitative data such as frequency and dispersion counts; it also provides concordance-based co-text and context for qualitative analysis (Hunston, 2002, 2010; O'Keeffe et al., 2007; Evison, 2010; Tognini Bonelli, 2010; Hasselgård & Johansson, 2011; Granger, 2012, 2015; Hasko, 2013; De Knop & Meunier, 2015; Gilquin & Granger, 2015). Thus, it can process large quantities of raw and annotated learner corpora and produce results more efficiently and accurately than manual work, such as that carried out in previous investigations (Hasselgård & Johansson, 2011; Granger, 2012, 2015; De Knop & Meunier, 2015; Gilquin & Granger, 2015;

Gries, 2015). Similar to any other type of mixed-methods research, by combining automatic computerized retrieval with interpretative analysis of learner language, LCR allows the linguistic elements of different levels to be investigated (Granger, 2002; Thornbury, 2010). Secondly, LCR makes use of large-scale organized and authentic language data to answer research questions (Granger, 2002, 2012, 2015; McCarthy & O'Keeffe, 2010; Hasselgård & Johansson, 2011; Hasko, 2013; De Knop & Meunier, 2015; Gilquin & Granger, 2015). Learner corpora are not only reliable resources for identifying linguistic patterns as well as the variabilities around them, but are also representative of the natural language data used by the members of a speech community (Granger, 2002; Leech, 2011). They are more authentic, compared with the introspective and experimental data used in previous SLA studies (Granger, 2009; Hasselgård & Johansson, 2011; Leech, 2011; Gilquin & Granger, 2015). Learner corpus data are authentic by default (Sinclair, 1996) and collected from natural learning settings where learners are using the target language for authentic communicative purposes (Sinclair, 1996; Ellis & Barkhuizen, 2005; Granger, 2012; Gilquin & Granger, 2015).

Compared with other corpus linguistic studies, LCR is considered to be more contextualized and theoretically informed. Contrary to general mega-corpora which are subject to criticism for a lack of contextual information, learner corpora can provide more contextualized data for the reason that they are generally compiled by the researchers themselves, who have detailed information about the learners, speech events and pedagogical contexts, and other contextual specifications (Granger, 2009; Evison, 2010; Koester, 2010; McCarthy & O'Keeffe, 2010; Hasko, 2013). Information about teaching methods, teaching materials, and learners' language proficiency can also be encoded in the metadata of the corpus (Granger, 2012). Furthermore, LCR utilizes corpus linguistic techniques under the guidance of SLA theories and also makes use of the theories when interpreting the corpus-derived results (Granger, 2012, 2015; Hasko, 2013; Callies & Paquot, 2015; Gilquin & Granger, 2015). Being descriptive in nature, corpus linguistic techniques tend to be criticized for a lack of theoretical grounding, and it is suggested that they should be complemented with theoretical linguistics, to seek explanations for the corpus-derived results (Schmitt et al., 2004; Gries, 2010, 2015; Gries & Ellis, 2015).

However, in LCR, the researchers' knowledge of SLA theories is a prerequisite, since they need them for the formulation of research questions and the interpretation of corpus-based results (Hasko, 2013). Since previous SLA studies have investigated the social, cognitive, and psychological factors in language learning, their insights are helpful to analyze learner language and interpret the data. In fact, corpus linguistic researchers have increasingly realized the value of SLA theories in interpreting results (Granger, 2002, 2012, 2015; Hasko, 2013; Gilquin & Granger, 2015).

Learner corpora or corpus linguistic methods are somewhat underused in current SLA studies, although SLA researchers seem to have become interested in using learner corpora and the corpus data are more available than the elicited data (Myles, 2008; Hasko, 2013). Three reasons may account for this. First, it may be because the corpus data are relatively new for SLA researchers, or because researchers are not trained to use corpus analysis tools and methods, so they lack relevant knowledge to have LCR work for them (Hasko, 2013). Second, there is a shortage of learner speech corpus data and longitudinal corpora to meet the requirement of SLA studies, as LCR is a recent endeavor in studying language learning and its development (Hasko, 2013; Gilquin & Granger, 2015). Moreover, although learner corpora offer a wide range of empirical materials for the investigation of different aspects of learner language and what may affect learner production, considering the dynamics and complexity of language learning, the causes of learners' actual learning difficulties are not always interpretable based on corpus data (De Knop & Meunier, 2015).

In addition, most current LCR is monofactorial, which means that the research tends to investigate one phenomenon from one perspective (Gries, 2015). However, language together with its development is a dynamic, complex system (Larsen-Freeman & Cameron, 2008a; Beckner et al., 2009; Hasko, 2013). Explanations for the occurrence of one or many of the features observable in learner language should include but not be limited to the following one single aspect, namely, first language transfer, common developmental features such as over-generalizing a particular morpho-syntactic rule in the learning process, different learning strategies, input bias, lack of register or genre awareness in language use, or being affected by contextual variables such as settings and task types (Barlow, 2005; Altenberg, 2011;

Hasselgård & Johansson, 2011; Gilquin & Granger, 2015). These aspects should be taken as dynamically interacting with one another over time (Larsen-Freeman & Cameron, 2008a; Leech, 2011; De Knop & Meunier, 2015). Another notable solution is to propose method integration, for instance, by complementing learner corpus data with psycholinguistic methods (Schmitt et al., 2004; Larsen-Freeman & Cameron, 2008b; Granger, 2012; Durrant & Siyanova-Chanturia, 2015).

4.4   Contrastive interlanguage analysis (CIA)

In learner corpus research, CIA, along with the integrated contrastive model and computer-aided error analysis, is the method that has been applied to analyzing learner language (Hasselgård & Johansson, 2011; Gilquin & Granger, 2015; Granger, 2015). As the most extensively acknowledged method in LCR, used for nearly two decades, CIA has two layers of meaning: one is about comparing a learner language corpus with a native reference corpus, and the other comparing different corpora produced by learners with different first language backgrounds (Granger, 2002, 2015; Altenberg, 2011; Hasselgård & Johansson, 2011; Flowerdew, 2014; Callies & Paquot, 2015; Gilquin & Granger, 2015). In the first type of CIA, the native speaker data are generally used as the benchmark for analysis, which aims to explore distinctive features of learner language at the lexical, grammatical, and discoursal level and provides information about what features differentiate learner language from native speaker data (Barlow, 2005; Hasselgård & Johansson, 2011; Gilquin & Granger, 2015). The second type of CIA can help us to capture the general process of learning another language, what features seem to be transferred from learners' first language, and what could be the characteristics of one particular nonnative variation (Barlow, 2005; Granger, 2009, 2015; Hasselgård & Johansson, 2011).

CIA is an improvement on contrastive analysis, which was prevalent in the 1940s and 1950s, and error analysis, widely used in the 1960s and 1970s (Hasselgård & Johansson, 2011). Contrastive analysis was restricted to the comparison of learner language with the language of native speakers, in order to identify what linguistic features are easy or difficult for learners to master. Based on elicited data or pre-electronic corpus data, error analysis aimed to identify deviant language uses, in order to avoid or eradicate them. However, it was soon replaced by performance analysis in the 1970s, because researchers at that time started to consider errors as a window to understand learning mechanisms and that they should be seen as evidence of progress in learning a second language (Yule, 2010; Hasselgård & Johansson, 2011). CIA expands the scope of contrastive analysis and error analysis, investigating not only the deviations and development in learner language but also overuses, underuses, and mother-tongue specific features by comparing different variations in language use (Hasselgård & Johansson, 2011; Gilquin & Granger, 2015). Moreover, CIA takes advantage of computerized large-scale authentic data gathered from a real communicative situation. As the major analytical method in LCR, CIA is also a mixed-methods approach. It involves both quantitative and qualitative comparisons between native and nonnative language or between different varieties of learner languages. Used to calculate overuse, underuse, or features that are salient in language varieties, corpus linguistic methods are mainly quantitative in nature because they are about the frequency of occurrence and the scope of distribution. However, qualitative interpreting analysis is required to investigate errors and developmental features (Granger, 2002, 2009, 2015; Hasselgård & Johansson, 2011; Gilquin & Granger, 2015).

CIA can be adopted to compare and contrast the production of formulaic language in a corpus of adult learner speech and a reference corpus of native speech both from a quantitative and a qualitative perspective. The reasons are as follows. First, contrastive design has been used for the study of speech fluency for quite a long time (Ejzenberg, 2000; Kormos & Dénes, 2004; Rossiter, 2009; De Jong et al., 2015). Second, contrastive analysis has been considered as the basic and best approach to uncovering the similarities and differences in different varieties of language use (Granger, 2002, 2015; Hasselgård & Johansson, 2011; Flowerdew, 2014; Callies & Paquot, 2015; Gilquin & Granger, 2015). Most importantly, a corpus of native speech is a good basis for comparison in the investigation of holistic production of formulaic language related to speech fluency. In fluency studies, native speakers have been considered as fluent speakers by default, and native speaker data can act as the baseline for the comparison of different levels of fluency (Riggenbach,

1991; Skehan, 2009; Foster, 2013). In fact, native speaker data have been widely considered as the yardstick for acceptable language use (Barlow, 2005; Hasselgård & Johansson, 2011; Graddol & Mesthrie, 2012; Gilquin & Granger, 2015) and it has been a crucial element in the study of the complexity, accuracy, and fluency of language performance (Skehan, 2009).

Granger (2015) insisted that the native and nonnative dichotomy should continue to be used in CIA, although there is some concern about using native speaker language as the norm. For one, there are variations in English language use even among native speakers (Ellis & Barkhuizen, 2005; Altenberg, 2011; Leech, 2011; Granger, 2015), and for another, nativeness has become a thorny issue since English has been used as a global language (Altenberg, 2011; Granger, 2015; Pan, 2015). In this study, native speakers of English are considered to be the users of English in the Inner Circle such as the United Kingdom (UK) and the United States of America (USA), whereas the learners of English from China mainland are clearly nonnative speakers of English, considering that China lies in the Expanding Circle where English is widely used as a foreign language (Kachru, 1985; Granger, 2002). According to Pan (2011), the policies in English language teaching (ELT) in China deliberately distance themselves from any particular variety of world Englishes so that neither American nor British English is taken as the norm in school syllabi. However, respecting authority and looking for norms for correct use, most English learners in China strongly believe that the English used in the inner circle should act as the norm and they aim for native-like English language proficiency (Hu, 2005; Bolton & Graddol, 2012). In addition, although three varieties of reference language have been used for purposes of contrast, namely, the traditional Inner Circle varieties, the Outer Circle varieties, or corpora of expert users' data in the Expanding Circle, all of these are implicitly expected to be representative of a native-like level of language proficiency (Granger, 2002, 2015).

It is important to contrast the production of formulaic language in learner speech with that in native speaker speech, for the following reasons. First, as reviewed in Chapter 2, learners' fluency problems related to the use of formulaic language are mostly assumed to be because they either have no store of the required formulaic language or have no automaticity in retrieving the stored linguistic knowledge (Towell et al., 1996; Fillmore, 2000; Lennon, 2000; Oppenheim, 2000; Ellis, 2003; McCarthy, 2010). Previous studies of formulaic language in learner discourse have mostly investigated over-, under-, or misuses (De Cock, 1998, 2000, 2004; Oppenheim, 2000; Götz & Schilk, 2011; Ellis, 2012), but there has been little large-scale empirical investigation of automatic use of formulaic language in adult learners' speech production (Wood, 2015). Thus, studying the production of formulaic language in a learner corpus and contrasting it with a corpus of native speech can verify or question the common assumptions in this area. Second, when identifying formulaic sequences, pairing them between a learner corpus and a reference corpus can screen out the sequences which may be considered less formulaic to either group of speakers (Schmitt, 2010; Myles & Cordier, 2017). That is because, on the one hand, learners' underuse or overuse of certain formulaic chunks may lead to skewed statistical calculation, but on the other hand, even among native speakers, the perception of formulaicity is different (Wray, 2008). Most importantly, this comparative analysis can offer evidence including which formulaic sequences are produced as wholes or contain pauses in learner and native speech, whether the use of formulaic sequences in the learner corpus reflects developmental features in learning, and whether the pausing patterns in formulaic language are different in these two types of spoken English.

Hasselgård and Johansson (2011) pointed out that CIA would be better complemented with the integrated contrastive model, which compares the language use between learners' mother tongue and their target language. This would reveal first language transfer and make better predictions about learning difficulties (Gilquin & Granger, 2015; Granger, 2015). Because of the existence of within-person fluency gaps, Segalowitz (2010) also emphasized the importance of using learners' first language speech samples as the baseline to investigate their L2 fluency features. He indicated that if the learners show the same fluency features as when they speak their native languages, the fluency problems concerned may be general phenomena in learners' individual styles of speaking. In this study, taking the integrated contrastive model would mean comparing Chinese learners' spoken English with their native spoken Mandarin Chinese. However, Mandarin Chinese and English belong to two different language families and they are known to be almost incomparable (Yule, 2010). Thus, it was decided not to use the integrated contrastive model but to use CIA, comparing Chinese learners' academic spoken English with native English speakers' academic speech.

4.5   Chapter summary

This chapter has provided the justification regarding the use of LCR as the research methodology and CIA as the method of data analysis. It has also made apparent the advantages and disadvantages in applying LCR as well as CIA to investigating SLA matters. To conduct CIA, two corpora are needed; an elaboration of the practical matters regarding compiling and annotating DSS and MiniM subsequently becomes the focus of the following chapter.

Chapter 5
Two Corpora of Academic Spoken English

5.1 Introduction

Based on the discussion in Chapter 4, LCR appears to be a most suitable research methodology for this study, as it can provide a plenitude of quantitative and qualitative evidence for the research questions posed. CIA has been decided on as the analytical method, one corpus of learner language and one reference corpus are thus needed. Accordingly, this chapter aims to enunciate the procedures of constructing the two speech corpora. Section 5.2 explains the building of a corpus of Chinese advanced learners' EAP speech, DSS, with several fundamental decisions elaborated at different stages of its construction. Section 5.3 discusses the comparability of and the selection criteria for the reference corpus, MiniM, and explains how it was built.

5.2 DSS

DSS consists of 89,633 words of classroom interactive speech, contributed by preliminary year students when they were taking the class of *Discussion and Seminar Skills*, an EAP course offered by the Centre for English Language Education

(CELE) at the University of Nottingham Ningbo China (UNNC) (Appendix 5.2[1]). As there is a lack of learner speech corpora that can provide evidence for the research questions of this study, the direct and main aim of building this learner corpus is to provide representative samples of Chinese learners' naturally occurring spoken English from which to obtain vigorous empirical validation regarding whether formulaic sequences are produced as wholes or interrupted by internal pauses. In the following subsections, first discussed are the principal considerations for the design of the corpus, and then presented are the procedures involved in recording, transcribing, and annotating the data.

5.2.1 The design stage

The factors that need to be seriously considered in the planning stage of building a speech corpus include the context of data collection, data types, the research subjects, the size of the corpus, and ethical matters (Thompson, 2004; Adolphs & Knight, 2010; Hasko, 2013). Thus, the following paragraphs address the reasons why the *Discussion and Seminar Skills* class at UNNC was chosen as the context of data collection, classroom-based interactive speech as the data to be analyzed and first year students as the participants, as well as explain the decision on the size of the corpus and how to protect the participants' identities.

Context of data collection

Collecting data from the *Discussion and Seminar Skills* class at UNNC is out of consideration for their authenticity and practicality (Ellis & Barkhuizen, 2005; Walsh, 2010). In a social context where English is used as a foreign language, learners have few opportunities to apply it in real-life communication (Granger, 2002; Graddol & Mesthrie, 2012). When English is hardly ever spoken outside classrooms, authentic language use data practically refer to the speech collected when students are carrying out an authentic classroom activity (Granger, 2002, 2012; Ellis & Barkhuizen, 2005). Thus, for Chinese EAP learners, the classroom appears to be the best location to collect naturally occurring speech samples (Ellis &

---

1   All the appendices are accessed by scanning the QR code in the CONTENTS, page 3; hereinafter the same applies in this book.

Barkhuizen, 2005; Walsh, 2010). Compared with other types of EAP courses, the *Discussion and Seminar Skills* class appears to be where learners produce naturally much more interactive speech. It is also believed that if data collection takes place in participants' familiar and relaxed classrooms, the data gathered should be most authentic and ecologically valid for the research (Tognini Bonelli, 2010). In addition, classroom-based speech is more automatic and less controlled, and insights from its study can have direct pedagogical relevance (Bygate, 1998).

The reasons why UNNC was selected as the location of data collection are as follows. First, established in 2004, UNNC is the first Sino-foreign university in China where English is used as the working language on campus (Shu & Chen, 2010; Levrai, 2013). Second, UNNC has been publicly acknowledged as having one well-established EAP base in China, where all Chinese first year students are required to take EAP courses offered by CELE (Levrai, 2013). Moreover, EAP courses at UNNC are considered new and innovative, having been considered a model for English language teaching and learning in China (Shu & Chen, 2010).

Data types

In previous fluency research, the tasks that are generally employed to elicit spoken data are reading, picture describing, story-telling, and interviews (Segalowitz, 2010). Reading tasks are easiest to administer, but speech processing in reading is now considered quite different from that in speaking. In picture description tasks, participants are generally asked to narrate a story based on a given picture or a silent film, so there are constraints on the topic and the meaning conveyed. It has been widely accepted that different task types affect fluency performance (Bygate, 1998; Skehan & Foster, 1999; McCarthy, 2009, 2010), but there are no agreed-upon criteria for the choice of the prompts for narration tasks (Segalowitz, 2010). In story-telling tasks, participants are usually asked to read or hear a story in their mother tongue and then to retell it in English. While sharing almost the same advantages and limitations as picture descriptions, story-telling tasks may also be affected by participants' individual differences in working memory, because of which, participants may behave differently when they do not have the relevant information physically present in front of them at the time of retelling (Segalowitz,

2010). Moreover, both picture describing and story-telling tasks are monologic in nature. In interviews, the participants are guided by a teacher or a researcher to talk about a certain topic. Imitating speaking activities in real life, this elicitation skill is claimed to have ecological validity, but the speaker may become intimidated or affected by the interviewer (Hilton, 2009). McCarthy (2009, 2010) pointed out that in everyday conversations all speakers are responsible for co-creating the smooth flow of talk; some of them may not intend to take the speaking turn but will give minimal responses by simply using backchannel signals. However, during the one-to-one interview where a teacher or a project investigator plays the role of the interviewer, he or she would follow a protocol of limited interaction and invite as much spoken data as possible from the interviewee. Therefore, responsibilities such as filling silence or avoiding long pauses is not shared, in which case, learners may be nervous because of their self-consciousness about their language use (Hilton, 2009). Accordingly, spoken data elicited from interviews would not be applicable to the study of learners' conversational fluency. In fact, the use of controlled elicitation skills for speech samples in previous research is mostly due to the belief that speech fluency is a temporal phenomenon (Segalowitz, 2010). With the changing viewpoint towards speech fluency, the data that are used for the seeking of evidence should be naturally occurring spoken English.

In previous SLA studies, the authenticity of the data exists on a scale ranging from being fully experimental to fully natural (Granger, 2002, 2012; Gilquin & Granger, 2015). The three types of production data generally used in the study of learner speech are naturally occurring language data, clinically elicited data, and experimentally elicited data (Ellis & Barkhuizen, 2005). The first type is also known as uncontrolled production data and collected in real-life communication. In clinical elicitation, learners are generally given a topic and they are expected to talk about it, with picture describing, narration, and interviewing as the representative forms; according to Segalowitz (2010), previous fluency studies mostly relied on this type of data. Experimental elicitation is where the researchers have close control over learners' production and it has a requirement on the application of specific linguistic forms. Most of previous SLA studies have chosen to use experimental and introspective data instead of natural language use data (Ellis & Barkhuizen, 2005;

Granger, 2012, 2015).

As clarified at the beginning of Section 5.2, the true primary reason for building DSS is that there is a lack of speech corpora that can be examined to answer the research questions. Based on the classification of production data listed in the last paragraph, the learner speech corpora in existence are mostly clinical, including speech elicited by reading aloud a text, describing pictures, learners' translation, or taking an interview (Sinclair, 1996; Granger, 2012), which are considered as peripheral types of production data, so they are broadly peripheral learner corpora (Granger, 2012; Gilquin & Granger, 2015). The two publicly accessible corpora of spoken English produced by Chinese students in China, College Learners Spoken English Corpus (COLSEC) (Yang & Wei, 2005) and Spoken and Written English Corpus of Chinese Learners (SWECCL) (Wen & Wang, 2008), are peripheral learner corpora, as the data in both corpora were elicited clinically. The spoken English in the former corpus was produced by college students sitting the College English Test (CET) Band Four and Band Six; the data of the latter corpus were contributed by year two and year four English major students who were respectively taking the Test for English Majors (TEM) Band Four and Band Eight. According to Sinclair (1996) and Granger (2002), such experimentally elicited data do not seem to meet the authenticity requirement for this study.

Based on the discussions above, only naturally occurring classroom interactive speech was considered qualified data for DSS, with oral presentations and group discussions being the two specific speech events. A dynamic systems perspective on fluency requires the use of authentic interactive speech as the data, as fluency is best captured in dyadic and multi-party conversations where learners are at ease talking naturally and show their true abilities of scaffolding and sustaining interaction (Riggenbach, 1991; Guillot, 1999; Ejzenberg, 2000; Morales-López, 2000; McCarthy, 2010). Moreover, classroom interactions are believed to contain more formulaic language than other spoken discourse at universities (Biber et al., 2004; Biber, 2006; Granger, 2012), and they are able to reveal learners' real ability in language use and provide information about their implicit linguistic knowledge (Ellis & Barkhuizen, 2005; Granger, 2012).

Participants

The population of DSS consists of fifty-six first year students at UNNC, who are all Chinese EAP learners participating in the *Discussion and Seminar Skills* class over two academic semesters. At the time the data collection started, the participants were more than eighteen years old and they were freshly enrolled at UNNC, with a minimum score of 115[1] for English achieved through the National Higher Education Entrance Examination, also known as *gaokao*. All of them are native speakers of Mandarin Chinese. They had not been to foreign countries for travel or study, except for two participants, one of whom travelled and the other studied outside China for a couple of months. They were either roommates or classmates, well known to each other. More information about these participants can be found in Appendix 5.2.1b. It is believed that the spontaneous speech produced by speakers who are familiar to each other presents more variations in language use than other kinds of conversation (Tognini Bonelli, 2010).

Recruiting such a population as the contributors of DSS is out of following considerations. Primarily, whether Chinese learners of English holistically produce formulaic language has not been empirically investigated with naturally occurring interactive speech. Validating this has eventful pedagogical implications because it can inform learning and teaching fluency of spoken English in China. However, no notable investigation of this issue can be retrieved from China Academic Journal Electronic Publishing House from 1994 to 2016[2]. Despite the fact that there are a couple of overseas studies concerning the speech fluency of Chinese learners of English who studied abroad, the number of participants investigated is rather small and the data used are clinically elicited (Larsen-Freeman, 2006; Wood, 2007). Moreover, learners at an advanced level of language proficiency are mostly neglected in previous SLA research (Granger, 2002, 2015; Gilquin & Granger, 2015).

Corpus size

The choice of the corpus size is mostly determined by the features of the

---

1　Available at https://www.nottingham.edu.cn/en/study/undergraduate/entry-requirements/mainland-Chinese/index.aspx, last accessed April 2019.
2　Available at http://www.china-k.net/, last accessed December 2016.

linguistic elements under investigation, the researchers' theoretical perspective, the level of detail required for the targeted linguistic phenomenon, and whether the analysis is more manual or automatic (Carter & McCarthy, 1995; Evison, 2010; Koester, 2010; Leech, 2011; Flowerdew, 2014). There are generally two mainstreams in compiling corpora: one is mega-corpora and the other small, specialized corpora (Koester, 2010). A large and wide-ranging corpus can provide more reliable and valid information about the frequent words and collocations (Leech, 2011) and is needed by lexicographers for the study of vocabulary coverage (Carter & McCarthy, 1995; Evison, 2010), but a very small corpus such as one thousand words may be enough for the investigation of focused discoursal or lexico-grammatical features such as the use of articles or pronouns (Carter & McCarthy, 1995; Evison, 2010; Koester, 2010; Granger, 2012). According to Flowerdew (2014), if a researcher takes a positivistic perspective, he or she will need a bigger size than the researchers who favor interpretative analysis. However, if a corpus is carefully built for the investigation of a special target, it does not have to be large (Tribble, 1997; Koester, 2010; Thornbury, 2010). Being specially targeted, small corpora can generate more reliable genre-specific results than general mega-corpora (O'Keeffe et al., 2007; Koester, 2010). Realistically, if the targeted linguistic items involve detailed analysis and manual annotation, the size tends to be small (Koester, 2010; Meunier, 2010; Flowerdew, 2014).

Small corpora have three notable advantages in corpus-based investigation. First, they are built for the investigation of special targeted research, so they are appropriate for carrying out specialized investigation (McCarthy & O'Keeffe, 2010). Second, contextualized, specialized small corpora are particularly valuable for the study of language development, as the quantitative results they generate can be complemented by qualitative analysis (Thornbury, 2010). The small-sized corpus compilers are often the analysts, so they have contextualized insights; being familiar with the contextual variables helps to interpret the results (Koester, 2010; McCarthy & O'Keeffe, 2010). Furthermore, small focused corpora are generally compiled with specific teaching or learning purposes, directly meeting the needs of teachers and learners. In the field of EAP, since there is a close link between linguistic patterning and the context of use, small contextualized corpora are preferred (Koester, 2010). In fact, small corpora are considered not only more manageable but also better suited for EAP learners or teachers (Koester 2010), whereas mega-corpora may generate too much data to be managed efficiently (Carter & McCarthy, 1995; Evison, 2010; Koester, 2010). It has been argued that the future of LCR will be based on small specialized corpora annotated with detailed contextual information (Meunier, 2010; Thornbury, 2010; Hasko, 2013).

There are some other aspects that require mention. First, it is not only the size, but also the design of the corpus that matters in corpus-based investigations (Koester, 2010). Second, the size of the data set does not necessarily reflect the level of representativeness (Granger, 2012; De Knop & Meunier, 2015). They are directly correlated only when the number of the participants who contribute to the corpus is taken into consideration (Granger, 2012). However, a corpus built by an individual researcher can be reasonably small due to limitations of time and effort in gathering and transcribing spoken data (Koester, 2010). For certain types of studies, a sufficient but manageable size seems a better option. For instance, Carter and McCarthy (1995) studied spoken English grammar based on 30,000 words of transcribed conversations, the size of the corpus of office talk in Koester (2006) was about 34,000 words, in Cutting (2000) it was reported to be 25,000 words of students' conversation, and Foster (2001) used approximately 20,000 words of elicited speech to investigate the use of formulaic language.

Ethical considerations

Strictly following university ethical guidelines and procedures, permissions to record the spoken data were first sought from the university and then from CELE. After the permissions were granted by the UNNC Research Committee, prospective participants were recruited on a voluntary basis and fully informed of the process of data collecting. Along with a questionnaire (Appendix 5.2.1a), they were also given an information sheet that explained the study, with explicit information about how recordings were to take place, how data were to be presented, what they would be used for, how they would be used, and who could access the data. In data transcribing and annotating pseudonyms were used to protect participants' identities. All participants consented to be recorded over two academic semesters by signing their names on consent forms. They were also paid a small inconvenience allowance for their contribution to the corpus.

5.2.2   Recording

To collect naturally occurring interactions, it was decided to videotape the entire session of two fifty-minute periods of the *Discussion and Seminar Skills* class in the first two weeks starting from November 2009, and then to audio-tape it until the last teaching week in May 2010. The reasons are as follows. Oral samples are commonly collected by either audio or video recording, but when collecting speech samples in classroom settings, audio recording is used more widely than video recording, because it is considered less intrusive and less likely to generate observer's paradox (Ellis & Barkhuizen, 2005; Friedman, 2012). However, using audio recording alone makes it difficult for the researchers to have an idea of contextual information and to identify speakers by simply listening to their vocalizations. Video recording can provide clues to identify speakers and offer detailed contextual insights of what participants are physically doing at the time of recording (Friedman, 2012), but ensuring good quality of videotaped data requires special setup, such as positioning four cameras in every corner of the classroom (Knight, 2009). However, having cameras set up in that way, normal classroom settings would have to be rearranged, in which case, the level of authenticity of data would be compromised. Thus, it was decided to complement audio recording with some single-camera video recording.

Three other strategies were adopted to ensure the quality of the speech data, namely, longitudinal design and recording the whole session, choosing a student helper from each group of participants, and using a small recording device. To minimizes the effect of the observer's paradox and to reduce possible affective influences such as anxiety and stress, the study is longitudinal in design and spans over two academic semesters. With this time length, participants would forget about being recorded, feeling at ease communicating with their classmates and using their normal language in their familiar classrooms (Wray & Bloomer, 2006; Walsh, 2010). Considering that the presence of the researcher and a recording device, audio or video, may make the learners aware that they are being observed, and possibly affect the authenticity and naturalness of the data (Ellis & Barkhuizen, 2005), a student helper was recruited from each group of participants to switch on and off the recording device when the class began and ended, without the presence of the researcher. Moreover, before the class started, a small, pen-like recording device was placed in the middle of the two connected desks around which the groups of participants usually sat. These two strategies, having student helpers and using small recording device, also help to minimize the potential disturbance to the normal scheduled classroom activities (Foster, 1996; Biber, 2006). However, there were occasions when the recording equipment was not brought to the class or not turned on by the student helper, or the participants were told by the class tutor not to record the session, so the actual times of recording were different, varying from six to eleven. Accordingly, the amount of recorded data for each session of the class was different (Appendix 5.2).

5.2.3 Transcribing and annotating

To meet the aims of the study and to remain faithful to the authenticity, the recordings were transcribed following four steps (Thompson, 2004; Adolphs & Knight, 2010; Koester, 2010). Three applications, Audacity[1], SoundScriber[2], and ELAN (Hellwig et al., 2002-2009), were used to process the speech. First, the original recordings of each session were played with Audacity several times for the selection of the to-be-transcribed speech events, namely, oral presentations and group discussions. The nonselected portion of the interactions was either poor in the quality of recording or contained insufficient learner speech. Altogether fifty-seven speech events were selected, twenty-four of which were oral presentations, and thirty-three were group discussions (Appendix 5.2). Second, following the transcription conventions described in Wray and Bloomer (2006), SoundScriber was used for the standard orthographic transcriptions after the selected segments were exported using Audacity. The reason for choosing SoundScriber was mainly due to its walk feature, allowing the speech segment to be played automatically and repeatedly while it was being transcribed. The data were typed down to a level of detail that

---

1 Audacity, downloaded from http://audacity.sourceforge.net, last accessed January 2013.
2 SoundScriber, downloaded from http://lsa.umich.edu/eli/micase/soundscriber.html, last accessed September 2011.

captured all recognizable words and word fragments. Speaker turns were represented in vertical alignment, that is, each speaker's turn was written in sequence below the previous turn (Wray & Bloomer, 2006). All audible hesitation and nonlexical fillers, backchannel cues, and exclamations such as *erm* and *uhm* were spelled out as they were pronounced by participants. Moreover, if there were contractions heard in the data, they were transcribed in the same way as they were contracted, such as *I'll*, *gonna* and *I'm*, in order to be faithful to the original data. If there were cut-off words, they were marked with a hyphen at the end of the last audible letter. Repetitions and false starts were transcribed exactly as they were uttered, and numbers were also spelled out as words, with standard hyphenation rules applied. Mandarin Chinese were spelled out in Pinyin. In the case when languages other than English and Mandarin Chinese were used, they were transcribed using an approximate phonetic transliteration. Moreover, as pointed out in the ethics considerations, all participants' names were changed to pseudonyms. Other symbols used in the transcriptions can also be found in Appendix 5.2.3. Third, ELAN was used to measure the duration of silent pauses and transcribe other contextual features. It was planned to time all occurrences of juncture and nonjuncture pauses longer than 200 ms, with the time duration inserted in brackets. Based on the discussion in Subsection 2.3.2, the pause exclusion criterion was originally set from 200 ms to three seconds. However, while transcribing, it was found that the participants still carried on the topic after pausing longer than 3 seconds and that they seemed to have needed more time than usually expected to formulate the following utterance, which was possibly because they were in their relaxed, comfortable classroom environment, so they may not have had much time pressure from the context. Therefore, the higher cut-off point was not set but whatever time it took in the data was calculated. The oscillographic picture manifested on ELAN can visually distinguish silent pauses from phonation such as filled pauses, cough, laughter, and other paralinguistic features. Once the segment between the two wavy portions was selected, the length of pauses would appear automatically in milliseconds. A buffer zone of a couple of milliseconds at either end of the selected stretch of wave form was reserved, in order to avoid the over- or under-calculation of the pause duration. The last step was to make sure the wavy portions were actual words rather than paralinguistic features such as cough or laughter, and the orthographic consistency was checked with the audiotapes played on ELAN. While the first half of DSS was being transcribed, all pauses of 200 ms or longer were timed using ELAN. At the later stage, however, it was realized that the exact length of pauses was not directly related to the aims of the undertaking, so the rest of the pauses were unanimously indicated by <9.99> instead of being measured as those in the first half. Furthermore, speaker turns were verified and the transcriptions with pausing details were double checked before the data were annotated.

After transcribing, each speech event was saved separately as one plain text, with each header containing the details of the group name, the date when the data were recorded, the ongoing speech event, and the participants involved. When pauses were annotated, they were first differentiated into within-turn pauses and between-turn pauses, and then marked with different brackets. The between-turn pauses were put in parentheses, and within-turn pause angle brackets. Moreover, all nonlexical fillers such as *huh* and *mhum* were enclosed in angle brackets. Paralinguistic features such as laughter and cough were enclosed in angle brackets, such as <laugh> and <cough>, and clearing the throat or snapping fingers was indicated as <CT> or <SF>. Moreover, indecipherable speech was annotated as <XX> and speech was uttered in languages other than English was marked with the initials for that particular language. For instance, Mandarin Chinese was indicated as <MC> and Japanese as <JP>. Unwanted speech such as interruption from other groups or the class tutor was removed and marked clearly with explainations attached in angle brackets. In order to enable corpus software to extract clusters across turn boundaries, the participants were also annotated with their pseudonyms in angle brackets such as <LL> or <TB>, so that they can be either included or excluded when WS6.0 is applied. Moreover, participants' background information including their date of birth, courses they were studying at that time, language learning background, time spent living or studying abroad, and the English tests taken was put in Appendix 5.2.1b instead of being annotated in the corpus. Part of speech (POS) or error tagging was not applied. The reasons for excluding these details were that, first, it was aimed to keep the data clean (Sinclair, 1996; Hunston, 2002), and second, they were hardly related to the research questions.

5.3   MiniM

Comprising 63,845 words of transcribed academic speech, MiniM (Appendix 5.3), the reference native speaker corpus used for this study, was adapted based on thirteen files selected from MICASE (Simpson et al., 2002). To ensure its comparability, the speech included in MiniM had to be discussions or oral presentations contributed by native speakers of American English who were also junior undergraduates. In the following two subsections, the selection criteria for the reference corpus and the procedures of its construction are introduced.

5.3.1   Selecting criteria for MiniM

Choosing part of MICASE, an already existent corpus of academic spoken English which is also publicly accessible, and rebuilding it as a reference corpus is out of the consideration for its comparability and practicability. When a reference speech corpus is selected, a number of aspects need to be considered, including the original purpose of its construction, the social contexts and the location of data collection, speech events, participants' academic position and their interpersonal relations, the variety of English, methods of recording, and their chronologies (Ellis & Barkhuizen, 2005; Čermák, 2009; Granger, 2012; Gilquin & Granger, 2015). The purpose of building MICASE is principally to study various aspects of academic speech (Simpson et al., 2002). This is comparable to the design of compiling DSS, which is to examine Chinese learners' spoken English in authentic academic settings, with the specific aim of investigating the correlations between the production of formulaic language and fluency of spoken English. Since the social dimensions of communication have a requirement on the use of a certain speech genre and linguistic expressions (Segalowitz, 2010), accordingly, the use of formulaic language in academic speech can only be compared when the data are collected from similar communicative contexts (Biber et al., 1999; Hyland, 2012). The speech that constitutes DSS was gathered from UNNC, an international university in China where English is the medium of instruction and the working language on campus (Shu & Chen, 2010; Levrai, 2013), whereas the data of MICASE were collected at a large research university in the USA (Simpson et al., 2003). As DSS is composed

100

of naturally occurring academic speech, with classroom-based oral presentations and group discussions as the two typical speech events, the comparable corpus is thus expected to contain similar types of authentic spoken data. Accordingly, only the part about these two speech events occurring in settings such as classrooms, laboratories or study rooms was selected from MICASE. Speech in both corpora was recorded when participants were talking to their fellow classmates or class instructors. Considering that all the participants of DSS are Chinese first year university students, all of the selected speech in MiniM was contributed by native speakers of American English who were junior undergraduates. Thus, the part of the speech contributed by near-native speakers, nonnative speakers, or native speakers of non-American English in the original thirteen transcripts was removed. In terms of recording, DSS was predominantly audio-recorded, and all the retrieved sound files making up MiniM are audio recordings. With regard to chronology, DSS is longitudinal, lasting seven months, but MiniM is cross-sectional.

5.3.2   Building MiniM

Thirteen files from MICASE were selected and re-annotated to form MiniM, with detailed processes carried out as follows. First, the files were selected based on the screening filters discussed in the last subsection. According to the information provided by the MICASE browse webpage[1], transcripts were selected based on two main categories: one is concerned with speaker attributes, categorized based on the academic position or role, native speaker status, and first language, and the other is about transcript attributes, subcategorized based on speech event types, academic divisions, academic disciplines, participant levels, and interactivity ratings. Only the files contributed by native speakers of American English who were also junior undergraduates were selected, with the interactivity rating considered. Second, each audio file was listened to; a file was ruled out if junior undergraduates, native speakers of American English made little contribution to it. Third, the selected files were edited, with all irrelevant contributions removed, that is, the part of the speech contributed by other groups of speakers was deleted. As in DSS, pauses in MiniM

---

1   Available at http://quod.lib.umich.edu/cgi/c/corpus/corpus?c=micase;page=mbrowse, last accessed September 2011.

were annotated so that WS6.0 can automatically run the corpus data separately either with pauses included or excluded. Fourth, in the original transcript of MICASE, pauses were indicated in four different ways. Those of four seconds or longer were timed and indicated in angle brackets, so a pause of five seconds was coded as <P:05>. Pauses of two to three seconds were indicated by ellipses. Pauses of one to two seconds were indicated either by commas or periods. Moreover, a comma was used to indicate a mid-utterance pause which was also not marked with an obvious intonational contour, and a period was used for the pause accompanied by a falling tone (Simpson et al., 2003). To maintain the consistency with DSS and to make it easy to run WS6.0, the pauses which were originally marked by commas were all changed to be marked by <0.18>, periods were changed into <0.19>, and ellipses <0.29>. Pauses of four seconds or longer were indicated as <LP>, short for <long pause>. Additionally, participants, filled pauses, and other contextual features were annotated in the same way as DSS. The original transcripts downloaded from the MICASE webpage contained relatively rich information, but to keep the cleanness of the data and to be consistent with DSS, only the file name, speech events, and the number of the required participants were kept in the header. As MICASE offers open access, the original metadata can be easily checked on its website.

5.4   Chapter summary

The chapter has discussed the design of DSS, including the context of data collection, data types, participants, corpus size, ethical issues, and the decisions regarding data recording, transcribing, and annotating. It is then followed by a discussion of the comparability, the selecting criteria, and the building process for MiniM. This chapter and Chapter 4 have provided the methodological basis for testing the Holistic Hypothesis; the details of the mixed-methods data analysis are reported on in the following chapters.

Chapter 6

Quantitative Analysis

6.1 Introduction

This chapter is predominantly concerned with quantitative analysis, with the aim of answering the first research question and laying the foundation for the qualitative analysis in Chapters 7 and 8. Section 6.2 starts with the operational preparations, explaining the factors and the criteria adopted to identify the formulaic sequences from DSS and MiniM. Section 6.3 introduces WordList and Concord, the two programs on WS6.0 used for the subsequent analytical procedures. Section 6.4 elaborates the seven steps undertaken to extract the formulaic sequences and to establish which of them are produced with or without pauses in both corpora and in which types of them pauses tend to occur more frequently than others.

6.2 Factors and criteria for identifying formulaic sequences

Which approaches are used to identify formulaic language is decided by what features need to be investigated to answer the research questions posed (Wray, 2009; Schmitt, 2010). It is methodologically valid and practical to complement corpus linguistic methods with a psycholinguistic approach to identifying formulaic sequences, as the main aim of this study is to test the Holistic Hypothesis, that is, to examine whether pauses occur in formulaic sequences. Corpus methods are used for automatic extraction and contrastive analysis of formulaic sequences based on structure, frequency, and dispersion, whereas the psycholinguistic approach is adopted to explore the occurrence of pauses in the extracted clusters (Schmitt, 2010; Gries, 2015; Gries & Ellis, 2015; Myles & Cordier, 2017). The following subsections accordingly discuss in detail the rationale behind the structures selected, the cut-off points for frequency and dispersion, and pauses as an additional necessary criterion.

6.2.1 Syntactic structures

It is decided to extract two-to-six continuous word combinations in this study, although the length of formulaic sequences can vary from being as short as one word to longer than ten words, and three- to five-word sequences are what the majority of previous work centered on, as discussed in Chapter 3. Two-word formulaic sequences are the focus of this study, whichs however, are generally neglected in previous studies because of their being too common and subsumed in clusters of a longer length such as three- or four-word clusters (Altenberg, 1998; Simpson-Vlach & Ellis, 2010). Dahlmann and Adolphs (2009) seems to be the only corpus-based investigation of the production of the two-word formulaic sequence *I think* in native speaker speech. However, as far as learner language is concerned, two-word clusters need to be seriously taken into consideration. The reasons are as follows. First, the length of formulaic sequences produced by learners tends to be shorter than those produced by native speakers (Wray, 2002; Wood, 2006). Second, learners have been found to be more efficient in processing two-word clusters such as *you know* and *go away* than the formulaic sequences of other lengths (Schmitt et al., 2004). Third, two-word clusters are indeed the most frequent category of clusters (Carter & McCarthy, 2006). On the other hand, taking six words as the high-end exclusion criterion is because the average length of fluent units or tone units for most speakers is six words maximum (Pawley & Syder, 2000). Few clusters have been found longer than six words in corpus-based studies. McCarthy and Carter (2002) found that only one seven-word cluster occurred with the required frequency in their data.

Therefore, six words seems a practical cut-off length (McCarthy & Carter, 2002; Gries, 2015). Contracted forms such as *it's* and *don't* are taken as one-word clusters, although they can be counted as two words (Lin & Adolphs, 2009). The primary reason is that they have been treated as single words in most previous studies (Bybee, 2002; McCarthy & Carter, 2002; Biber et al., 2004; Carter & McCarthy, 2006; Biber & Barbieri, 2007; Biber, 2009; Götz & Schilk, 2011). Second, WS6.0, the corpus analysis software chosen to process the data, automatically treats contractions as one word. Moreover, when the speech of DSS was transcribed, contractions were written faithfully based on how they were pronounced in actual classroom-based interactions. In both corpora, for instance, if the textual representation is *don't*, it indicates the words *do* and *not* have been reduced as one word *don't* by the participants in the original recordings; otherwise, they must have been typed separately as two words, *do* and *not*.

The reasons for investigating continuous formulaic sequences only are as follows. First, spontaneous speech relies more on the use of continuous word combinations, which seem to be more directly linked to holistic production than non-continuous clusters (Schmitt, 2010; Strik et al., 2010; Gray & Biber, 2013). Second, the syntactic structure for speech formulae appears relatively fixed (Fillmore, 2000; Pawley, 2007). Most importantly, learners seem to have been more efficient in learning continuous formulaic sequences (Biber, 2009). As to the formulaic frames with open slots, it is difficult to tell whether adult learners' uses have more to do with holistic processing or they are more likely to be constructed online based on grammatical rules (Myles & Cordier, 2017). In addition, it is also intended to be practical and to limit the scope of the targets to be investigated, so the structures that regularly occur in a relatively fixed sequence are primarily considered.

The decision not to consider structural or meaning integrity is mainly because formulaic sequences may behave differently from human intuition, expectations, and understandings of language use (Biber et al., 1999; Adolphs, 2006). A dynamic systems perspective on the study of language requires investigating the data as they are and not ignoring any different or deviant forms (Larsen-Freeman, 2012). Moreover, as pointed out in Chapter 3, formulaic sequences do not necessarily have structural or semantic integrity. Many frequency-driven clusters are not complete either in meaning or in structure (Biber et al., 1999; Carter & McCarthy, 2006; Myles & Cordier, 2017). A great number of them are sub-phrasal and sub-clausal clusters such as *of the* and *but I don't*, but they have been repeatedly found to be widespread in previous studies (Biber et al., 1999; Adolphs, 2006). They may not necessarily have psychological salience, but they are indeed the basic building blocks of language and can perform discoursal functions, including bridging two different chunks (Biber et al., 2004; De Cock, 2004; Carter & McCarthy, 2006). As a matter of fact, they do have phonological and pragmatic integrity, which can be examined in terms of the possible occurrence of internal pauses and the context-based interpretation (McCarthy & Carter, 2002; Myles & Cordier, 2017). Most importantly, these fragmentary structures account for a major portion of the clusters extracted from DSS and MiniM (Appendices 6.4.1-3).

In the subsequent analysis, for descriptive purposes, formulaic sequences are categorized using their grammatical structures such as preposition-based or noun phrase formulaic sequences. This has been considered methodologically clear and valid (Biber et al., 1999; Carter & McCarthy, 2006; Hyland, 2008; Erman, 2009). Primarily, the boundaries of fluent speech units are more or less equivalent to those of phrases (Underhill, 1994; Grant, 2001; Chung, 2005; Levis & Wichmann, 2015), and phrases are believed to be the basic level of linguistic representation where forms reliably map onto meanings (Ellis, 2008; Sinclair, 2008), the taxonomies of which appear stable and uncontroversial (Carter & McCarthy, 2006). Although a large number of previous studies have classified formulaic sequences based on their functions (Altenberg, 1998; McCarthy & Carter, 2002; Biber et al., 2004; Simpson, 2004; Biber & Barbieri, 2007; Hyland, 2008, 2012; Simpson-Vlach & Ellis, 2010; Götz & Schilk, 2011), many of them actually perform overlapping functions, and their classifications are deemed problematic and imprecise (Nattinger & DeCarrico, 1992; Biber et al., 2004; Simpson, 2004; Simpson-Vlach & Ellis, 2010). Most importantly, when formulaic sequences are retrieved by WS6.0, some of them are inevitably grammatically incomplete, making it difficult to attribute the function to each cluster (Biber et al.; 1999; Carter & McCarthy, 2006; Hyland, 2008; Biber, 2009). It is also decided to use word classes such as nouns, verbs, and adjectives to describe the constituent elements of formulaic sequences. The descriptive terms are mostly adopted from Carter and McCarthy (2006), a recent reference for the corpus-based grammar of spoken English, and should be enough for this study, because the grammar of academic English is indicated to be in common with that of the English language in general, with no structure found unique in academic registers (Biber, 2006; Carter & McCarthy, 2006).

6.2.2 Frequency

After the length and the continuity are decided, frequency is used as the third screening filter. The reasons are as follows. First, frequency can act as an indicator of what patterns are regular or preferred in the cases where it is difficult to establish the norm for formulaic sequences, or where there are multiple structures available to express the same meaning (Pawley & Syder, 1983; Carter & McCarthy, 2006; Schmitt, 2010). Second, high frequency formulaic language is not only believed to form the basis for the development of lexico-grammatical knowledge but also to be more entrenched in learners' linguistic knowledge (Ellis, 1996; Leech, 2011; Gries & Ellis, 2015). Frequency may also be the measure that determines the processability of a formulaic sequence, as learners seem to have been more likely to process and automatize high frequency, meaning-transparent formulaic sequences than those of low frequency, to which they are rarely exposed (Ellis et al., 2008; Simpson-Vlach & Ellis, 2010; Conklin & Schmitt, 2012; Gries & Ellis, 2015; Myles & Cordier, 2017). Moreover, Skehan (2009) pointed out that the frequency of the lexis is the factor that influences learners' fluency performance. In fact, high frequency formulaic sequences are advised to be learned first due to their usefulness for comprehension and production (Leech, 2011; Gries, 2012).

Considering that DSS and MiniM are different in size, and that the two-word clusters are more common in the corpora than those of three to six words, it is decided to use different retrieval thresholds: nine times will be chosen as the minimal frequency threshold for the two-word clusters in DSS, three for their counterparts in MiniM; five times will be used for the three- to six-word clusters in DSS, but for their equivalents in MiniM, as long as they occur more than once, they will be included. Moreover, they are normalized for comparison. This is because first, the choice of the cut-off point for frequency has been arbitrary, and it is mainly decided by the sizes of the corpora involved and the goals of the research (Altenberg, 1998; McCarthy & Carter, 2002; Simpson, 2004; Simpson-Vlach & Ellis, 2010). In mainstream studies of formulaic sequences, the threshold frequency has been four (McCarthy & Carter, 2002), ten (Biber et al., 1999; Simpson-Vlach & Ellis, 2010), twenty (Simpson, 2004; Hyland, 2008), or forty times per million words (Biber et al., 2004). In some studies, instead of using one unitary frequency standard, different cut-off points of frequency have been adopted to retrieve the clusters of different lengths; otherwise, too many or too few clusters might be generated (Biber et al., 1999; Biber & Barbieri, 2007; Chen & Baker, 2014). Especially in CIA, frequencies are suggested to be normalized for comparative purposes when the involved corpora are of different sizes (Adolphs, 2006; Leech, 2011; Hyland, 2012; McEnery & Hardie, 2012; Gries, 2015). One million words has been commonly used as the basis for comparison, but this study uses 100,000 words, because it is closer to the size of the corpora and thus considered more appropriate than the usual norm (Adolphs, 2006; Leech, 2011).

The extraction being purely frequency-driven at this point is intended to include any variability and to avoid researcher subjectivity in picking and choosing certain types of formulaic sequences according to their intuition, excluding the clusters that are thought to have questionable formulaic status (De Cock, 2004; Biber, 2009; Götz & Schilk, 2011). The automatically extracted clusters may not only contain syntactically incomplete sequences but also those consisting of repetitive uses such as *no no no*. The reasons for including the former category in the target list have been elaborated in Subsection 6.2.1. Clusters involving repetitions have generally been eliminated in previous studies, because they tend to co-occur with hesitations and are considered meaningless at the semantic level (Altenberg, 1998; McCarthy & Carter, 2002). Considering that this study examines speech fluency, as long as the clusters consisting of repetitions or other types of hesitant speech meet the frequency and the dispersion requirements, they are included in the target list.

However, for the conventionality of formulaic language in a genre, frequency cannot be the only statistical indicator. First, it has been pointed out as not always a reliable criterion in the identification of formulaic language in learner language, given that a formulaic sequence may be frequently used by native speakers but not necessarily by learners, or vice versa (Myles & Cordier, 2017). Furthermore, unless a corpus is about learners' own output, a frequent cluster may not necessarily sound formulaic to learners (Gries, 2015). Frequency is also constrained by the size of a corpus. Some well-established formulaic sequences may have a low frequency of occurrence (Schmitt, 2010; Leech, 2011). Although MI scores are widely utilized as a complementary indicator for measuring the formulaicity between the components of low frequency clusters, learners have been found to be insensitive to MI scores (Ellis et al., 2008; Siyanova-Chanturia et al., 2011b), and the scores are not always reliable when measuring the clusters consisting of three or more words (Hyland, 2012; Gries, 2015). Consequently, dispersion is brought in as the fourth filter and discussed in the next subsection.

6.2.3 Dispersion

The reasons for bringing in dispersion as an indicator of formulaicity are as follows. Along with frequency, dispersion is not only a measure for the conventionality of formulaic language but also an indicator of preference in use (Leech, 2011; Myles & Cordier, 2017). But different from frequency, which generally asks how often a cluster occurs in a corpus, dispersion concerns in how many of the linguistic contexts that make up a corpus a cluster is encountered. Dispersion across corpora answers particularly whether or not a cluster has broad conventionality (Gries & Ellis, 2015). In CIA, the value of dispersion can reveal what common formulaic sequences are used in both native speech and learner speech, as native speakers and learners may have different formulaic language stored in their mental lexicon (Ellis et al., 2008; Wray, 2008; Schmitt, 2010), and learners may produce deviant or idiosyncratic forms of formulaic sequences (Myles et al., 1998; Ejzenberg, 2000; Myles & Cordier, 2017). As a cluster may have the same frequency in two corpora but be distributed in a different manner, a lack of filtering using dispersion as a criterion may produce skewed generalization (Gries, 2015). Moreover, investigating the dispersion and the frequency of formulaic language in use can help to explain speakers' motivations to communicate and their relations to the concerned social contexts (Segalowitz, 2010).

The cut-off values used for dispersion in previous studies appear to have been randomly decided and varied (Chen & Baker, 2014). In some studies, it has been suggested that formulaic language should be distributed in at least five different texts (Biber et al., 1999; Biber et al., 2004; Biber, 2009), but three different texts has also been used as the threshold for small specialized corpora (Biber & Barbieri, 2007; Chen & Baker, 2014). Moreover, Hyland (2008) used ten percent of texts as the selecting criterion. This is to say, if a corpus comprises twenty texts, only a cluster that occurs in two or more texts meets the requirements. On the other hand, a wider spread is recommended if a study seeks for a general list of formulaic language. To compile such a list that is relevant to the teaching of EAP courses, the cut-off point for dispersion of the formulae in academic speech in Simpson-Vlach and Ellis (2010) requires that they should occur in four out of five of the academic divisions that made up the corpora.

The above-mentioned cut-off standards are typically applied to written texts. For speech corpora, the way of calculating dispersion needs to be adjusted. As each text is generally written by one participant, the restriction of the clusters occurring in three or five texts actually indicates that three or five different writers are involved. In a spoken register, taking the transcribed text files comprising DSS for example, each text is contributed by three or more participants. Thus, the dispersion value regarding the spoken discourse should be calculated based on the number of the participants who are involved in each transcribed text file rather than the sheer number of text files making up one speech corpus. An examination of the dispersion value is thus required to ascertain how many speakers contribute to each speech text file. In this study, only the clusters that are used by more than three speakers and appear in both the DSS and MiniM are counted. As to be demonstrated in Subsection 6.4.1, if the dispersion value of a cluster is marked as one in either DSS or MiniM, a second step is scheduled to check how many speakers have used it. Only the cluster that is confirmed to have been used by four or more participants will be further investigated. Actually, Schmitt and Carter (2004) pointed out that a formulaic sequence is supposed to appear in more than two different participants' speech.

Although the corpus methods based on structure, frequency, and dispersion can identify efficiently the clusters with fixed structures, they seem to have challenges in retrieving automatically the formulaic sequences with structural variations (Schmitt,

2010). Moreover, it has been pointed out that using a corpus-based approach alone to extract formulaic language from orthographic transcriptions can cause some problems (Dahlmann & Adolphs, 2009; Lin, 2010, 2012). To cope with the issues, and along with other justifications provided below, the psycholinguistic approach is thus adopted, with pauses bought in as a necessary criterion for the identification (Bybee, 2006; Myles & Cordier, 2017).

6.2.4 Pauses

The reasons why pauses are one crucial factor in analyzing formulaic sequences are as follows. Primarily, natural pauses are not expected to occur in formulaic language (Chambers, 1997; Pawley & Syder, 2000; De Jong, 2016), which forms the basis of the Holistic Hypothesis, but native speakers and learners are found to have produced formulaic sequences with pauses (Schmitt et al., 2004; Dahlmann & Adolphs, 2007, 2009; Erman, 2007; Gao & Fan, 2011; Wu, 2012). Only by examining pausing and the production of formulaic sequences in native and learner speech, can it be seen which types of formulaic sequences tend to be used with or without pauses by both groups of speakers. Second, pauses need to be taken as an essential and necessary criterion of identifying formulaic language in learner speech, since the structures of learners' formulaic sequences do not appear to be quite the same as those in native speech (Pawley & Syder, 1983, 2000; Ejzenberg, 2000; Wray, 2002, 2008; Myles & Cordier, 2017). Based on the review in Chapter 3, learners may have only acquired part of formulaic language, and accordingly, produce shorter or incomplete formulaic sequences; some of them may not have the holistic awareness that formulaic sequences would be preferably used as single units (Wray, 2002; Schmitt et al., 2004; Ellis et al., 2008; Ellis, 2012). As to the formulaic sequences with structural flexibility, learners may have even more challenges in the process of automatizing them, thus presenting different levels of developmental features in production (Myles et al., 1998; Schmitt et al., 2004; Schmitt, 2010; Myles & Cordier, 2017).

There are many causes regarding why pauses may occur in formulaic language. The most direct one seems to be that formulaic sequences either have not been conventionalized in the speech community or not been fully automatized by language users (Pawley & Syder, 2000; Wood, 2001, 2004, 2006, 2010; Erman, 2007; Myles & Cordier, 2017). Given the complexity of speech production, pausing may also be evidence of online planning pressure as well as cognitive stress in speech formulation and articulation (Bygate, 1998; Biber et al., 1999; Segalowitz, 2000; Ellis, 2003; Schmitt et al., 2004; Erman, 2007). Furthermore, they may be caused by individual speakers' pausing preferences or other external factors, including the time available for planning, rhetorical requirements, or unfamiliarity with the subject matter (Zellner, 1994; Guillot, 1999; Pawley & Syder, 2000; Segalowitz, 2010). Filled pauses including repetitions and false starts are considered as testaments to the attempt that speakers are making to monitor their speech online, reformulating the speech, or trying to prevent their speaking turns from being taken over by another participant (Biber et al., 1999; Guillot, 1999; Yule, 2010; Foster, 2013).

Pauses analyzed in Section 6.4 in this chapter as well as in Chapters 7 and 8 include silent pauses which are longer than 200 ms, nonlexical fillers, drawls, repetitions, false starts, and repairs (Riggenbach, 1991; Zellner, 1994; Freed, 2000; Carter & McCarthy, 2006). They are widely regarded as the boundary markers for fluent speech units, so they are carefully marked and annotated in a way that they can be either ignored or included when formulaic sequences are extracted from DSS and MiniM (Pawley & Syder, 2000; Wood, 2006; Myles & Cordier, 2017). It has been consistently supported that formulaic sequences constitute fluent speech runs between pauses, and that they are embedded in fluent units, but in learner speech, a fluent unit is not simply equivalent to one formulaic sequence (Raupach, 1984; Oppenheim, 2000; Pawley & Syder, 2000; Myles & Cordier, 2017). To include as many formulaic sequences as possible, pauses are thus ignored at the first-time extraction in this study. Due to the automatic calculation of WS6.0, if pauses were not ignored, there is a high probability that the sequences with them would have been left out. However, when the formulaic sequences are extracted for the second time, pauses are included, which are then aligned with the pause-ignored clusters retrieved from the first extraction. Pairing the pause-included with the pause-excluded clusters will generate results about which formulaic sequences have internal pauses.

6.3   Programs of analysis

WS6.0 has been widely used in corpus-based studies by many different language students, teachers, and researchers (McCarthy & Carter, 2002; Evison, 2010; Scott, 2015). This software package makes it possible to analyze linguistic elements both from a cross-corpus and a within-corpus comparative perspective (Scott, 2015). Two main programs, WordList and Concord, of WS6.0 were used to process the corpus data in this research. WordList enables automatic retrieval of individual words or clusters, providing information of their frequency, distribution in texts, and the percentage they take in a corpus (Scott, 2015). A frequency list shows how many instances of a word or a cluster appear in a corpus. The distribution of words or clusters in texts is marked by the value of dispersion, referring to in how many texts a word or a cluster occurs in a corpus. The percentage can either indicate the proportion of the occurrence of a word or a cluster in relation to all the words in the texts, or that of the number of the text files where a word or a cluster occurs in relation to the overall text files from which the word list is created. Moreover, both words and clusters can be sorted based on frequency or in alphabetical order. In this study, as the two corpora involved have been well annotated with pauses, WordList is applied directly to extracting formulaic sequences, with pauses ignored for the first extraction but included in the second extraction, according to the designated length, frequency of occurrence, and dispersion.

Concord is the most comprehensive program to display all the relevant concordance lines of a given word or cluster (Scott, 2015), offering co-texts and contexts to examine its actual uses, including collocates and colligations (Hunston, 2002; Granger, 2009, 2012; Evison, 2010; Gries, 2012; Hasko, 2013). The investigated word or cluster in the center is called the node and is displayed in a vertical arrangement, with the preceding and following co-texts presented on the computer screen. The span size of the node is generally three to five words to the left and to the right (Hunston, 2002; Gries, 2012), and the original source text of the investigated word or cluster can also be traced using Concord (Scott, 2015). However, this program simply generates all the instances of the searched linguistic item in the co-texts (Scott, 2015), and it is the researchers who observe the patterns in their immediate linguistic contexts and explicate the linguistic features observed (Gries, 2010; Hunston, 2010; McCarthy & O'Keeffe, 2010). In this study, Concord is used to generate the concordance lines, to check dispersion, to refine frequency, and to explore the patterns of pausing in and around formulaic language.

6.4   Procedures of quantitative analysis and results

Based on the discussion in Section 6.2, formulaic sequences studied in this book are restricted to continuous two-to-six-word clusters that occur with the designated frequencies and are used by more than three speakers in DSS and in MiniM. Altogether seven steps are taken to explore whether the extracted formulaic sequences are produced as wholes by learners and by native speakers, and if not, which of them are more likely to be produced with or without pauses. The steps are illustrated below, with the results presented in the subsection after.

6.4.1   Procedures

In the first step, with pauses ignored, five cluster lists in DSS, namely, two-word, three-word, four-word, five-word, and six-word, and five correspondent lists in MiniM were automatically extracted using WS6.0. Due to the different sizes of the two corpora, different cut-off frequencies were used to retrieve clusters of different length and later normalized for comparison. For two-word clusters, the minimal raw frequency threshold was set on nine times in DSS, and three in MiniM; for three-to-six-word clusters, it was five times in DSS and more than once in MiniM. This was accomplished by following five steps, four of which are displayed in the screen prints titled PrtScs 6.1, 6.2, 6.3 and 6.4 in Appendix 6.1. First, WordList on the main panel of WS6.0 was selected and then "Customise" under Settings in the menu list was chosen (PrtSc 6.1). Second, on Advanced Settings, Tags & Markup was clicked, with the two symbols, <*> and (*), typed in the blank marked as "Mark-up to ignore" (PrtSc 6.2). Third, "New…" under File in WordList was chosen, with the texts from DSS or MiniM respectively imported, and the two frequency-based index files for both corpora were created (Appendices 6.2 and 6.3). Next, the "Clusters" option under Compute in the menu list of the index file was selected (PrtSc 6.3). Lastly, the number from two to six in the slots designed for the selection of the cluster size was respectively entered, with nine or five in the slot for the minimum frequency decided on and the option of "omit any containing #" chosen, and the "OK" button was clicked at the bottom of the setting entitled "Cluster choices" (PrtSc 6.4). Each of the cluster lists was then exported to be saved one by one according to the lengths of the clusters in Excel files after the names of DSS2wCs PsIgnored, DSS3wCs PsIgnored, DSS4wCs PsIgnored, DSS5wCs PsIgnored, DSS6wCs PsIgnored, MiniM2wCs PsIgnored, MiniM3wCs PsIgnored, MiniM4wCs PsIgnored, MiniM5wCs PsIgnored, and MiniM6wCs PsIgnored. In these file names, for instance, 2wCs was short for two-word clusters and PsIgnored for "with Pauses Ignored". This way, if the spreadsheet is entitled "MiniM6wCs PsIgnored", it is about the six-word pauses-ignored clusters extracted from MiniM. These ten lists were saved separately in Appendices 6.4–6.13.

The second step was normalizing the frequency of each cluster per 100,000 words in both corpora. For two-word clusters, the normalizing cut-off point was decided on ten times per 100,000 words, and for three- to six-word clusters, the minimum sufficient condition was more than five times per 100,000 words, the reasons for which have been discussed in Subsection 6.2.2. The normalized frequencies are automatically calculated in the Excel spreadsheet by first dividing the raw frequency of each cluster by the total number of the words in either of the corpora, and then multiplying the results by 100,000; they are presented in the last column of the Appendices 6.4–6.13.

In the third step, the clusters with the required normalized frequency generated from DSS were paired with their counterparts from MiniM. This was the first time that between-group comparison was conducted in the analysis, with the aim of selecting the clusters that occurred in both corpora with the designated normalized frequency. First, two contrasting cluster lists, entitled DSS2wCs PsIgnored and MiniM2wCs PsIgnored, were aligned in the same Excel spreadsheet; using the DSS list as the baseline, each cluster with the required frequency was copied into the blank of the "search" function, and then, "find next" was clicked, to check whether it had a counterpart in MiniM. It was found that 469 two-word, 154 three-word, and 19 four-word clusters met the criteria, as displayed in Appendices

6.14–6.16, respectively titled as 2wCsinBoth PsIgnored, 3wCsinBoth PsIgnored and 4wCsinBoth PsIgnored. No five- or six-word cluster was found in either corpora with the required frequency. Thus, the rest of the steps introduced in the following paragraphs are only applied to two-to-four-word clusters.

The fourth step was checking the dispersion value of each cluster generated from the third step, with the aim of excluding the clusters that were used by fewer than four speakers. As discussed in Subsection 6.2.3, the clusters selected must be used by more than three speakers, so those occurring in three or fewer participants' speech were deleted. For the 469 two-word clusters, all of them in both corpora meet this criterion, although while checking, the cluster *the hydrogen* appeared suspicious. As can be seen in Appendix 6.14, its displayed number under Texts is two in DSS and one in MiniM, which means that *the hydrogen* appears in two texts in DSS and one in MiniM, so there is a possibility that this cluster might have been used by two or three participants. An examination of its co-texts in DSS reveals that *the hydrogen* was used by three participants under the pseudonyms of JJ, TC, and JM in the text marked as <J20100331J-GD-4>, and it was used by one speaker indicated as TT in <T20100331T-GD-3>; in MiniM it was used by two speakers indicated as SB and SD in <2-2SGR200JU125-5>. Thus, this cluster was actually used by six different speakers, although occurring in only three texts.

With regard to the three-word and four-word clusters, as indicated in Appendices 6.15 and 6.16, the dispersion value for each frame is zero, so the check of dispersion was focused on the specific items listed under the frame. Take the three-word frame *I think* * for instance, although the number under the "Texts" is zero, a list of specific three-word clusters such as *I think the*, *I think it* and *I think that* are provided in the "Lemmas" slot and their frequencies are marked in their subsequent square brackets. Thus, the dispersion value for each specific three-word or four-word cluster can actually be found in the "Texts" slot. With frames discarded, 152 three-word (Appendix 6.17) and 14 four-word specific clusters (Appendix 6.18) were examined for their dispersion values. In the three-word cluster list, one dubious item was *lot of time*, which also made up a four-word cluster *a lot of time*, whose dispersion value is one in DSS and one in MiniM. An investigation of its context reveals that it was only used by two speakers. Therefore, *lot of time* and *a lot of time* were deleted from the lists. After these four steps, with pauses ignored, each cluster list contains only those that meet both the required frequency and dispersion criteria. The remaining are 469 two-word, 151 three-word, and 13 four-word clusters, respectively presented in Appendices 6.4.1–6.4.3.

In the fifth step, WordList on WS6.0 was used once again to extract automatically two-to-four-word clusters from DSS and MiniM, but this time, with pauses calculated. Similar to the process of generating pauses-ignored clusters in the first round, WS6.0 can easily manage this by not inputting anything in the blank of "Mark-up to ignore" in Tags & Markup on the panel of Advanced Settings (PrtSc 6.5) and not ticking the option of "omit any containing #" on "Cluster choices" (PrtSc 6.6). The cut-off frequency point was decided on once, with the aim of including any possible equivalent to the clusters that have been generated following the first four steps. These cluster lists were also exported to be saved respectively in the Excel spreadsheet based on their lengths, titled DSS2wCs PsIncluded, DSS3wCs PsIncluded, DSS4wCs PsIncluded, MiniM2wCs PsIncluded, MiniM3wCs PsIncluded, and MiniM4wCs PsIncluded (Appendices 6.19–6.24).

The sixth step was about comparing and refining within individual groups the frequency of each cluster with and without the inclusion of pauses, to confirm whether it was accurately calculated and to reveal which clusters were produced with or without pauses for each group. First, within the learner group, the frequency of each pause-ignored cluster, which remained after the first four steps conducted above, was compared with its pause-included equivalent extracted following the fifth step. This is to find out for the learners which clusters have the same or different frequencies when pauses are considered, or in other words, which clusters are not possibly interrupted by pauses and which are. The same comparative procedure was then conducted with the native speech, to find out what was the case with the native speaker clusters. The frequency differences calculated by comparing the pause-ignored with pauses-included clusters at this point reveal which clusters are most likely to be interrupted by pauses, but they do not necessarily all result from the occurrence of internal pauses. The reason is that, when the mark-up for pauses and other paralinguistic features was ignored, WS6.0 may have automatically included the sequences that occurred across words, units, or turns, and mistaken them as clusters; detailed examples are provided in Appendices 7.2a and 7.2b in Chapter 7.

The refining process was thus conducted to verify whether the frequency of each cluster was about the actual instances that occurred in DSS and MiniM, and to eliminate the three types of frequency discrepancies caused by the automatic cross-word, cross-unit, and cross-turn calculation using WS6.0. It was conducted following three steps. First, the pauses-ignored two-word, three-word, or four-word clusters were sorted based on frequency. Second, the WordList setting was changed, and the pause mark-ups including <*> and (*) in the blank of "Mark-up to ignore" under Tags & Markup on Advanced Settings were deleted. Third, each cluster in the pauses-ignored list on WordList was right-clicked, with the option of "Concordance" chosen (PrtSc 6.7). By doing this, the concordance lines of this cluster were generated under Concord, as shown on the right side of PrtSc 6.8. Following these three steps, the concordance lines generated only include the instances of the cluster that were produced as wholes, that is, without pauses.

By comparing the frequency of a cluster displayed on the pause-ignored cluster list and the number of concordance lines listed on Concord, it can be clearly seen how many instances of this cluster were free from internal pauses (PrtSc 6.8), which conversely indicates how many of them were either produced with pauses or the frequency was over-calculated. If the frequency of a cluster remains the same regardless of the consideration of pauses, or in other words, when a cluster is free from internal pauses, all of its concordance lines are displayed on Concord. If the frequency differs, simply right clicking and choosing "Concordance" will not be able to generate all of the concordance lines, as these two actions can only produce the lines in which the cluster is used as one holistic unit. For instance, the frequency of *because of* in the pauses-ignored cluster list was 42, to verify whether this was the actual number of the instances that occurred, the cluster *because of* was right clicked and run by Concord. It can be seen that 41 concordance lines were generated (PrtSc 6.8). This clearly demonstrates that 41 instances of this cluster were produced free from internal pauses, but one instance of *because of* was missing. Subsequently, a new search with a pause marked in the cluster, *because * of*, was conducted by clicking "New…" under File on Concord (PrtSc 6.9). Double clicking the line of *because * of* (PrtSc 6.10) produced its context in the source text presented below.

<TB> (0.33) give up the country give up the profit from this country because=

<TT> =of course not of course not=

<TC> =just as XX mentioned that the US market becomes smaller and smaller <0.55> you you have to <0.32> enter those <0.20>

As can be seen, the components of this instance, *because* and *of*, were in fact produced by two different speakers, <TB> and <TT>, so the actual occurrence of *because of* as a unit is 41 times, and the number 42 indicated in the pauses-ignored two-word cluster list were over-calculated.

With regard to the three-word clusters, pauses might occur at two different locations. If * refers to the location of a pause and ABC represents a three-word cluster, the possible placement of pauses can be either A*BC or AB*C. Thus, in the case where the number of concordance lines generated was different from the frequency of a three-word cluster that displayed in the pauses-ignored list, a further search of A*BC and AB*C was conducted. For instance, to verify the frequency of the three-word cluster *I think the*, which is 43 in the pause-ignored cluster list, first, *I think the* was right-clicked, and "Concordance" was chosen to generate its concordance lines (PrtSc 6.11). Displayed were 36 lines; the rest not being shown suggests that they are either interrupted by pauses, or, as in the case of *because of*, the frequency might have been over-calculated. Since *I think* has been established as a two-word cluster free from internal pauses (Appendix 6.25), the pattern of *I * think the* can be disregarded. A second search of this cluster thus focused on *I think * the*, with "New…" under "File" (PrtSc 6.11) clicked. PrtSc 6.12 reveals that six of them were interrupted by pauses, but one *I think the* was still missing. Thus, a third search of *I think * * was conducted, with the aim of generating a wider context to locate where the missing item was. As can be seen in PrtSc 6.13, in line 137, *I think* and *the* were spoken by the two speakers, <JY> and <JJ>. The actual context is presented below:

<JY> (9.99) <er> <9.99> no no not totally <9.99> yeah it may have some: benefits for the: economy <9.99> <er> but <er> generally I think

119

<JJ> (9.99) the question is only ask about the [[tourism
<JM>   [[tourism =

While refining the frequency of the clusters such as *how can you* and *you think about*, both A*BC and AB*C forms were examined. Following the same lead, in the four-word clusters, the internal pauses may occur at three different locations: if ABCD were used as a representative form for a four-word cluster, A*BCD, AB*CD, and ABC*D were respectively adopted to start a new search.

After the frequencies of the clusters in all groups were compared and refined, the results are now crystal clear and the conclusion can be safely drawn: the same frequencies show clearly which clusters were produced as wholes in learner and native speech, and the frequency discrepancies are the number of the instances of the clusters that were produced with pauses. With respect to the learner speech, the results show that 178 two-word, 68 three-word and 9 four-word clusters present the same frequencies, but the frequencies of 291 two-word, 83 three-word and 4 four-word clusters are different (Appendices 6.25–6.27). As to the native speech, 308 two-word, 112 three-word and 12 four-word clusters have the same frequencies, but 161 two-word, 39 three-word and 1 four-word clusters show the different frequency information (Appendices 6.28–6.30). These are also summarized in Figure 6.1.

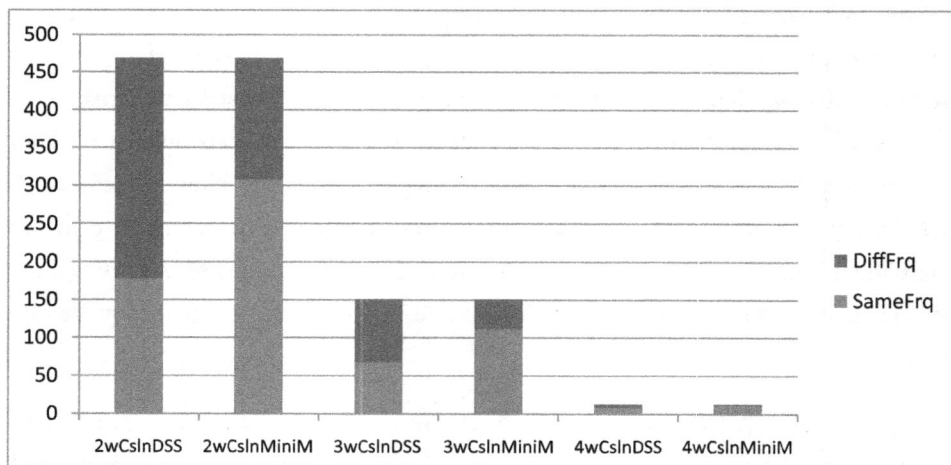

Figure 6.1   Quantitative results of within-group comparison

6.4.2   Quantitative results

Cross-checking the cluster lists generated above, this step finalized the results regarding which clusters showed the same frequencies in both corpora, which clusters had the same frequencies in one corpus but not in the other, and which clusters had frequency differences in both corpora, which accordingly concluded in which corpus and in which instances of the clusters pauses occurred. The results are summarized into four categories (Figure 6.2), with percentages provided in Table 6.1 and specific clusters provided in Appendices 6.4.4–6.4.7. As can be seen, 150 two-word, 56 three-word, and 9 four-word clusters have the same frequencies in DSS and MiniM (Appendix 6.4.4); the relevant numbers are indicated under the abbreviation HoInBo in Table 6.1 and Figure 6.2, signifying that the clusters were holistically produced in both corpora. The frequencies of 28 two-word and 12 three-word clusters are the same in DSS but different in MiniM (Appendix 6.4.5), indicated as OHoInD in the table and in the figure, suggesting that these clusters were only produced without pauses in DSS. Moreover, 158 two-word, 56 three-word, and 3 four-word clusters display different frequencies in DSS, but they have the same frequency information in MiniM (Appendix 6.4.6). They are indicated as OHoInM and mean that the clusters were comparatively only produced as wholes in MiniM. Lastly, the frequencies of 133 two-word, 27 three-word, and one four-word clusters are different in both corpora (Appendix 6.4.7); the numbers are indicated under nHoInbo, denoting that these clusters were not holistically produced in either of the corpora.

Table 6.1   **Percentages of two-to-four-word clusters that were produced as wholes in DSS and MiniM, with pauses in either of them, and with pauses in both**

Clusters	HoInBo	OHoInD	OHoInM	nHoInBo
2wCs	32%	6%	34%	28%
3wCs	37%	8%	37%	18%
4wCs	69%	0%	23%	8%

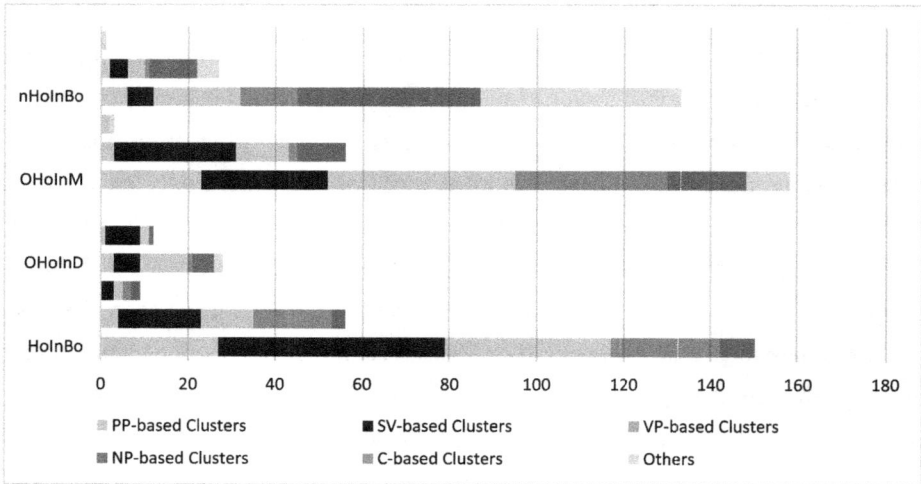

Figure 6.2   Between-group comparison of different types of clusters

As shown in Appendices 6.4.4–6.4.7, the clusters of each category appear different in terms of grammatical structure. As to the two-word formulaic sequences, six types can be identified. The most frequent ones are prepositions followed by determiners, such as *of the*, *to the*, and *in the*; known as prepositional clusters, preposition-based clusters, or the PP-based for short, they have been considered as the most frequent academic bundles (Biber et al., 1999; Carter & McCarthy, 2006; Hyland, 2008; Biber, 2009). Subject verb clusters, or the SV-based, are the second most frequent structure, referring to the combinations of pronoun subjects and verbs such as *I think*, *it is*, and *we can*, with verbs being lexical, auxiliary, or modal (Carter & McCarthy, 2006; Hyland, 2012). The third type is the verb phrase clusters, hence the VP-based, including verb phrases such as *want to*, *will be*, and *talk about*, or verbs followed by articles or determiners, such as *is a*, *is the*, and *have a* (Carter & McCarthy, 2006). Noun phrase clusters or NP-based clusters rank fourth; they center around noun phrases such as *the first*, *a lot*, and *the problem*, and are either followed by a relational clause or preceded with a modifier. Being register-specific, noun phrases have been largely ignored in previous studies (Hyland, 2012; Chen & Baker, 2014), although they are considered common in spoken discourse (Biber et al., 1999; Carter & McCarthy, 2006; Hyland, 2008). The clusters consisting of conjunctions co-occurring with pronouns, adverbs, or part of noun phrases are treated as the fifth type, hence the conjunction-based or C-based as indicated in Figure 6.2 or Tables 6.2–6.3, including *and the*, *and it*, and *if you*, which are also the crucial structure in spoken English (Carter & McCarthy, 2006). The sixth and also the last group, indicated as "Others" in the figures and tables in this section, is about the different uses of *that* co-occurring with other linguistic elements, which are generally used to introduce a relative or a nominal clause, such as *that is*, *that the*, and *is that*. To make it easy to calculate and group the rest of the remaining few retrieved from DSS and MiniM, repetitions such as *the the* and other combinations including *you a* and *them to* are also included in this last group.

The structures of three- and four-word clusters are categorized based on those of the two-word clusters and appear similar to the findings concluded in Carter and McCarthy (2006: 829-834). As to the three-word clusters, the SV-based clusters are found to have occurred extensively, consisting of subject verb combinations followed by other elements, such as *I think the*, *I think it's*, and *you want to*, or preceded by conjunctions or other lexical items, including *and I think*, *so I think*, and *I I think*. Another common group is made up of noun phrases, hence the NP-based, for instance, *a lot of*, *lot of people*, and *one of the*. Clusters consisting of verb phrases, that is, the VP-based clusters, such as *talk about the*, *would like to*, and *want to say*, also occur frequently. Most frequent four-word clusters include NP-, VP-, and SV-based clusters, such as *a lot of people*, *going to talk about*, and *I would like to*.

Table 6.2   Numbers of different types of clusters in each category

Types	HoInBo			OHoInD			OHoInM			nHoInBo		
	2w	3w	4w	2w	3w	4w	2w	3w	4w	2w	3w	4w
PP-based	27	4	0	3	1	0	23	3	1	6	2	0
SV-based	52	19	3	6	8	0	29	28	0	6	4	0
VP-based	38	12	2	11	2	0	43	12	1	20	4	0
NP-based	25	18	2	1	0	0	35	2	0	13	1	0
C-based	8	3	2	5	1	0	18	11	0	42	11	0
Others	0	0	0	2	0	0	10	0	1	46	5	1

Note: 2w, 3w, and 4w are respectively short for two-word, three-word, and four-word clusters.

Table 6.3　Percentages of different types of clusters that were produced as holistic units

Clusters	Total	HoInBo	OHoInD	Percentage	OHoInM	Percentage
PP-based	70	31	4	50%	27	83%
SV-based	155	74	14	57%	57	85%
VP-based	145	52	13	45%	56	74%
NP-based	97	45	1	47%	37	85%
C-based	101	13	6	19%	29	42%
Others	65	0	2	3%	11	17%

Pauses were found in all types of the clusters. Based on the detailed calculation presented in Tables 6.2 and 6.3 as well as in Figure 6.2, SV-based clusters are the type that are most likely produced without pauses in DSS and in MiniM, whereas the conjunction-based clusters and those consisting of *that*, repetitions, or other elements, indicated as "C-based" and "Others" respectively in the tables above and Figure 6.2, are most likely disrupted by internal pauses. The percentages each type of holistically produced clusters accounts for differ. As can be seen, the predominant majority, 85%, of the SV-based were found as wholes in MiniM; by contrast, more than half (57%) of them were produced without pauses in DSS. A significant majority (83% and 85%) of the PP- and NP-based and well over two-thirds (74%) of the VP-based clusters were uttered without pauses in MiniM; in DSS, just half of the PP-based, and slightly under half (47% and 45%) of the NP- and VP-based clusters were found free from internal pauses. The holistically produced conjunction-based clusters in MiniM were more than twice those in DSS, but their overall numbers were small.

In summary, either in DSS or in MiniM formulaic sequences were not entirely produced as holistic units. Among the two-word clusters that met the requirements of structure, frequency, and dispersion, learners placed pauses in the instances of nearly two-thirds of them, whereas native speakers produced approximately two-thirds of the equivalents completely as wholes. As to the three-word clusters, the majority of them had the instances that were produced with pauses by learners, whereas native speakers produced a significant majority of them entirely without pauses. Regarding the four-word clusters, more than half of them were produced without pauses in DSS and in MiniM, but the total number of the clusters involved was quite limited. Cross-checking the occurrence of pauses in the two-word and three-word clusters, we found approximately one-third of the clusters were entirely used as holistic units by both groups of speakers, nearly another one-third of them that had instances with pauses in DSS but not in MiniM, and in the remaining one-third, most of the clusters had instances that were produced with pauses in both corpora, with a small number of them produced as single units in DSS but having several instances with pauses in MiniM. Furthermore, pauses occurred in the clusters of different structures. In both corpora, the SV-based were most extensively produced as wholes; the clusters consisting of conjunctions or *that* co-occurring with other elements appeared most likely to be produced with pauses. Regarding PP-, NP-, and VP-based clusters, significantly more instances of them were uttered as holistic units in MiniM than in DSS.

6.5 Chapter summary

To answer the first research question, that is, whether learners or native speakers would place pauses in formulaic sequences, and if they did, in which formulaic sequences they tended to pause, the screening filters and the relevant criteria used for the identification of formulaic sequences in the two corpora were first discussed. WordList and Concord used for analysis were then introduced. Following seven steps, both learners and native speakers were found to have placed pauses in all types of formulaic sequences. Instances of the SV-based category were extensively produced as wholes; those consisting of conjunctions, *that*, repetitions, or other elements were most likely to be produced with pauses. Moreover, native speakers clearly produced substantially more clusters of all types as holistic units than learners did.

The results of the analysis in this chapter merely provide quantitative information of which formulaic sequences were produced without or with pauses. A closer contextual analysis is needed to investigate the patterns of internal pausing, the causes of its occurrence, and whether there is any group or individual difference in pausing in formulaic sequences. Apart from these, how pauses behave in and around high frequency formulaic sequences is needed in order to assess the Holistic Hypothesis comprehensively. These two inquiries are addressed respectively in the next two chapters.

Chapter 7

Formulaic Sequences with Internal Pauses

7.1　Introduction

Based on the quantitative results obtained in the last chapter, internal pausing, or pausing in formulaic sequences, occurred in DSS and in MiniM. This chapter is thus dedicated to exploring the patterns of internal pausing, the possible causes of its occurrence, and the individual and the group differences in pausing in the production of academic formulae. It is organized as follows. Presented first are the procedures undertaken to analyze the clusters that have instances produced with pauses, and then in respective corpus the meticulous investigation of internal pausing and five types of formulaic sequences, namely the PP-, NP-, VP-, SV-, and conjunction-based. The examined instances are generally provided with more than three words on both sides as their co-texts. Clusters of two words are the focus, primarily because they are indeed the lion's share in both corpora and most readily retrieved by WS6.0. The justifications for targeting them have been provided in Chapter 6. To limit the scope of the analysis, the recurrent clusters of *that* and other elements categorized under the sixth type in the last chapter are excluded from the following investigation.

7.2   Analytical procedures

In both corpora, the patterns of internal pausing, the causes, and the individual and the group differences in the pausing behavior related to the production of formulaic sequences were investigated following four steps. First, to calculate the frequency discrepancies, with the frequencies of the pause-ignored clusters contrasted with those of the pause-included ones in each Excel spreadsheet. Second, the clusters were sorted in the order of the just-calculated differences, marked in different colors, and investigated qualitatively in their co-texts and contexts. Integrated with the same practice at the sixth step of the quantitative analysis elaborated in Subsection 6.4.1 in the last chapter, any over- or mis-calculation caused by the automatic run of WS6.0 was eliminated.

As can be seen in Appendices 7.2a and 7.2b, cross-word, cross-unit, and cross-turn calculations are the three potential causes of the over- and mis-calculated frequencies. Cross-word calculation is a result of ignoring the unintelligible speech or paralinguistic features annotated in the angle brackets between two words; it is considered merely noise to holistic production, since the components of the relevant instances do not occur next to each other. Cross-unit calculation occurs between two obviously different syntactic units when the contribution from a class tutor or a group member is included by WS6.0, or when annotated contextual information such as participants' writing or addressing questions is overlooked because of the automatic retrieval. Some of the instances involving cross-unit calculation might have been produced as wholes if without the interruption from other speakers, as shown in the clusters *get the*, *the problem*, *you know*, and *kind of*. Cross-turn calculation is due to WS6.0 taking the words that span different speaker turns as belonging to the same cluster. Some instances of the kind may be in fact the evidence of participants co-constructing speech flow, as demonstrated in the examples of *because of* and *the second*. As to some, their components may be simply part of different speaking turns, as can be seen from the instances of *be a* and *it is*. Because any contribution from the participants, indecipherable speech, turn-taking, and observable paralinguistic features are clearly annotated, these over- and mis-calculated instances can be directly recognized in the transcripts of both corpora.

After the over- and mis-calculated instances were eliminated, clusters that still presented different frequencies in DSS and in MiniM were investigated for their internal pausing, along with their grammatical structures, co-texts in the concordance lines, and the source texts. The refined frequencies are indicated as RIg (refined frequency, with pauses ignored) and RIn (refined frequency, with pauses included) in the frequency columns in the appendices (Appendices 7.2a, 7.2b, 7.3.1–7.3.5, 7.4.1a, 7.4.1b and 7.4.2–7.4.3), from which it can be seen the overwhelming majority instances were in fact produced holistically. That is to say, internal pausing only occurred in a limited number of the instances of the clusters retrieved. The speakers who produced the clusters were also identified, considering individual speaking styles, preferred pausing patterns, and human agencies are not only influential factors on performance fluency but also provide insights into the underlying processes of language development (Segalowitz, 2010).

7.3 Clusters in DSS

As indicated in Figure 6.1 and Appendices 6.4.4–6.4.7 in Chapter 6, nearly two-thirds of the clusters extracted from DSS have instances that were produced with pauses. Following the procedures elaborated in Section 7.2, this section highlights the analysis of the instances with internal pauses in the learner corpus and is divided into the following five subsections mainly based on the number and the behavior of the internal pauses, including whether they co-occurred with other hesitation phenomena in the co-texts.

7.3.1 Clusters with one internal pause

Of all five types of the listed clusters, instances with one internal filled or unfilled pause, or one drawl are noticeable (Appendix 7.3.1). As to the PP-based clusters *to the* and *of this*, the placement of internal pausing seems controversial. On the one hand, it appears to act as a boundary marker, separating the VP- or NP- from its following NP-based clusters (Grant, 2001; Gilbert, 2005). The fluent units that preceded pausing were two VP- and two NP-based clusters: *is opposite to, talk to, original place to*, and *the production of*. After pausing, both *to* and *of* were followed by holistically produced and structurally complete NP-based clusters, namely *the word*, *the place*, *the government officials*, *this good*. Since prepositions are normally constrained by their preceding nouns, adjectives, or verbs, Biber et al. (1999) suggested that they tended to make up holistic units with their preceding elements. Noticing the close relation between *of* and its preceding nouns, Chung (2012) specifically pointed out that it should be pronounced as a unitary unit with its nouns preceded. It thus seems appropriate for the learner to have placed a pause after *of* and kept *the production of* holistically. However, she also suggested that pauses should be placed before other prepositions, such as *on*, *in*, *to*, *into*, *by*, *over*, *down*, and *up*. According to Grant (2001) and Gilbert (2005), pauses are more likely to be placed before prepositional phrases. Accordingly, the probable holistic units of the instances involved would be *to the word*, *to the government officials*, *to the place*, and *of this good*.

Moreover, pausing in relation to PP-based clusters may have been affected by their following NP-based clusters. It would not be surprising if there were pausing after *to the* and *of this*, since the determiners, *the* and *this* in these cases, were the starting elements of NP-based clusters. Being highly frequent in spontaneous speech, generally followed by the lexical words or the noun head, they can be considered as the major locations of online planning pressure (Biber et al., 1999; Yule, 2010). Pausing after these particles may thus have been used to plan for the following constituents of the NP-based clusters or to hold the speech floor. A similar pausing pattern was found in the instances of *the same* and *the business*, where pauses were placed after *the*, the respective holistic units in the preceding co-texts being *compared to the* and *talk about the*. Regarding the instances *the government*, *the government officials*, *the best one*, *the hydrogen vehicles*, *a new website*, and *our group name*, pauses also occurred after the articles *the* and *a*, or *our*, a possessive determiner. These again suggest that the speakers may be formulating speech online. As formulaic sequences are widely embedded in fluent units as the basic units of communication in speech and they are not necessarily syntactically complete, the presentation of their phonological coherence would be considered more crucial than that of their grammatical completeness or meaning integrity (Myles & Cordier, 2017).

Three patterns of pausing were found in the VP-based clusters. Regarding the instances of *is a*, *is not*, *is more*, *are more*, and (*will*) *not be*, the components before the pause involved copular or modal verbs, namely, *is*, *are*, and (*will*) *not*, and they seem to have formed fluent SV-based clusters with their preceding words, *that is*, *it is*, *which is*, *a healthy mind is*, *there are*, and *they will not*. As to some of *is a*, *have the*, and *it's like*, their second halves, namely, *a*, *the*, and *like*, seem to have been linked to their following words and constructed syntactically complete NP- or PP-based clusters: *a lot of competition*, *the right time*, *like an outline*, and *like discrimination*. These two patterns of pausing may be associated with demarcating the boundaries of clusters, as their respective components seem to have made up holistic units with their preceding or following words. Pauses were additionally found in some instances consisting of the infinitive *to* and verbs, for example, *to be*, *to do*, *to say*, *to find*, and *to have*. As can be seen, the co-texts before pausing were respectively *allow them to*, *how to*, *we are going to*, *then to*, *going to*, *use the Google Street View to*, *she really wants to*, *they have the priority to*, *we strongly suggest you to*, and after pausing *be married*, *do big business*, *do some proposal*, *say something a little*, *find some solutions*, *find public areas*, *have a large bar of chocolate*, *have better chances*, and *have these solutions*. This pausing behavior generally involved two types of VP-based clusters: one consisting of a verb followed by a noun phrase and an infinitive clause, and the other a verb followed by an infinitive clause.

The instances of SV-based clusters that contained one internal pause include *we can*, *we should*, *you have*, and *they have*. As all the listed subjects were realized by pronouns, pausing after them could be an indication that the speaker was planning what to say next (Biber et al., 1999). As can be seen, the two modal verbs *can* and *should* apparently modified their following lexical verbs, having constituted extended complex VP-based clusters, *can change the bribery into another way* and *should not concentrate on*, and the two *haves* were followed by noun phrases which served as their object complements, namely, *have chocolate* and *have right to get married*. However, there has been discussion regarding the occurrence of pauses after the subject. On the one hand, the subject generally takes a simple structure in conversation and is realized by nominative pronouns; signaling the beginning of a clause, the subject is considered as where the speaker conducts speech planning and pausing after the subject could reduce the online planning pressure (Biber et al., 1999). On the other hand, also because of the simple subject, verbs tend be attached to the subject as one unit, so the subject and the verb together would constitute the point of planning for the remaining clause (Biber et al., 1999). That is to say, SV-based clusters tend to be treated as single units. If the first pausing pattern observed from the VP-based clusters in the last paragraph is synthesized here too, pausing or no pausing in the SV-based structure seems to be related to the syntactic complexity of the subject and of the verb. Even when the subject was a full noun phrase, containing lexical words as the noun head, and if it were followed by a copular verb, the subject and the verb would have been produced as a whole.

As to the conjunction-based clusters, since conjunctions such as *and*, *but*, *when*, and *if* are common clause-introducing words and believed to be built into the following clauses, pauses are supposed to occur before conjunctions (Pawley & Syder, 2000; Chung, 2012), but in actual analysis, Freeborn (1995) and Biber et al. (1999) noted otherwise. One of the main findings from Chapter 6 indicates that the conjunction-based clusters are especially likely to contain internal pauses, so the instances of *but we*, *if we*, and *because there* are provided here as examples. Different from the SV-based clusters, the component elements of the conjunction-based clusters can be clearly distinguished from one another as two different grammatical constituents (Freeborn, 1995; Grant, 2001). In fact, pausing after conjunctions may have the same trigger as pausing after the subject, since conjunctions also generally occur at or towards the beginning of a clause or turn and they are likely to be the major point of online planning pressure (Biber et al., 1999). There is a high probability that pauses may occur in between a conjunction and its following element. Consequently, it remains yet to be explored which pausing pattern is frequently adopted by the speaker, especially when the conjunction-based clusters consisting of the conjunction and the subject are immediately followed by verbs: would pauses be placed between the first or the second two constituting components, or would the connected conjunction- and SV-based clusters be produced as wholes? This needs to be checked in the native speech.

7.3.2　Clusters interrupted or surrounded by two or more pauses

As to the instances scattered with pauses, four patterns of pausing were observed: some of them had two types or more of internal pauses; some had pauses before, in, and after them, that is, they not only had one internal pause, but one of the components was also immediately followed or preceded by filled or unfilled pauses, repetitions, or repairs; some had two internal pauses, and additionally were preceded or followed by hesitations or reformulations in the co-texts; some had three internal pauses, yet still with multiple pauses occurring in the immediate contexts (Appendix 7.3.2). Specifically, in the instances of *to the*, *as the*, *to go*, and *who are*, one silent pause occurred with one filled pause or a drawl. Regarding *to the* and *as the*, the prepositions appear to be part of the VP-based clusters that occurred before the pauses, including *turn to*, *expand to*, and *regard them as*, and the article *the* along with its following lexical items seem to have completed the NP-based clusters such as *the broadband assets*, *the whole world*, and *the same people*. Similar to the finding observed from the first two instances of *to the* in Subsection 7.3.1, these PP-based clusters may in effect have been part of the VP- and NP-based combinations, so pauses here seem to be marking the boundaries of different grammatical constituents (Zellner, 1994; Grant, 2001; Gilbert, 2005). Such pauses would not have a negative impact on perceived fluency if their durations were not longer than 400 ms or they had not co-occurred with other dysfluencies (Freed, 2000; Pawley & Syder, 2000). Regarding the instances of *to go* and *who are*, with the words occurring before, their first halves seem to have formed the NP-based clusters *chance to* and *the people who*, whereas the second halves made up holistic VP-based clusters *go to school* and *are running it* with their following words. As to the instances of *should be* and *to say*, although three types of pauses occurred in between the components, the units formed with the preceding and the following elements were respectively complete SV-based clusters *we should* and *they would like to*, followed by the VP-based clusters *be against them* and *say something about topic B*. These pauses therefore on the one hand indicate the great planning pressure learners might have experienced while formulating the speech online, and on the other hand witness the effort they may have exerted to produce holistically the involved VP-, NP-, and SV-based clusters before or after the pauses.

Regarding the instances of *you have*, *very good*, and *because there*, the occurrence of multiple pauses in front of *you*, between *you* and *have*, and after *have*, together with the placement of the two internal pauses in *very good* and *because there* suggests that learners seem to be formuláting speech online, but the immediate contexts also provide evidence of learners' strategic pausing and their attempt at producing holistic NP-based clusters such as *the determination*, *a very good impression*, and *our McDonald's restaurants*, and the SV-based cluster *there are a lot of*. The occurrence of multiple pauses in and around *to the*, *on the*, *the second*, *the government*, and *some other* not only reveals that learners appear to be under pressure while planning speech on the spot but also that they seem to have had difficulty in retrieving nouns or adjectives to formulate complete NP-based clusters, as in the examples of *the licensing of*, *the foreign countries*, *the country's condition*, *the second question*, *the government*, and *some other strategies*.

For learners, producing NP-based clusters as holistic units appears to be especially challenging. Even in the instances of the VP-based clusters *to do*, *have the*, *be the*, and *can make*, the occurrence of pauses seems to be in fact caused by a search for the nouns intended to complete the NP-based instances such as *some short period of working*, *the data*, *the transportation of a lot of people*, and *great benefits*. There are also cases where learners seem to have given up the attempt at retrieving the nouns, as in the instances of *to the* and *to go*: the former was followed by a drawl and a long pause; in the case of the latter, after a drawl and a short pause, the speaker seems to have used *so* as a transitional marker to start a new topic. Moreover, not only were pauses placed in the instances *have the*, *the government*, *the people*, *the public*, and *the country*, in their co-texts there are nouns that were spelled out partially or in the wrong form, namely, *the social respon- -pon- -ponsibility*, *the careness*, *the traditional of the*, *mas- ma- majority*, *the po- process*, *publicities to the*, and *Chinese po- policies*. These indicate that learners may have just partially or incorrectly completed the automatization process of the concerned NP-based clusters (Ellis, 2012; Myles & Cordier, 2017).

Learners also seem to have experienced difficulties in retrieving some verbs and modifying elements. The verb-related retrieving difficulties can be found in the instances of *to the*, *they have*, *the people*, and *them to*, where apart from their internal pausing, repetitions, wrong word forms, partially spelled-out verbs, and other hesitation phenomena can be observed, for instance, *a way to <9.99> <er> the culture to to for the communication culture, they <0.24> have <0.31> they had <0.46> evacu- <0.97> evacu-, they <0.42> have <0.53> complicate <0.48> <er> they may <0.84> they may, for the <uhm> people to <9.99> define <9.99> and to iden- to identify*, and *them <0.20> to <er> <er> <0.21> ensure their health*. As to the difficulty in formulating the modifying elements, evidence can be found in the internal pauses of *be a, the final, it's not, it has*, and *very good*, as well as in the repetitions, partially spelled-out adjectives, adjectives with the wrong forms, and multiple pauses in the co-texts, for example, *be: <0.43> a little in danger, the <9.99> <er> final disadvantage, highly explo- explosive, it's <0.21> not <0.53> <er> so related, it <0.35> has already <0.24> been beneficial*, and *some <0.73> very <er> good university*. These again suggest that learners might have just automatized part of or erroneous VP- or NP-based clusters.

There are some more instances of *on the, it's not, the problem* and other NP-based clusters listed on the last page of Appendix 7.3.2, where the occurrence of internal pauses, reformulations, repetitions, grammatically incorrect word forms, as well as multiple pauses in the co-texts clearly indicates that fluent speech units in learner speech can be very short. These also suggest learners may have encountered overwhelming online planning pressure or difficulties while retrieving the relevant nouns, verbs, and adjectives for the holistic production of PP-, NP-, VP-, and SV-based clusters. The causes may include learners' incremental acquisition of formulaic sequences, lack of the needed automaticity or the holistic awareness for speech production.

7.3.3　Clusters involving repetitions

Pauses also occurred in the instances where part of the cluster, the entire cluster, or the cluster along with its preceding or following words was repeated, as shown in Appendix 7.3.3. Partial repetitions were found in the instances of SV-, conjunction-, and NP-based clusters, namely, *they have, when they, the first, very good*, and *the whole*. As the pronoun *they* and the verb *have* are rather common in speech, there is little chance that they would be difficult to be retrieved from the mental lexicon; however, they might have been the major point of planning pressure. With repetitions, the speakers would be able to relieve the pressure (Biber et al., 1999), formulating subsequent, relatively longer fluent VP- and SV-based clusters, such as *have already gained much priorities than the*, *have high wages and*, and *they feel very difficult*. In the same cluster *they have*, the respective repetition of *they* and that of *have* both occurred. This not only reinforces that the speakers may have been at the planning point for the subsequent clause (Biber et al., 1999), but also shows learners' individual variability in holistic production, considering that they probably have different automatization processes of acquiring the same cluster (Myles & Cordier, 2017). In addition, partial repetitions indicate learners may have encountered unusual challenges in producing holistic NP-based clusters, as shown, the repetition of *first*, *good*, and *whole* in *the first solution*, *very good salaries*, *the whole China*, and *the whole process of management* occurred.

Repeating the whole cluster was found in the instances of *a problem*, *to their*, and *can make*. Along with the internal pausing in the co-texts, the location and the frequency of the occurrence of other pauses, the repetitions not only manifest the efforts the learners might have exerted to search for the required noun or the verb, but also indicate the holistic awareness the speakers have of these clusters. As can be seen, when the instances were uttered the first time they were surrounded by pauses, such as *<0.21> that's a <0.50> problem, to <9.99> their <er>*, and *can <0.20> make <0.21> <er>*, but when they were repeated, no pause occurred in them. Moreover, what followed the repetitions were relatively long and undisturbed stretches of fluent speech, namely, *problem that is a problem*, *to their to the high calories to the high energy*, and *you can make your own video*. These evidently demonstrate that repetitions can improve performance fluency. The repeated production of the whole clusters can also be seen in the immediate contexts of *we know* and *they want*: a repetition of *but how* and *what purpose they* occurred in each preceding co-text. Not only that, these two clusters were produced as holistic units both times, which undoubtedly means they were treated as single units. If the occurrence of the internal pauses in the two just-discussed SV-based instances was taken into consideration, the repetitions might have been motivated by a need to plan the rest of the utterance (Biber et al., 1999) or used to emphasize the questions regarding *how* and *what purpose.*

Some instances of *not the, to go, them to,* and *for one* were found straddling repetitions. Their first and the second elements were respectively correspondent to the last and the first word of the clusters, namely, *the last one but not, go to, to them, to make them,* and *one hundred sellers compete for.* As to *the last one but not,* it may have been involved a degree of fossilization. Based on the co-texts, it appears to have been used erroneously twice; the expected expression should have been *last but not least.* With regard to the rest of the instances just listed, when they were produced the first time, they seem to have had more pauses in or around them and been related to comparatively shorter fluent units than they were reproduced. Such repetitions indicate not only learners' attempts at producing the cluster as one single unit but also that they could facilitate the learners to speak the same chunk with a relatively more coherent contour. Furthermore, they might have functioned as a rhetoric strategy, emphasizing the message conveyed.

7.3.4 Clusters involving repairs or restarts

There were some instances the internal pausing of which also involved repairs or restarts, specifically falling into four types: they were either linked to a change of lexical selection, grammar correction, adding new component elements such as a noun or a verb, or topic-shifting (Appendix 7.3.4). The co-texts of the clusters *to the, can you, do we, to do,* and *of it* suggest that repairs may have been used to reformulate the meaning of the utterance with different lexical words. As can be seen, their first halves seem to be the last words of the preceding chunks, *but the solutions we have to, the the the the society want to, we can, we <1.94> do <0.29>, and what we should do is to contribute to, do anything to,* and *and it create a custom of,* whereas the second half of each instance was the first word of the repaired unit after the internal pause, namely, *the solutions are what we should, the the government want to control the society, you can not name the road, we don't have to do the bribery we, do something in turn to make our society own society better, do some huge cases to show that why would you,* and *it create a atmosphere of such.* In these cases, repairs seem to also have facilitated the production of longer fluent stretches of speech. As to the instances of *from the* and *in this,* the repairs

136

may have been intended for the correct use of the prepositions *of* and *on*. As can be seen, *the effect from* was repaired by *the effect of*, and *this is what happened in* was replaced by *this is what happened on* after the filler *er*, as the two chunks were then followed by a noun phrase, *oil crisis*, and a specific date, *March twenty-three*. Repairs may also have been used to supplement the missing elements. Take the instance of *as the* for example, the repaired unit after the internal pausing was *the same products and same food to the*, which clearly indicates that the nouns *products* and *food* were added after *the same* in the previous chunk, *to give the same as*. The same phenomenon was found in the co-text of the second instance of *to do*, where *do anything to* may have been a repair of *to anything*, with *do* added before *anything*, considering that the preceding unit is *and you don't have to anything*. In terms of the cause that may have been related to a shift of topic, it is noticeable in the instances of *of it*, *it's a*, and *the only*: their first component elements appear to be part of the previous units, *lot of*, *it's*, and *but the*, but they seem to have been cut off, with the second halves restarted with different meaning units, namely, *it will*, *a lot of student if not*, and *only in the two twenty two thousand two*.

Apart from the internal pauses and the reformulations, filled pauses, different lengths of silent pauses, repetitions, and lexico-grammatical errors occurred in the co-texts of the majority instances discussed in this subsection. Except for the examples provided above, other observable evidence included a partial and false start of an adverb, as in *very environmen- not environmental friendly*, applying wrongly the third person singular to a verb, as in *it create*, using the incorrect plural form, as in *a lot of student*, and inaccurately using numeral expressions, as in *March twenty-three* and *two twenty two thousand two*. As spoken language takes place in real time, reformulations, repetitions, hesitations, and incomplete utterances commonly co-occur (Biber et al., 1999; Carter & McCarthy, 2006), but an exceedingly large number of these dysfluencies indicate that learners do seem to have been under the unusual pressure of online planning and experienced considerable difficulties in speech formulation. On the other hand, the above-discussed repairs, including changing lexical choices, correcting lexico-grammatical errors, and making up for the missing elements, as well as other dysfluencies clearly show that different learners are at different levels of holistic production of these clusters. Repairs may also be considered as a testament to the trade-offs between speech accuracy and fluency. They may impair fluency when noticeably used with other hesitations to reformulate the speech for the sake of lexico-grammatical accuracy (Skehan, 1996, 2009; Chambers, 1997; Ellis, 2003), but when applied to facilitate the natural production of speech, they can actually create a positive impression about perceived fluency (Segalowitz, 2010). As the examined instances seem to have sporadic pauses in and around, these repairs might have been more related to conveying of messages than to a contradiction of distributed attention on fluency or accuracy.

7.3.5 Within-individual differences

There were cases where the same cluster was used by the same speaker, who placed pauses in one or two instances but holistically uttered the rest in the co-texts or other contexts (Appendix 7.3.5). For example, some instances of NP-, PP- and SV-based clusters, namely, *the government*, *the public*, *a way*, *how many*, *up a*, *they are*, *that is*, and *not just*, were produced with and without pauses almost in the same utterance or in the same speech event respectively by GDTB1, GDTT5, GDJJ4, GDJJ6, GDTT3, GDJJ5, GDTT4, and GDTT2. As to some instances of *by the*, *the people*, *have to*, and *think about*, they were used with or without pauses by the same speakers indicated respectively as GDTT1, GDJJ3, GDJJ1, and GDJJ2 in different contexts. These within-individual differences can be accounted for as follows.

First, the occurrence of internal pauses in some instances along with other hesitating phenomena in the co-texts seems to reinforce that learners may be formulating speech online and having difficulty in retrieving the required nouns and verbs for the NP-, PP-, SV- and VP-based clusters from their mental lexicon. As can be seen, the surroundings of *the government*, *a way*, *that is*, *not just*, *by the*, *the people*, and *have to* were dotted with pauses or other dysfluencies, supporting that learners in general did seem to produce short fluent speech runs. Instead of producing *improve the government system* as a whole, the speaker paused after *the* and separated the VP-based cluster *improve the* from its object NP-based cluster *government system*, breaking the structure into two smaller units, although a second but coherent instance of this cluster in its close context indicates that the speaker seems to be able to produce the entire cluster as a holist unit. Another case in point is

138

the instances of *up a*: the speaker produced *fill up a tank of hydrogen* holistically, but she paused after *up* when uttering *fill up a cell of oil*. This again shows that learners paused in the clusters made up of different grammatical constituents, producing short fluent clusters.

Second, some cases of internal pausing indicate that learners may deliberate where they pause to emphasize or to breathe, or may be due to their individual preferred pausing scheme. For example, the participants seem to be able to produce the instances of *how many* and *think about* without any pauses, which is testified not only by their multiple times of holistic production in the co-texts or close contexts, but also by the relatively long fluent speech runs preceding or following them, but they paused in them anyway. In this case, internal pausing might have served the purpose of emphasizing the words that precede or follow it (Guillot, 1999). A close examination of these pauses in the audio data, however, revealed that there was no obvious stress on or other prosodic change in the words before or after them, and these internal pauses thus would not have been used for rhetorical effects. Considering the high frequency of occurrence of these two clusters in DSS as well as their ubiquity in everyday language, learners can actually produce them as wholes without any difficulty. This seems to echo that speakers may have their own preferences in terms of where they decide to pause and how they manipulate pauses, or that they have their preferred pausing styles in general (Zellner, 1994; Segalowitz, 2010).

Moreover, internal pauses may be used to keep the conversational floor. Pausing at an unexpected point such as at a non-grammatical juncture has been pointed out to be a common floor-holding strategy (Guillot, 1999; Yule, 2010). While producing *the public*, the speaker GDTT5 paused after *the* in two of the instances, but she had produced the cluster effortlessly and holistically in the previous context, and also in the following co-text, which seems to have excluded the assumption that pausing at the beginning of a noun phrase, in this case, pausing after *the*, might be a time-buying strategy used to relieve planning pressure (Biber et al., 1999). Moreover, since no obvious, unusual prosodic properties like rising or falling tones, stressing, or drawling was observed in the original audio data, the two internal pauses might simply signal that the speaker may not have finished his or her turn, wishing to continue the conversation.

7.3.6　Summary and conclusion

Altogether five categories of internal pausing were examined in DSS. In the first category where the instances had one internal pause, first, it appears that its occurrence needs to be carefully investigated in the contexts, especially when there is the presumption that some PP- or NP-based clusters are supposed to be produced as holistic units. Situated in a wider co-text, some internal pauses may have been used to mark the boundaries of the preceding or following NP-, PP-, SV-, or VP-based clusters, and some may have been linked to online planning pressure. Regarding the occurrence of pausing after the determiners in PP- or NP-based clusters or that in the VP-based clusters involving the infinitive *to*, the causes seem especially complicate. Thus, why the internal pauses of these kinds occur and whether similar causes would arise need to be explored in the reference corpus. Furthermore, whether SV- and conjunction-based clusters, especially when they are interconnected, have the similar patterns of pausing needs to be checked.

The second category was about the instances having two or more internal pauses, and those that not only had internal pauses but also were surrounded by other dysfluent phenomena. The occurrence of multiple pauses and other dysfluencies in the co-texts clearly shows that learners produced shorter fluent units. It partly indicates that learners may have treated where they placed pauses as the location where they could stop to formulate the subsequent speech content or separate such as the NP- from VP-based clusters, and partly that they may have conducted online planning, making efforts to produce holistic NP-, VP-, or SV-based clusters but having difficulties in doing so. There was substantial evidence of difficult production of nouns, verbs, and adjectives for the investigated NP- and VP-based clusters. The partial or erroneous production suggests that learners may be at different developmental stages of automatization process, because of which, they may not have achieved the fully automatized level of holistic production or had the awareness of producing them as wholes.

In the third and fourth categories where the instances also involved repetitions, repairs, or restarts, these pauses seem to be more than just manifestations of learners' online speech planning. They also indicate learners' attempts at retrieving adjectives, nouns, or verbs, as well as their developmental processes of automatization in acquiring the clusters. Both repetitions and repairs can be used as a time-gaining device for speech planning since they seem to have prompted the production of subsequent longer fluent speech runs. Partial repetitions as well as repairs show that learners may not have automaticity in producing the clusters as single units. Conversely, repeating an entire cluster or also with its co-text suggests learners may have the holistic awareness regarding its production. Moreover, there are instances where repetitions might have been used for the purpose of emphasis. The instances involving either repairs or restarts also provide evidence for topic-shifting, but the trade-off between accuracy and fluency seems indistinct.

The last category shows there were within-individual differences in pausing. Although some of the instances had internal pauses, the same clusters also had others used holistically by the same speakers in the co-texts or close contexts. When the instances that had internal pauses were compared with those that were produced without pauses, the placement of internal pauses can be seen to be influenced by learners' pressure of ongoing planning, individual preferred pausing schemes, or conversational strategies. Apart from reinforcing that learners tend to speak with short fluent units, the occurrence of internal pauses as well as multiple types of other pauses in the co-texts may serve as evidence that learners had tried but failed to produce the involved extended clusters as single units. Indicated by fewer pauses and relatively long stretches of fluent speech, there were also cases where learners placed a pause in a certain cluster, although they had already used it as a whole in the immediate context and seem to have been well able to do so.

As the patterns of internal pausing and the causes of its occurrence seem varied, it is necessary to investigate the five categories of internal pausing and the production of formulaic sequences in the native academic speech. For example, regarding the instances of PP-based clusters such as *to the* and *on the*, would they be produced holistically or with pauses occurring in, before, or after prepositions in MiniM? In DSS, some instances of the PP-based clusters are in fact part of the extended VP- and NP-based combinations, would pauses be found in between these two types of clusters, or would they occur after the main verbs, leaving their following prepositions with the NP-based clusters constituted as holistic units? When the PP-based clusters are followed by NP-based clusters, where would pauses occur, would they be also placed after articles or determiners in MiniM? Regarding the clusters consisting of verbs followed by the infinitive *to*, would the pause be placed before or after *to*? Moreover, would SV- and conjunction-based clusters be broken down into smaller units, with pauses placed in between their constituting components, or would those consisting of conjunctions followed by the SV-based clusters be produced as wholes? Are there also within-individual differences in pausing such as the same speaker using the same cluster but placing the pause differently in the co-text or other context? The next section thus aims to explore these issues in MiniM.

7.4   Clusters in MiniM

As can be seen in Figure 6.1 and Appendices 6.4.4–6.4.7, approximately one-third of the clusters in MiniM have instances that were produced with pauses. With a slight modification of the categories that are applied in Section 7.3, internal pausing found in the native speech is regrouped as follows in Subsections 7.4.1–7.4.3: the first group is about the instances that had one internal pause (Appendices 7.4.1a and 7.4.1b); the instances with two or more internal pauses, those having one internal pause but with one or two more pauses occurring in the co-texts, and those involving repetitions, repairs, or restarts are organized as the second group (Appendix 7.4.2); as in DSS, clusters that showed within-individual differences in pausing are categorized separately as the third group (Appendix 7.4.3).

7.4.1   Clusters with one internal pause

To echo the first category of internal pausing in DSS, this section is concerned with all five types of clusters that had one internal pause and divided into two subtypes: in one subtype, internal pausing may have served as a boundary marker for its preceding or following fluent unit (Appendix 7.4.1a), while in the other subtype, the causes of its occurrence appear ambiguous (Appendix 7.4.1b). Regarding some of the instances of PP-, SV- and VP-based clusters, *on the*, *do you*, *it is*, *are you*, *has the*, and *get the*, the internal pauses may have been employed as boundary markers, since they obviously occurred at the clause or phrase junctures, separating the preceding fluent units from the ones that followed. As shown, their first components can be clearly identified as the constituents of their preceding clauses, namely, *business goes on, you need something to do, like <xx> talked about it, if they offered it, I don't think they are, where the king has*, and *so whatever channel it is that I get*, whereas their second components were the apparent starting words for the following holistically produced NP- or SV-based clusters: *the women, you go crazy, is that like on human lifetime, is that like a good thing, you know, the king*, and *the guy*. Moreover, same as what was found in DSS, some instances of the PP-based clusters were also part of the extended combinations of VP- and NP-based clusters. As can be seen, the respective co-texts of *to the* and *with the* were *move to the suburbs* and *deal with the harassment of defenders*. In these two instances, pausing after *to* or *with* seems to have separated the VP- from the NP-based clusters.

Other patterns of internal pausing and the causes of the occurrence observed in DSS are distinguishable in MiniM (Appendix 7.4.1b Type B). Firstly, regarding some other instances of PP-based clusters, *for the* and *over the*, pauses occurred after the prepositions *for* and *over*, and were followed by full NP-based clusters. This pausing behavior appears different from the claim that pauses need to be placed before prepositional phrases (Grant, 2001; Gilbert, 2005; Chung, 2012). However, as shown, the units that followed, *the heavy metals in N-H-three* and *the democratic state of Brazil*, were produced without pauses, and the preceding co-texts before the internal pausing were long fluent chunks consisting of more than seven words. Considering human working memory limitations on speech processing, pausing before structurally complete noun phrases may be a strategy used for breathing or other organic, physiological, or cognitive reasons (Pawley & Syder, 2000), or reinforce that more processing effort is needed to plan the nouns (Seifart et al., 2018). In relation to the preposition *of*, one exception can be found in the instance of *percent of*, however, pausing in between *percent* and *of* seems to have separated two relatively short but structurally complete clusters: one is NP-based, *twenty percent*, and the other PP-based, *of AIDS cases*. This appears to echo that pauses are expected to be placed before prepositions (Grant, 2001; Gilbert, 2005), but contradictory to the claim that pauses would be preferably placed after *of* when this particular preposition is preceded by noun phrases (Chung, 2012).

As to the NP-based instances of *the one*, *the government*, and *the public*, they were in fact preceded by the PP-based ones, which seem to have constituted generally somewhat fluent units, including *for the*, *I mean it'll always be on the*, *because a large majority of the*, and *down to the*. This shows that pauses may occur after the fluently produced PP-based clusters and that the beginning of an NP-based cluster is indeed a major point of planning pressure, since pausing after *the* seems to do with the formulation of the remaining noun phrase. When the NP-based clusters are preceded by optional modifiers, pauses may occur in between, with the determiner and the noun head produced as a holistic unit. As to the instances of *all the*, *just the*, and *just a*, pauses occurred after *all* and *just*, and the articles *the* and *a* seem to have formed coherent NP-based clusters along with their following content words, namely, *the other ones*, *the sake of tradition*, and *a really awesome nucleophile*. Another two instances related to the NP-based clusters are *people who* and *who have*, which were immediately and fluently followed by verbs, as the co-texts were *I have a couple people who quit* and *you have a group of people who have competing interests* respectively, and they seemed to have mainly constituted an extended NP-based cluster modified by an attributive clause. On the one hand, pauses can occur before *who*, since this word seems to have formed a fluent SV-based cluster with its following element, *who quit*. On the other hand, they could occur after *who* since it was used to introduce the attributive clause. Pausing here may have helped the speaker to plan for the subsequent clause including the verb phrase, *have competing interests you're never gonna get anything done you're gonna be*.

Regarding some instances of the SV-based and some of the VP-based clusters that immediately followed a subject, *people are*, *who are*, *was a*, *is more*, *be the*, *have the*, *have no*, and *take a*, the second halves of them seem to have constituted holistic VP- or NP-based clusters with their following predicative adjectives or the remaining verb or noun phrases, namely, *are subject to threats*, *are supposed to have power*, *a lot of the physicians who were scared*, *more substituted*, *the frequency of the genotype*, *the highest priority*, *the knowledge of*, *no idea*, and *a Spanish class*. The quantitative results in Chapter 6 reveal that SV-based clusters are most likely to be produced as wholes, but as can be seen, when the subject was a complicate full noun phrase, and when the verb was copular and followed by a predicative adjective, pauses did occur after the subject, stead of having kept the SV-based cluster as a fluent unit. However, when the verb, be it copular or transitive, has a simple structure and is followed by a NP-based cluster, pauses occurred in between, leaving the SV-based cluster as a holistic unit. Furthermore, when the verb is an auxiliary verb in negative constructions and used with lexical verbs, pauses may be placed in between the components of SV-based clusters, as can be seen from the pausing after the pronoun subjects in the clusters *I don't* and *you don't*, the extended units of which were *I don't think* and *you don't know*. Thus, the few occurrences of the internal pausing in SV-based clusters seem to be affected by the complexity of the subject, the verb, and what is followed after the verb.

As in DSS, the patterns of pausing regarding the VP-based clusters appear varied. For example, instances of *to do* and *think about* were part of *has to do with* and *has to think about*, but in the former, pausing occurred in between *has to* and *do with*, and in the latter, after *has to think*, leaving the preposition *about* to form a PP-based cluster with its following lexical items, *about like what you write*. As indicated in the co-text, in between the words *think* and *about*, <IC>, used to mark that an instructor's speech was deleted, occurred after the internal pause, which shows the occurrence of this pause was more likely due to individual choice rather than being interrupted by the classroom instructor. As to the instances of *to have* and *to make*, pauses were placed after *to*, the preceding co-texts being *have one recessive allele to* and *you're trying to*, whereas the verbs, *have* and *make*, seem to have constituted the VP-based clusters with their subsequent elements, *have the trait* and *make soluble*. Same as the finding in DSS, the respective structures for these two clusters were verbs followed by the infinitive. Based on these, pauses did occur in between the infinitive *to* and verbs, or after the co-occurrence of these two elements, but there is also a possibility that pauses would be placed before the clusters consisting of *to* and verbs. As to the instance of *can be*, pausing occurred after the modal auxiliary *can*, so the subject and part of the verb phrase constituted a holistic unit, *it can*, with the copular verb and its followed noun phrase making up another holistic unit, *be the path*. Such pausing behavior seems to have contested the widely accepted use of modal auxiliaries, which are generally assumed to occur with other verbs and build up complex VP-based clusters (Biber et al., 1999). However, in spontaneous speech, pausing may just be unplanned, so the speaker might have placed this pause in *can be* simply because of the biological constraints. However, a close examination of the context indicates that the speaker may have been thinking in process, as he seems to be working on a deduction to a chemical problem.

Pauses were also found in the conjunction-based clusters in MiniM, including *if you*, *when you*, *because it's*, *because there's*, and *but the*, which seems contradictory to the claim that in speaking pauses are supposed to be placed before conjunctions (Chung, 2012). Of the instances listed, the second halves seem to have made up holistically produced SV- and NP-based clusters with their following words, namely, *you know*, *you assume*, *it's more substitutive*, *it's a part of your every life*, *it's not as positive because it has the negative*, *there's it*, *the philosophy class*, and *the majority don't go*, which apparently echoes that as the clause-introducing words, the conjunctions may have been the point of ongoing planning pressure (Biber et al., 1999). Moreover, some of the holistic units were extended SV-based clusters consisting of the simple subject, the copular verb, and the predicative, supporting that native speakers tend to produce the clusters of this type as single units and that they produce longer fluent units than learners.

7.4.2 Clusters with two or more pauses or involving other dysfluency features

What is reported in this section aligns with the analyses of the second, third, and fourth categories of internal pausing in DSS discussed in Subsections 7.3.2–7.3.4 (Appendix 7.4.2). First, two or more internal pauses were found in the instances of PP- and VP-based clusters: *on the*, *about the*, *from the*, *be more*, *is just*. Similar to the finding in DSS, these pauses may have served as boundary markers. As to the instances of *on the* and *about the*, *on* and *about* were produced holistically with their preceding components as VP-based clusters *depending on* and *talk about*, whereas the second halves of them, the article *the* appears to have formed coherent NP-based clusters *the number of hydrogens* and *the giants*. The two clusters were categorized as preposition-based but in fact part of verb phrase and noun phrase combinations. Multiple pauses in between these units seem to reinforce that a structurally complete noun phrase, that is, consisting of a preceding determiner and a noun head, may have been preferably produced as a holistic unit in MiniM. As to the instance of *from the*, the second half with its following elements seems to have constituted a holistically produced NP-based cluster, *the middle nineteen nineties*, whereas the first halves of the instances *be more* and *is just* along with their preceding words, namely, *can it be* and *the second factor is*, seem to be treated as holistic SV-based clusters.

Apart from having one internal pause, instances of PP- and NP-based clusters such as *about the*, *from the*, and *the people* were directly preceded by another pause. They were further preceded by fluent speech runs consisting of seven or more words, *you know how you said you sent an email, basically found that the P-H is going to increase*, and *here's another example of when they caught*, and followed by holistically produced NP-based clusters, *the announcement*, *the left side of the*, and *people who were violating the human rights and*. Instances of *with the* and *the one* were not only interrupted but also surrounded by pauses. After multiple pauses occurring in and around *with the*, *<0.18> and then <0.18> with <0.18> the <0.18> science <0.18>*, what followed was a long stretch of fluent speech, *Lutheran science gives power to the intellectuals and*, probably with *Lutheran science* as a reformulation or a much clearer identification of the preceding noun phrase, *the science*; after similar pausing in and around *the one*, *<um> <0.18> the <0.18> one <0.18>*, a structurally complete noun complement clause, *that most people in Brazil the way they get AIDS is through blood transfusions*, was followed. The occurrence of these pauses seems mostly related to the effort required to retrieve the following nouns, which seems to support that the beginning of a noun phrase is one crucial point where the speaker is experiencing planning pressure (Biber et al., 1999). When compared to the findings about learners' fluent units, which are discussed in 7.3, these clearly show that native speakers produced evidently longer fluent units. As to the instances of *it is*, *is a*, *has a*, apart from one internal and one immediately preceding pause, other pauses occurred closely in the co-texts, but the fluent units that preceded or followed still appeared much longer than their counterparts in DSS. In addition to one internal pause, the instances of *with the*, *that's the*, and *have the* were directly followed by one more pause, and further by discourse markers, partial repetitions, false starts, and restarts, which indicate native speakers may have had some difficulty in retrieving the nouns to complete the involved

PP-, SV-, and VP-based clusters. Furthermore, evidence of difficulty in searching for verbs to formulate SV-based clusters is marked in the instances of *I don't* and *because they*, as they were followed by incomplete verbs as in *if I wanna sp-* and *they l- they want to.*

Repetitions were found regarding the instances of NP- and SV-based clusters. In the case of *on the*, the two words, *on* and *the*, clearly formed their own units separately, with *on* teaming with its preceding words as *I guess maybe that later on*, and *the* supposedly constituting its own NP-based cluster, but as shown, *the* was repeated, followed by a partially spelled word, *monas-*, and then a change of the subject, *the Franciscans*. Repeating *the*, the beginning of a full noun phrase, is considered a common practice of relieving planning pressure (Biber et al., 1999), but the partial start of the following lexical word and then the reformulation suggest the speaker may have had a failed attempt at retrieving the noun from memory for this NP-based cluster and abandoned the previous piece of discourse, starting afresh. On the other hand, repeating an entire cluster occurred to the instance of *the one*. Although pauses occurred in and right after it, *<um> <0.18> just the <0.18> one <0.18>*, when it was repeated, it was produced holistically along with its following PP-based cluster, *the one with the leaving group right*. This shows that repetitions can improve the fluency of speech production. Additionally, three instances of repetitions concerning SV-based clusters were found in the co-texts of *to the*, *want to*, and *because it's*: there was partial repetition as in *that are genen- genetically identical*, and the entire repetition of *does the other* and *it's just*, respectively showing that repetitions may occur while speech planning is conducted online and that the SV-based clusters tend to be treated as single units in speech processing.

Clusters involving repairs and restarts are also noticeable. As to *the hydrogen*, which had one internal pause and one pause that followed, its repaired equivalent seems to have contained much more specific information than the previous instance. Accordingly, multiple pauses and repairs may have occurred for the topic-related, cognitive reason. Evidence of reformulating SV-based clusters can be found regarding the instances of *it is*, *it will* and *it's the*. The first halves of them were part of the preceding SV-cluster, where the second elements of them seem to have begun a new clause. The instance of *just the* seems to have involved a reformation of the subject for the ongoing turn. As to the instances related to *if you* and *because it's*, specifically *if <0.18> you <0.18> like* and *<0.18> it's <0.18> like*, it seems that the whole cluster was respectively replaced by *if there's* and *there's not as m-* in their following co-texts, where a shift in topic occurred. Restarts or repairs also took place in the co-texts of *I don't*, *the most*, *to help*, and *it's the*. In addition to the internal and the preceding pauses, *I don't* was further preceded by a reformulation of the meaning conveyed, *the instruc- it was a G-S-I*; based on the context, the speaker seems to have been intended to point out who the instructor was but for some reason he spoke of the course code instead. The reformulation, the partially produced noun, and multiple pauses in the co-text are a clear indication of thinking in process. As to *the most*, apart from the internal pause, it was also preceded by a false start, *i-*, and a partial repetition, *the mo-*. The speaker seems to have emphasized the word *most*. Moreover, there was trace of changing VP-based clusters in the co-text of *to help* and *it's the*: in the former *who's* was reformulated as *who strives to*, and in the latter, *reproduced like* was rephrased as *reproducing itself*. It needs pointing out though, regarding all the instances discussed above, except for the repetitions, repairs, or restarts, they all had one internal pause and at least another pause that immediately preceded or followed. Biber et al. (1999) pointed out that these dysfluencies often co-occur under the real-time production constraints. Nevertheless, it would be safe to conclude that native speakers may not always have the automaticity of producing holistic formulaic sequences in spontaneous speech.

7.4.3 Within-individual differences

Native speakers were also found to have paused in some instances of a cluster but produced others as single units in the co-texts or contexts. Notable examples included two SV-based clusters, *I don't know* and *I don't think*, two VP-based clusters, *want to* and *going to*, and two NP-based clusters, *the one* and *the people* (Appendix 7.4.3). Due to the nature of spontaneous speech, the main cause seems to be online planning of what to say next. For example, of the five listed instances of *I don't know* taken from the same text file, the speaker <SB> paused in one but produced the rest holistically on the other four occasions. In the co-texts of these instances, multiple types of pauses occurred and relatively frequently, other dysfluent features including hesitations, an attempt to produce a verb or a determiner, reformulations, and repeats were observed, and the fluent units were relatively short. These indicate the speaker may have encountered real-time pressure and that his or her planning may not have been able to catch up with the production (Biber et al., 1999). As to the eight instances of *I don't think*, two of them had internal pauses but at different locations, *but i <0.18> <IC> don't think* and *but i don't <0.18> think that*, three of them contained the initial repetition, *i <0.18> i just don't think, i i don't think that you,* and *i <0.18> <ugh> i just don't think*. Biber et al. (1999) suggested that the beginning of a clause is generally the point where speakers tend to have severe planning pressure, and it thus seems common to pause in or repeat part of this cluster, considering that it is generally followed by the construct of a clause and obviously effort-consuming. Regarding the pausing in *want to*, the within-individual difference may have also been caused by the planning pressure, indicated by the multiple pauses and the reformulation in the co-text.

Pausing may have been used as a conservational strategy, and this could be another explanation of why within-individual differences occurred in the pausing of some clusters. As to the instances of *going to* produced by <SA>, one of them was found to be interrupted by an internal pause and also preceded by two more pauses, as in *<0.19> am <0.18> i going <0.18> to want to be S-N-one or S-N-two*, but the rest were either produced without pauses or contracted as *gonna* embedded in the co-text. As can be seen, in the holistically produced instances *am i going to* and *am i gonna*, two of them were preceded by a pause, one by a pause and a repetition of *am*, and that last one was coherently attached to its preceding co-text, and on the other hand, all of them, including the one with the internal pause, were followed by coherently produced stretches of speech. Considering that all the involved instances occurred in an interrogative clause, the location where pauses occurred, namely before *am*, is the general point where online planning might have been conducted; pausing in this one particular instance may be chiefly related to rhetoric matters, where the speaker seems to be slowing down the speed of speaking in order to clarify the question posed.

As to the five *the one* instances produced by <SD>, two of them had an internal pause, additionally with one preceded by hesitations, followed by another pause and further by its repeated unit along with a PP-based cluster as its postmodifier, *<um> <0.18> just the <0.18> one <0.18> the one with the leaving group right*, and the other interrupted by one interlocuter marked as <SUC> but still continued with a PP-based cluster, *<yeah> <0.18> for the <0.18> <SUC> one with the halide <0.19>*. Regarding the instances of *the people*, the one that had an internal pause was preceded by another pause but followed by an attributive clause consisting of more than seven words, *<0.18> the <0.18> people who were violating the human rights and*. Primarily, the pausing difference in these instances seems to be caused by thinking in process. Based on the contexts, the speaker who produced *the one* seems to be contemplating the chemical questions discussed in the conversation, and the one who produced *the people* provided a detailed example regarding the issue of human rights; one seems to be retrieving specialized lexical words such as *the leaving group* and *halide*, and the other retrieving certain lexico-grammatical patterns to complete a complex relative clause: both of them thus seem to be under great planning pressure. As discussed above, pausing after the determiner *the* could be motivated by the need to buy time to relieve the planning pressure, formulating what nouns follow. Another possible cause of the pausing differences, especially in the instances of *the people*, might be that the speaker might have aimed to hold the speech floor. As can be seen, the speaker was trying to elaborate the examples, if he or she had paused in between the noun phrase and its following relative clause, there is a chance he or she would lose the floor. Placing pauses at the point where the meaning is clearly incompletely conveyed, in this case, in the noun phrase, could be a strategy used to keep the floor.

7.4.4   Summary and conclusion

Although smaller in number, all patterns of internal pausing that occurred in DSS were found in MiniM. Some instances of the clusters had one internal pause, and some had two or more. In addition to having one internal pause, the co-texts of some instances had one or two more pauses, repetitions, repairs, or restarts. Within-individual differences were also observed in the production of some clusters. As in the findings from DSS, the possible causes of the occurrence of the internal pausing in MiniM include marking syntactic boundaries, online planning pressure, difficulties in planning the next noun or verb, repetitions, reformulations, a shift of topic, individual pausing preferences, and holding the conversational floor. Several occurrences in MiniM are probably due to working memory limitations, for rhetorical effect or for cognitive reasons, as they were placed in between units of connected speech consisting of more than seven words or seemingly for the purpose of deliberating, emphasizing, or clarifying, which is not manifest in the instances examined in DSS.

In response to the questionable pausing behavior observed from Section 7.3, findings from this section are not yet conclusive. First, it is still unclear in both corpora which pattern of pausing would occur more frequently especially when the VP-, PP-, and NP-based clusters are interlocked. Some PP-based instances are also part of connected VP- and NP-based clusters in MiniM, but the placement of pauses seems inconsistent. Pauses were also found in the NP-based clusters, which may have been initially taken as part of the PP-based clusters, whereas the PP-based clusters may have actually constituted the VP-based clusters with their preceding verbs, that is to say, with their preceding verbs, the prepositions and *the* or other determiners may have been produced as holistic units, although it appears in the native speech that structurally complete NP-based clusters were widely produced as wholes. As to the clusters consisting of verbs and the infinitive *to*, pauses were found placed before, in, or after it. Regarding the SV-based clusters, the occurrence of internal pauses seems to be affected by the syntactic structure of the subject or the verb, or even what follows the verb, but when the SV-based clusters are preceded by conjunctions, it needs further validation whether pauses tend to occur before or after the conjunctions, or after the combined units made up of the conjunction and the pronoun subject.

Because of these remaining issues, pausing and the production of different types of clusters require further investigation. Moreover, the analyses demonstrated so far are only concerned with the instances that had internal pauses. Based on the results summarized in Chapter 6, for learners, approximately one-third, and for native speakers, nearly two-thirds of the clusters were produced completely without pauses; even among those that had instances with internal pauses, the majority were in fact used as single units. Considering learners' developmental processes of acquiring formulaic sequences, the next chapter is thus to explore pausing and the production of high frequency clusters in DSS and then compare them with those in MiniM.

7.5   Chapter summary

This chapter has investigated the patterns of internal pausing and the possible causes of its occurrence in the two corpora. Internal pauses were examined based on their behavior, such as occurring alone in clusters or being accompanied by other pausing and hesitations that immediately preceded or followed the investigated PP-, NP-, VP-, SV-, and conjunction-based clusters. Five categories of internal pausing were analyzed, and the causes of the occurrence were found various. Apart from serving as boundary markers for two neighboring grammatical constituents in their wider co-texts, internal pauses in both corpora may occur noticeably because of speakers' online planning pressure, difficulty in lexical retrieval, or individual preferred pausing schemes, or because pauses are used to perform discoursal functions. More internal pauses in learner speech appear to be caused by difficulties in online speech formulation, a lack of automaticity or holistic awareness in production, but in native speech, they seem more likely to be related to individual pausing preferences, conversational strategies, and topic-related cognitive issues.

Chapter 8

High Frequency Formulaic Sequences and Pauses

8.1 Introduction

To continue testing the Holistic Hypothesis and resolve the issues left from Chapter 7, this chapter reports on the investigation of pausing in and around the high frequency clusters extracted from both corpora. Four two-word formulaic sequences from each of the five grammatical categories, namely PP-, SV-, VP-, NP-, and conjunction-based, are selected, with the VP-based specifically focusing on those consisting of verbs and the infinitive *to* (hence *verb to* clusters), and the last category the conjunction pronoun clusters. The analysis of each cluster is divided into two parts: one where it is produced as a holistic unit and the other with pauses. The holistic production of each cluster is analyzed based on whether it is immediately bounded by pauses on both sides, whether it involves repetition, whether it has pauses on the right or the left side, whether it is embedded in an extended longer cluster, or whether it has been contracted as one word. The analysis is first performed based on the concordance lines generated from DSS and from MiniM separately, which is then compared and contrasted between the corpora for similarities and differences, with explanations and justifications posited. Apart from pausing and the linguistic features in the co-texts, when necessary, the speaker who produced the cluster, the frequency of the word that preceded or followed the pausing as well as other paralinguistic features are also considered.

For descriptive purposes, the symbol ‖ is used to signal the location of pausing. Similar to the previous use of the contractions but with a slight modification, noun phrases, verb phrases, and prepositional phrases are respectively represented by NP, VP, and PP. Lexical verbs are marked as *verb* when they occur in patterns such as *verb the NP*, *verb in the*, and *if you verb*, the passive form of which is shortened as *verb-ed*. Nominative pronouns are marked as *pron* when they are found in the patterns such as *I think pron* or *pron want to do*, and abbreviations *conj, prep, adj,* and *adv* are correspondently adopted for conjunctions, prepositions, adjectives, and adverbs when they collocate with the cluster under discussion. Lastly, parentheses ( ) are used to indicate that the element concerned is absent, cut short, or left out.

8.2 Prepositional clusters

Prepositional clusters, also referred to as the PP-based clusters in this book, are one paramount grammatical type that is well worth detailed investigation, despite the fact that they have always been neglected for a lack of semantic or syntactic wholeness (Gries, 2008; Simpson-Vlach & Ellis, 2010). They not only occurred with high frequencies in DSS and in MiniM (Appendices 6.4.1-3), but also indeed express various relations such as directions, possession, time, and space (Carter & McCarthy, 2006). Moreover, the findings of the pausing patterns regarding the PP-based clusters in Chapter 7 are varied and leave open the question of which one occurs more frequently: are pauses preferably placed before prepositions so that the entire prepositional phrases are treated as holistic units, or after prepositions, leaving the following NP-based clusters as single units? There is another possibility that pauses are placed after the prepositions and determiners, with the core components of the NP-based clusters produced as wholes. When the clusters are preceded and also followed by other elements, pauses may occur somewhere in the co-texts, and the PP-based clusters may be contained in longer fluent units.

As the typical two-word PP-based clusters consist of prepositions followed by the article *the*, they are indicated as *prep the* in the following analysis. The four clusters to be analyzed below are *of the*, *to the*, *in the*, and *on the*. The classification of pausing regarding *of the* is more detailed than the other three, as *of* is believed to have different linguistic behavior from others (Chung, 2012). Since both the refined and the normalized frequencies for the clusters have been already provided in Chapter 6 (Appendices 6.4.1-6.4.3), Table 8.1 along with those for the other grammatical structures (Tables 8.6, 8.11, 8.16 and 8.21) includes only the frequency ranking in the pause-ignored cluster lists or wordlist indexes. For these four PP-based, the ranking was taken from the pause-ignored, two-word cluster list of DSS and that of MiniM, marked as FRD and FRM, respectively (Appendices 6.4 and 6.9).

Table 8.1　Frequency ranking of four prepositional clusters

Clusters	FRD	FRM
of the	2	8
in the	6	5
to the	4	13
on the	27	9

8.2.1　*Of the*

Based on the frequencies presented in Appendix 6.4.7, in DSS, *of the* occurred 300 times when pauses were ignored; when pauses were included, it occurred 287 times. This indicates that the cluster was overall produced without pauses but its thirteen instances probably had internal pauses. As pointed out by Carter and McCarthy (2006), the preposition *of* is commonly used in extended NP-based clusters, *of the* in DSS as well as in MiniM was found to be the main constituting component of a long sequence represented by *(the) NP of the NP*. Given the high frequencies of occurrence in both corpora, *the NP of the NP* and *NP of the NP* were analyzed separately. The patterns of pausing are summarized in Table 8.2, each with the number of the instances that are categorized as an individual pattern indicated under the slot marked as FOD and FOM, respectively referring to the frequency of occurrence in DSS and MiniM. Detailed co-texts for each instance are provided in Appendices 8.2.1.1–8.2.1.11.

Table 8.2   Pausing patterns of *of the* in DSS and MiniM

of the	FOD	FOM
|| *of the* || and repeating	18	3
the NP of the NP		
A: *the || NP of the || NP*	11	0
B: *the NP || of the NP*	8	4
C: *the || NP of the NP*	20	0
D: *the NP of the || (NP)*	9	1
E: *the NP of the || NP*	21	2
F: *the NP of the NP*	58	25
NP of the NP		
A: *NP || of the NP*	5	1
B: *NP of the || (NP)*	12	3
C: *NP of the || NP*	23	4
D: *NP of the NP*	69	42
Other *of the* clusters		
A: || *because of the || NP*	5	0
B: *because of the || NP*	7	2
C: || *because of the NP*	5	0
because of the NP	3	2
D: *instead of the NP*	2	1
in terms of the NP	6	0
verb of the NP	0	6
E: Other structures	0	3
of || the	13	8
because of || the (||) NP	2 (3)	0
(the) NP of || the (||) NP	2 (6)	8
Misuse of *of*	5	0

Evidence of holistic production of *of the* in DSS is provided in the Appendices 8.2.1.1–8.2.1.4. As shown, there were instances that manifested as a short fluent speech unit despite being surrounded by pauses (lines 1–3), followed by repairs (lines 4–5), or involving repetition (lines 5–18) (Appendix 8.2.1.1). Apart from being preceded and followed by pauses, the instances in lines 1–3 were further preceded and followed by noun phrases, the wider co-text of which is marked as *NP \|\| of the \|\| NP*. The symbol \|\| is used to indicate the location of pauses here and in the following analyses, as already pointed out at the very beginning of this chapter. In line 4, *of*

157

the seems to be a repaired chunk for *some of <xx>*, which occurred in its distant context; it was immediately preceded by a prepositional phrase and further followed by a shift of topic. As to the instances that involved repetition, different levels of repetitive use, namely *of* in lines 5–11, *the* in line 7 and the entire cluster in lines 11–18 were observed. Some of them were followed by pauses and hesitant noun phrases (lines 7–11 and 17–18), but some seem to have facilitated the production of the following noun phrases (lines 6 and 12–16). Except for lines 12–13, the repetition of which appears to be the repaired chunk for the preceding prepositions, the rest of the instances were further preceded by noun phrases. The occurrence of multiple pauses in the *of the* co-texts in lines 1–11 on the one hand indicates the production of short fluent speech units and serves as evidence that the learners may have had difficulty in formulating speech, but on the other hand, the instances of *of the* being kept together in these short fluent units seem to have reinforced its holistic status.

With regard to *the NP of the NP*, its pausing falls into six main types (Table 8.2, Appendix 8.2.1.2). The first pausing pattern (type A) is marked as *the || NP of the || NP*, indicating the part of *NP of the* was produced without pauses, and that it was preceded by pauses and further by *the* on the left side, and on the right side it was followed first by pauses and then the remaining components of the second noun phrase, indicated as NP. On the right side, almost half of the pauses were placed at the points as marked in the just-mentioned pattern, that is, in between *the* and its following components that made up the first noun phrase (lines 1–5), and the rest were placed in the content words of the noun phrase, as indicated in lines 6–11. The second type (type B) is indicated as *the NP || of the NP ||*, meaning that pauses occurred first after the first noun phrase *the NP*, and occurred again after *of the NP*. Except for the instances in lines 1–2, the rest were immediately preceded by verb phrases (lines 3–5) or noun phrases (lines 6–8). Indicated as *the || NP of the NP*, the third type (type C) suggests either that pauses were placed after the first *the*, with the rest of the cluster *NP of the NP* produced as a whole (lines 1–13), or that pauses were placed in the first noun phrase, with the rest of the chunk kept holistic (lines 14–17). The instances of the first NP being indecipherable (line 18), grammatically incorrect (line 19), or incomplete (line 20) were also included in this pausing pattern. In the fourth type (type D), *the NP of the* was produced without pauses, but with the remaining component of the second noun phrase being missing, because it was either taken over by repairs (lines 1–2), pauses and repairs (lines 3–7), or contribution from other group members (lines 8–9). In the fifth type (type E), *the NP of the* was first followed by pauses and then by hesitant but nevertheless structurally complete noun phrases. Types D and E are respectively marked as *the NP of the* ‖ (*NP*) and *the NP of the* ‖ *NP*. Moreover, in type E in the second noun phrase, pauses occurred in between *the* and the remaining component of the noun phrase in lines 1–9; in lines 10–19, pauses were placed in the phrases when the content words seem to be retrieved; in lines 20–21, the first noun phrase does not seem to be grammatically correct. In the last type (type F), the entire *the NP of the NP* structure was produced holistically, although in a couple of instances, pauses or hesitations were found in their immediate co-texts. Furthermore, apart from being a stand-alone holistic unit (lines 1–10), following verbs and prepositions, *the NP of the NP* made up extended fluent units such as *verb the NP of the NP* (lines 11–29) and *prep the NP of the NP* (lines 30–41).

Four pausing patterns are found in the instances consisting of *NP of the NP* structure (Table 8.2, Appendix 8.2.1.3). The first type includes five instances marked as *NP* ‖ *of the NP*. This means that *of the NP* was used holistically but preceded by pauses. In the first two lines, pauses occurred in between the first noun phrase and *of the NP*; the first noun phrase was also preceded by verbs, forming a *verb NP* ‖ *of the NP* structure. In the remaining three lines, the occurrence of pauses seems to have been caused by the retrieval of the content words for the noun phrases. The second pattern is marked as *NP of the* ‖ (*NP*), where *NP of the* was produced holistically but followed by contribution from the group members (lines 1–2), hesitations (lines 3–8), restarts (lines 9–11), or indecipherable speech (line 12), because of which, the second supposedly complete noun phrase appeared to have been cut off. The third type is marked as *NP of the* ‖ *NP*, showing that pauses were placed after the chunk *NP of the*; some of them were further followed by relatively coherent noun phrases (lines 1–16), and some of them had pauses before the content words of the noun phrase were retrieved (lines 17–23). In the fourth type, all of the sixty-nine *NP of the NP* instances were free from internal pauses, although some of them were surrounded immediately by pauses on both sides (lines 1–6), preceded by pauses only (lines

1–20), or embedded in the structures such as *prep NP of the NP* (lines 33–48) and *verb NP of the NP* (lines 49–59). Moreover, the last three instances involved repairs (lines 67–69). In most of the instances that evolved from *NP of the NP* structure, the preceding nouns before *of the* were used to indicate numbers or amounts, such as *all*, *most*, *part*, *one*, *some*, and *percent*.

Three other noticeable cluster groups are *because of the* (*NP*), *in terms of the* (*NP*), and *instead of the NP* (Appendix 8.2.1.4). The pausing patterns of the twenty *because of the* (*NP*) instances are further categorized into three types, types A, B and C, and the rest are included under type D. Type A is marked as ‖ *because of the* ‖ *NP*, where five *because of the* instances were both preceded and followed by pauses, one of which was then followed by reformulation (line 1) and four by hesitant noun phrases (lines 2–5). Type B is indicated as *because of the* ‖ *NP*; seven instances of *because of the* were followed by pauses, hesitant but structurally complete noun phrases. In type C, all eight instances of *because of the NP* were holistically produced, with four preceded by pauses. In line 7 in type B and line 4 in type C, when *because of the* was first used, it was followed by a pause, but then it was repeated, with *because of the NP* holistically produced. This on the one hand indicates that learners tend to produce shorter clusters such as *because of the*, but on the other hand, reinforces the idea that repeating can be used as an effective strategy for the production of longer fluent chunks. Such uses occurred previously in Appendix 8.2.1.1 and were also found in the instances of the cluster *in terms of the* (*NP*), where the speaker seems to have attempted *in terms of the* for the first time, and then continued with the holistic *in terms of the NP* structure (lines 3–4). In addition, except for the hesitation when *ter-* was used in the first line, other instances of *in terms of the* and *instead of the* were produced holistically.

Quite a small number of the instances of *of the* were produced with pauses or inappropriately. Thirteen instances had internal pauses, which can be patterned on the whole as *because of* ‖ *the NP* (lines 1–5), *the NP of* ‖ *the* ‖ *NP* (lines 6–12), and *NP* ‖ *of* ‖ *the NP* (line 13) (Appendix 8.2.1.5). This shows: first, pauses occurred between *because of* and its following noun phrases; second, the instances of *the NP of* in lines 6–12 were used as wholes; third, learners may especially have had difficulty in producing the second noun phrase as a holistic unit. Furthermore, *of* in five instances seems to have been used incorrectly: it may have been unnecessary in lines 1–4 because its preceding word was either a transitive verb or another preposition, and it should have been replaced by *between* in line 5 (Appendix 8.2.1.6).

In MiniM, the *of the* frequencies were 99 and 107 when pauses were and were not included, respectively, so the predominant instances were produced without pauses, and eight of them were not (Appendix 6.4.7). Holistic production of this cluster is presented as four categories and their pausing patterns are aligned to those in DSS (Table 8.2). In the first category, when *of the* first appeared in line 1, it had pauses on both sides; its repetitive use in line 2 was immediately linked to its following noun phrase. In line 3, *of the* was followed by a hesitant noun phrase, with pauses placed in the content words that appear to have formed the phrase. The preceding *of the* seems to be a false start of *of the*. Moreover, they were further preceded by noun phrases, and along with the co-texts, they can be patterned as *NP ‖ of the ‖ of the NP* (lines 1–2) or *NP of the ‖ of the NP* (line 3) (Appendix 8.2.1.7).

The second category is about pausing and *the NP of the NP* structure. Four pausing patterns of this structure in DSS are found in MiniM, namely, *the NP ‖ of the NP*, *the NP of the ‖ (NP)*, *the NP of the ‖ NP*, and *the NP of the NP* (Table 8.2, Appendix 8.2.1.8). The pattern of *the NP ‖ of the NP* had four instances. Three of them had pauses occur at the point indicated in the pattern, that is, in between the first noun phrase, *the NP*, and the second half of the structure, *of the NP* (lines 1–3). One had a pause placed when the content word of the first noun phrase was being retrieved (line 4), and the partial start of the word, *cult-*, indicates that the speaker probably had difficulty in retrieving this word. There was one example of the pattern *the NP of the ‖ (NP)*, where the expected noun phrase was cut short by contribution from another interlocutor. Two cases are marked as *the NP of the ‖ NP*, which can be further specified as *the NP of the ‖ NP ‖* in the first line, but in the second line the occurrence of the pause after *the NP of the* seems to have been caused by the difficulty in formulating the content word for the second noun phrase, indicated by the false start *co-*. Twenty-five instances of *the NP of the NP* were used holistically. Specifically, four of them had pauses as boundary markers on both sides (lines 1–4), seven were preceded by pauses (lines 5–11), nine made up the *prep the NP of the NP* cluster (lines 12–20), and the rest were embedded in other structures (lines 21–25).

161

Other instances consisting of noun phrases and *of the* are patterned as *NP of the NP* (Appendix 8.2.1.9), and all four types of pausing that occurred in DSS are found in MiniM (Table 8.2). First, there was evidence of difficulty in lexical retrieval, as the first noun involved was partially started and then followed by its complete formulation (line 1). This type of pausing is marked as *NP* ‖ *of the NP*. The second pattern *NP of the* ‖ (*NP*) had three examples. The content of the second noun phrase being missing seems to be due to contribution from another interlocutor (line 1), repeating (line 2), or topic-shifting (line 3). Four instances are marked as *NP of the* ‖ *NP*, three of which had pauses after *NP of the*, and one had a pause in the content words that made up the second noun phrase. Forty-two *NP of the NP* instances were produced without pauses; they were either bounded by pauses on both sides (lines 1–6), preceded by pauses (lines 7–13), or formed the *verb NP of the NP* structure (lines 14–25) or others (lines 26–42).

As in DSS, the typical cluster groups *because of the* and *instead of the* also occur in MiniM (Table 8.2, Appendix 8.2.1.10). Except for the first two *because of the* instances (lines 1–2), which were followed by reformulations, the rest of the instances of *because of the NP* and *instead of the NP* were uttered without pauses (lines 3–5). What was found different from DSS is that first, in MiniM the cluster *of the* was used after verb phrases, forming the patterns such as *get out of the NP* and *think of the NP* (lines 6–11), and second, *of the NP* was used as an independent cluster without being preceded by any noun phrase (lines 12–14). These instances are marked under type E in Table 8.2. Additionally, eight *of the* instances had internal pauses: one was preceded by an adjective (line 1), and the rest are marked as *NP of* ‖ *the NP*, following the marking scheme used for the instances of this prepositional cluster (lines 2–8) (Appendix 8.2.1.11), which further indicates a close relationship between *of* and its preceding noun phrases.

8.2.2 *To the*

The calculated frequencies of *to the* were 265 and 245 respectively when pauses were excluded and included in DSS (Appendix 6.4.7). This shows that a preponderant number of the instances in learner speech were used holistically, and only a small number may have been produced with pauses. Its holistic production is classified into six types, as listed in Table 8.3, ranging from types A to F in Appendix 8.2.2.1. All instances in type A were bounded by pauses on both sides, so they are indicated as ‖ *to the* ‖. Moreover, apart from being preceded by pauses, one was further preceded by an adverb (line 1), four first by noun phrases and further by verb phrases (lines 2–5), and one by a verb (line 6). On their right side, one was followed by reformulation (line 1), one by the contribution from a group member (line 2), and the rest by pauses (lines 3–6); three of them were further followed by noun phrases (lines 4–6). As can be seen, the *to the* instance in lines 4–5 was part of a larger structure *verb NP* ‖ *to the* ‖ *NP*, and in line 6 was part of *verb* ‖ *to the* ‖ *NP*. Despite the occurrence of the multiple pauses in the co-texts, no pause was found in between *to* and *the* in this type, which suggests that *to the* may have been already treated as one single unit. Type B is about different levels of repetitions. *To, the, to the,* or *to the* together with the words in its co-texts was found to have been repeated, leading to different outcomes. After repetition, the *to the* instance was followed by repairs in line 1 and by hesitant noun phrases in lines 2–5 and 21. In lines 6–7, their following utterances were cut off probably due to the contribution from other interlocutors. In lines 8–20 and 22–37, repeating *the, to the,* and *to the* along with the words in the co-texts seems to have facilitated the production of longer fluent units. There were cases where the first use of *to the* was followed by repairs; after it was repeated, the cluster was still followed by the noun phrases that had internal pauses (lines 38–41). The pausing of type C is marked as *to the* ‖ *(NP)*, suggesting that there should have been noun phrases following *to the*, but there were not. Six *to the* instances were followed by topic shifts (lines 1–6); another six were interrupted by the group members (lines 7–12), although two of them were further followed by hesitant complete noun phrases after the interruption (lines 9–10). In lines 13–14, the components of the noun phrases involved were unintelligible. The elements preceding the instances of *to the* in this group included verbs (lines 1–4, 9–10 and 13–14), nouns (lines 5–7 and 11), and adjectives (lines 8 and 12), respectively making up the structures such as *verb to the* ‖ *(NP)*, *verb NP to the* ‖ *(NP)*, and *adj to the* ‖ *(NP)*. In type D, the pausing pattern is marked as *to the* ‖ *NP*. It shows that on the one hand the instances of *to the* were immediately preceded by the elements including adverbs, adjectives, verbs, or nouns, and on the other hand, pauses occurred after *to the*, which were further followed by noun phrases. They made up the patterns including *according to the* || *NP* (lines 1–3 and 36), *adj to the* || *NP* (lines 5–8 and 35), *verb to the* || *NP* (lines 9–20 and 27–31) and *verb NP to the* || *NP* (lines 22–26 and 33–34). Furthermore, although marked as *to the* || *NP*, pauses were in fact placed at two locations: the majority occurred in between *the* and its following noun phrases (lines 1–26), and the rest were located in the noun phrases when the noun heads were retrieved (lines 27–37). The pattern type E is indicated as || *to the NP*, meaning that all instances in this group were uttered as wholes, although preceded by pauses. Eight of them were further preceded by verb phrases, whose patterns are marked either as *verb NP* || *to the NP* (lines 1–6) or *verb* || *to the NP* (lines 7–8), and others were further preceded by nouns (lines 9–13) or adjectives (lines 14–15), respectively patterned as *NP* || *to the NP* and *adj* || *to the NP*. In type F, *to the NP* was embedded in longer fluent chunks, including *verb to the NP* (lines 1–55), *verb NP to the NP* (lines 64–90), *adj to the NP* (lines 56–63 and 91–106), *NP to the NP* (lines 107–111), and *according to the NP* (lines 112–116).

Table 8.3   Pausing patterns of *to the* in DSS and MiniM

to the	FOD	FOM
Holistic use		
A: || *to the* ||	6	2
B: repeating	41	4
C: *to the* || (*NP*)	14	4
D: *to the* || *NP*	37	2
E: || *to the NP*	15	2
F: *to the NP*	119	73
to || *the*	20	2
Misuse of *to*	13	0

The outliers of the holistic production fell into two types: internal pauses either occurred in between *to* and *the*, or the use of *to* was not grammatically correct. Twenty *to the* instances had internal pauses (Appendix 8.2.2.2). Moreover, two of them were followed by repairs (lines 1–2), but on their left side, they were preceded by verbs, keeping *verb to* as a holistic unit. In lines 3–8, the instances were followed by noun phrases, although two of them seem to have been incomplete and hesitant (lines 3–4); they were also preceded by verb phrases, the overall pausing pattern of which is thus marked as *verb to* || *the NP*. Another five *to the* instances were part of the *verb* || *NP to* || *the NP* structure (lines 9–13), where *to* appears to have been more closely adhered to the preceding noun phrases than to those that followed, as indicated by the location of pauses in these concordance lines. One instance formed the prepositional phrase *from* || *NP to* || *the NP* (line 14), whose pausing pattern is similar to the verb phrases just mentioned. In lines 15–16, with its following elements, the article *the* constituted structurally complete noun phrases such as *the word* and *the culture*, and the co-texts in lines 17–19 were scattered with pauses, indicating the pressure on formulating speech online. In line 20, although the repetitive use of *to the* seems to have enhanced speech fluency, the use of *to* in this context appears grammatically incorrect. Misuse also occurred when *to* was immediately connected with *the* and other words, as shown by the thirteen instances in Appendix 8.2.2.3: *to* should have been replaced by *of* in lines 1–4, by *on* in lines 5–7, by *from* in line 8, and by *for* in line 9; in the remaining four instances, *to* was surplus, as the verb preceding was either a linking verb (line 10) or transitive (lines 11–13).

In MiniM, the frequencies were 87 and 89 respectively with or without the inclusion of pauses in calculation. This suggests that all instances were used holistically except for two outliers. Following the categories in DSS, all six types of its holistic use are found in MiniM, as indicated in Table 8.3. Detailed evidence is provided in Appendix 8.2.2.4. As can be seen, the first pausing pattern || *to the* || occurred in two instances. Both were preceded by pauses but further by verb phrases on their left side, and on their right side, they were also followed by noun phrases, so the structure for such use can be patterned as *verb* || *to the* || *NP*. In the second type, either *the* or *to the* was repeated, but repetition did not always lead to successful production of longer fluent units. The first two instances seem to have achieved the aim (lines 1–2) whereas the other two did not (lines 3–4). With regard to the third type *to the* || (*NP*), the noun phrases appear to have been cut off by repairs (lines 1–2) or followed by intelligible speech (lines 3–4); no contribution from the group members was observed. However, on their left side, three of them were preceded by verbs, making up the patterning *verb to the* || (*NP*) (lines 2–4). Two instances were also included in the fourth pattern *to the* || *NP* (type D), both of which were preceded by adjectives, and on their right side, they were first followed by pauses, and then by noun phrases. Thus, the pausing pattern of these instances can be expanded as *adj to the* || *NP*. The fifth pattern, || *to the NP*, had two examples: on the left side, one of them was further preceded by a noun phrase and then a verb phrase, and the other was preceded by a preposition phrase; on the right side, both of them were followed by pauses. Thus, *to the NP* seems to have been treated as an individual unit in these two lines, although one being part of *verb NP* || *to the NP* (line 1), and the other *prep NP* || *to the NP* (line 2). In the last type (type F), *to the NP* was embedded in larger fluent units, including *verb to the NP* (lines 1–34), *verb NP to the NP* (lines 35–45), *adj to the NP* (lines 46–57), and others (lines 58–73).

MiniM had two instances disrupted by internal pauses (Appendix 8.2.2.5). The first instance formed the pattern *to* || *the NP*. As discussed previously in Section 7.4.2, the occurrence of a false start and multiple pauses in the co-text suggests that this internal pause may have been triggered by online planning pressure and most probably difficulty in lexical retrieval. The second instance was embedded in the *verb to* || *the NP* structure, which also occurred in DSS. As already discussed in Section 7.4.1, this pause may have been used as a boundary marker to separate the VP-based and its object NP-based cluster.

8.2.3 *In the*

The frequency of *in the* in DSS calculated when pauses were ignored was 220, and it was 213 when pauses were included (Appendix 6.4.6). This indicates that all but seven *in the* instances were produced without pauses. Same as *to the* discussed in the last section, the holistic production of *in the* is categorized into six types, ranging from types A to F (Table 8.4). The co-texts are provided in Appendix 8.2.3.1. As displayed, the first pattern || *in the* || had twelve instances. In addition to being both preceded and followed by pauses, four of them were further followed by topic-shifting (lines 1–4), and eight by hesitant but complete noun phrases, which formed the || *in the* || *NP* structure (lines 5–12). The elements on their left side were various: two instances were located at the beginning of a new turn (lines 2 and 12), and the rest were preceded by a noun phrase (lines 1 and 6–7), a conjunction (lines 3–4), an adjective (line 5), a verb (lines 8–9 and 11) and a preposition (line 10). Type B is about different levels of repetition. Repeating *in* (lines 1–9), *the* (line 10), *in the* (lines 11–18), and *in the* with its subsequent word *two* (lines 19–20) seems to have facilitated the learners with the production of grammatically complete fluent speech units, but in lines 21–23, the repetitive use of *in* was still followed by pauses and hesitant noun phrases. On their left side, the majority repetitions were preceded by noun phrases (lines 1, 3–8, 11–14, 17–18 and 22–23), some of which also had verbs (lines 1, 3 and 6) and prepositions (lines 4 and 7) placed before the noun phrases. The rest either occurred at the beginning of a new turn (lines 2 and 15–16) or were preceded by conjunctions (lines 9–10 and 19–20). The pausing of type C is marked as *in the* ‖ (*NP*), where the absence of the following noun phrase seems to have been caused by repairs (lines 1–3), interruptions (lines 4–5), or indecipherable speech (lines 6–8). Their preceding co-texts consisted of verbs (lines 1–2 and 5), nouns (lines 4 and 7–8), and adverbs (lines 3 and 6). In type D, the *in the* instances directly followed their preceding words, which mostly consisted of noun phrases (lines 1, 10–15 and 25–30) or verb phrases (lines 2–9 and 17–24) but were followed by hesitant but nevertheless structurally complete noun phrases, so the pausing of most instances was expanded as either *NP in the* ‖ *NP* or *verb in the* ‖ *NP*. Pausing regarding the structure *in the* ‖ *NP* also fell into two subtypes: in one subtype, pauses occurred in between *in the* and its following noun phrases (lines 1–17), and in the other, they involved retrieving the content words for the noun phrases (lines 18–36). In type E, all instances of the *in the NP* cluster were used as wholes, with fifteen of them bounded by pauses on both sides (lines 1–15) and nineteen preceded by pauses (lines 16–34). Moreover, eleven of them seem to have been used as turn-openers (lines 1–6 and 16–20), three were repaired speech for their preceding units (lines 7–8), and thirteen were further preceded by noun phrases (lines 10–14 and 25–32). In the last type, some *in the NP* instances made up longer fluent units such as *verb in the NP* (lines 1–14), and some of them were embedded in wider co-texts, indicating time (lines 15–34), locations, or directions (lines 1–14 and 35–67), or others (lines 68–94).

Two groups of outliers reveal that this cluster was not always used holistically by the learners. First, as shown in Appendix 8.2.3.2, *in* and *the* were separated by pauses; the preceding elements before *in* were a noun phrase (lines 1–2, 4–5 and 7), a verb (line 3) and an adjective (line 6), but *the* was followed directly by noun phrases after pausing (lines 1–6). In line 7, pauses not only occurred after *in* but also in its following noun phrase. Pausing can be patterned either as *NP in || the NP* in lines 1–2 and 7 or *verb NP in || the NP* in lines 4–5. Moreover, the first two instances of this category were used to indicate time (lines 1–2), and the rest locations. Second, six instances involved misuse of *the* or *in* (Appendix 8.2.3.3). In lines 1–2, *the* seems to have been unnecessary, as its following nouns were the names of countries, Brazil and America. In lines 3–4, *in the* should have been replaced by *on the*. Furthermore, it would be more appropriate to use *at* in line 5, and *with* in line 6.

Table 8.4 Pausing patterns of *in the* in DSS and MiniM

in the	FOD	FOM
Holistic use		
A: || *in the* ||	12	1
B: repeating	23	7
C: *in the* || (*NP*)	8	6
D: *in the* || *NP*	36	6
E: || *in the NP*	34	19
F: *in the NP*	94	101
in || *the*	7	0
Misuse of *in*	6	0

Including or excluding pauses, this cluster in MiniM had the same frequencies, both of them being 140 (Appendix 6.4.6). This indicates that all of them were produced without pauses. Although smaller in number, but similar to those in DSS, the pausing patterns are also organized into six groups (Table 8.4). As can be seen in Appendix 8.2.3.4, in the first type, although surrounded by pauses, *in the* was further followed by a noun phrase and preceded by a verb phrase, forming the pattern *verb || in the || NP*. The second type involved repeating *in* (lines 1–2), *the* (line 3), and *in the* (lines 4–7). By doing so, except for the first line, the second attempt in the other lines appear to have helped to produce the subsequent fluent speech units. Before repeating, except for the instance in line 3 which was located at the beginning of a new turn, the preceding elements of the rest were a verb (line 1), a conjunction (line 2), and noun phrases (lines 4–7). In type C, the noun phrase after *in the* was cut off because of a topic shift (lines 1–5) or contribution from group members (line 6). On the left side, it was preceded either by nouns (lines 1–2), adjectives (lines 3–4), a conjunction (line 5), or a verb (line 6). In type D, the speakers either paused after *in the* (lines 1–2) or showed hesitation when retrieving the content words for the following noun phrases (lines 3–6); on their left side, four instances were preceded by noun phrases (lines 2–5). Type E is about the holistic use of the *in the NP* cluster. Six of the instances were isolated from their surroundings with pauses occurring on both sides, and thirteen of them were preceded by pauses. Moreover, four of them were placed at the beginning of a turn (lines 1–2 and 7–8), two were preceded by clear boundary markers indicating that the previous turn had been finished (lines 3–4), three by conjunctions (lines 9–11), one by an adverb (line 13), one by a preposition (line 19), and others by noun phrases (lines 5 and 14–17) or verb phrases (lines 6, 12 and 18). Similar to the findings in DSS, in the last type, 101 instances of *in the NP* either formed larger structural units or were used to express notions such as time or locations. For instance, eleven of them made up the cluster *verb NP in the NP* (lines 1–11), seven were used to describe time (lines 12–18), and a large number of them were used to indicate locations (lines 19–60).

8.2.4 *On the*

The frequencies of *on the* were 89 and 86 respectively in DSS with pauses excluded and included (Appendix 6.4.7), which means three instances may have had internal pauses whereas the rest were used as wholes. As with *to the* and *in the*, pausing behavior regarding the holistic production of *on the* is categorized into six types (Table 8.5), with detailed examples provided in Appendix 8.2.4.1. Five *on the* instances belonged to the first pausing pattern, namely, || *on the* ||; accordingly, pauses occurred both before and after *on the*. Except for the last instance, which was followed by a change of topic, the rest was followed by noun phrases; on their left side, three of them were further preceded by verb and noun phrases (lines 1–3) and two by conjunctions (lines 4–5). It can be seen the wider co-texts for the first three instances made up the pattern *verb NP || on the || NP* (lines 1–3). The second type involves repeating *on* (lines 1–2) or *on the* (lines 3–8). By repeating, six of them seem to have increased the length of the following fluent speech runs (lines 1–6), although two of them involved the wrong use of the noun concerned (lines 5–6). Moreover, in lines 7–8, repetitive use was followed by contribution from another interlocutor. The pattern of type C is marked as *on the || (NP)*, indicating that the main components of the noun phrases after *on the* were missing. The causes seem to have involved a reformation (line 1), an interruption (line 2), and indecipherable speech (lines 3–4). The preceding co-texts consisted of an adjective phrase (line 1) or a verb phrase (lines 2–4); the extended structure for the instances in lines 2–4 can be patterned as *verb on the || NP*. As in the fourth pausing pattern for *in the* and *to the*, *on the* instances in type D can also be marked as *on the || NP*, having two sub-categories: pauses either were placed in between *on the* and its following noun phrases (lines 1–13) or occurred when part of the content words were being formulated (lines 11–17). Moreover, most of the instances in this category were embedded in the *verb on the || NP* structure as they were preceded by verb phrases (lines 2–15). As to type E, *on the NP* instances had pauses occurring before and after them, suggesting they may have been treated as individual units. The four-word cluster *on the other hand* is a typical and specific example of this category (lines 4–6). In the last type, the noun phrases involved were used to express locations, directions, time, or manners. Apart from being used as holistic units, some *on the NP* instances were part of larger fluent units such as *verb on the NP* (lines 1–24) and *NP on the NP* (lines 25–31).

Table 8.5   Pausing patterns of *on the* in DSS and MiniM

on the	FOD	FOM
Holistic use		
A: || *on the* ||	5	1
B: repeating	8	5
C: *on the* || (*NP*)	4	1
D: *on the* || *NP*	17	4
E: || *on the NP*	6	14
F: *on the NP*	43	71

170

Continued

on the	FOD	FOM
on ‖ the	3	3
Misuse of on or the	3	0

As to the instances that were not used holistically, the occurrence of the internal pause was partly a result of repairs (line 1), or because *on* and *the* seem to have formed the pausing pattern *verb on ‖ the NP* (lines 2–3) (Appendix 8.2.4.2). Pausing between the VP-based clusters and their object NP-based clusters has already been discussed in Chapter 7 in both learner and native speech, which appears to be a common practice. Second, either *on* or *the* was used incorrectly in the co-texts. As indicated in Appendix 8.2.4.3, *on* in the first line should have been replaced by *to*, and in the second line by *in*; *the* in the third line should have been deleted, saving *on average* as one unit.

In MiniM, the frequencies of this cluster were 99 and 96 respectively with the exclusion or inclusion of pauses. All six types of the holistic use found in DSS occurred in MiniM (Table 8.5), although some types had only a few instances (Appendix 8.2.4.4). For instance, either type A or C had one example to indicate the correspondent pausing pattern, but the instance in type A seems to have been part of ‖ *on the* ‖ *NP* structure, since it was placed at the beginning of a speaking turn but further followed by a noun phrase. The one in type C appears to have been part of *verb on the* ‖ (*NP*), as it was preceded by a verb phrase but followed by indecipherable speech. As to type B, repeating *the* (line 1) or *on the* (lines 2–5) seems to have facilitated the production of the rest of the noun phrases. Moreover, all of its repetitions were preceded by verb phrases. In type D, pauses occurred in between *on the* and its following constituents in lines 1–3, and in line 4, *on the* was followed by contribution from another interlocutor. On their left side, two of them were preceded by verb phrases (lines 1–2), one by a verb phrase collocating with a noun phrase (line 3), and one by an adverb (line 4). Consequently, the extended structure for the first two instances was *verb on the* ‖ *NP* and for the third one was *verb NP on the* ‖ *NP*. As in DSS, the pattern of type E demonstrates that the cluster *on the NP* stood alone as an intact unit, with six instances preceded by boundary markers (lines 1–6), five by verb phrases (lines 7–11), and three by prepositional phrases (lines 12–14), the co-texts of which in the last two categories were respectively patterned as *verb || on the NP* (lines 7–10), *verb NP || on the NP* (line 11), and *prep NP || on the NP* (lines 12–14). In type F, *on the NP* instances were embedded in other lengthy fluent units such as *verb on the NP* (lines 1–19) and *verb NP on the NP* (lines 20–37), and some instances were used to express relations such as locations or directions (lines 38–71).

Three *on the* instances had pauses in between their components (Appendix 8.2.4.5). In the first two instances, *on* seems to have been more attached to its preceding words, making up an adverb phrase, *later on*, and a verb phrase, *goes on*, whereas *the*, with its following elements, made up noun phrases used in different clauses (lines 1–2), so pauses at these two locations may have served as boundary markers. In line 3, *on* seems to be part of a verb phrase, *depending on*, and *the* part of a noun phrase, *the number of hydrogens*, whose pausing pattern is *verb on || the NP*. Thus, pausing at this point seems to have separated different grammatical constituents.

8.2.5 Summary and conclusion

The predominant majority of *of the* instances were produced holistically. They were either bounded by pauses or involved in repetitions, or used as part of the structures including *the NP of the NP* and *NP of the NP*, or as part of those preceded by *because, instead, in terms*, and verb phrases. Some instances had internal pauses or have *of* misused. Comparatively more instances in learner speech were found to have pauses on both sides or involved repeatss than in native speech, suggesting that learners tend to produce shorter fluent units, have individual variation in automatizing this cluster, and have more difficulty in producing the extended *of the* clusters as wholes. As to *the NP of the NP*, the pausing patterns *the || NP of the || NP* and *the || NP of the NP* occurred only in DSS; although differing in proportion, the rest of the patterns that were applied to DSS learner speech were adopted by the native speakers in MiniM. These reinforce that fluent speech units in learner speech are shorter than those in native speech and learners have different developmental processes of automatizing clusters. Moreover, pauses seem to be more likely to occur in the second noun phrase than in the first one, or in other words, the first half of the chunk, *(the) NP of*, tends to be produced holistically. This echoes Chung's

(2012) claim that pauses are preferably placed after *of* when it co-occurs with noun phrases. Regarding the instances that had internal pauses, in both corpora, *of* seems to have made up the fluent *the NP of* cluster with its preceding elements, whereas *the* constituted a second *the NP* with its following noun phrases. Such uses in MiniM outnumbered those in DSS, indicating the preposition *of* indeed may have a closer relationship with its preceding noun phrases and that *the NP of* would be commonly kept as one unit in native speech. In learner speech, difficulty in retrieving noun phrases appears to be the cause of the occurrence of the pauses in *of the*. Native speakers may have had similar difficulty while planning noun phrases, reflected by the use of the pausing patterns *NP of the* || *(NP)* and *NP of the* || *NP*. In addition, although *of the* in DSS occurred almost three times as frequently as it did in MiniM, the pattern *verb of the NP* was only found in the latter.

As to the other three *prep the* clusters examined, their instances were also predominantly produced as holistic units. The first two patterns of pausing occurred frequently in DSS, which not only again indicate that learners had pressure on lexical retrieval, leading to their fluent runs being relatively short, but also present the close relationship between the three prepositions, *to*, *in*, and *on*, and *the*, since they consistently co-occurred despite being surrounded by pauses, or their co-texts were full of hesitations and other dysfluencies. When these *prep the* clusters supposedly or actually collocated with noun phrases, many instances were immediately preceded by lexical elements. In learner speech, pauses seem to occur more frequently after *prep the* than before it, supporting that the beginning of an NP-based cluster, in this case, *the*, is indeed the main point of online planning pressure; that is to say, learners may have difficulty when searching for the content words to complete the noun phrases followed. Nevertheless, more than half of these *prep the NP* instances were produced without pauses in DSS. In MiniM, most of *prep the NP* instances were used wholes; if pauses occurred, they would be placed before *prep the NP* structure. Many instances of *prep the NP* were in fact found to be embedded in clusters of four or more words in both corpora. Some internal pauses in the three *prep the* clusters may have actually been used to set the boundary for different grammatical constituents, as their components respectively appeared related to the preceding or following units; more of them in DSS were found to be marks of online planning pressure. Furthermore, including *of the*, misuse or overuse of the prepositions or *the* was found in DSS, which, same as different levels of repetition, can evidence that individual learners may have different automatizing processes leading to formulaicity.

8.3 Subject verb clusters

With regard to the subject verb clusters, or the SV-based, it has been established that they tend to be used as wholes in both corpora, and as can be seen in Chapter 6, the vast majority of them were holistically produced in MiniM, in contrast to more than half in DSS. Based on the findings from Chapter 7, where pauses tend to occur when the SV-based are preceded by conjunctions remains to be answered. Moreover, it is worthwhile to compare between corpora how pauses behave in or around the high frequency clusters of this type. To fulfill these tasks, selected are *I think*, *you know*, *it is*, and *they are*. Table 8.6 includes their frequency ranking in the pauses-ignored, two-word cluster lists taken from Appendices 6.4 and 6.9. It is believed that words that are extensively used in a register tend to be contracted (Erman & Warren, 2000; Foster, 2001), so the contracted forms of *it is* and *they are*, namely *it's* and *they're*, are also considered in the discussion, with their ranking taken from the pause-ignored wordlist index of DSS (Appendix 6.2) and that of MiniM (Appendix 6.3). Based on the pausing patterns used to describe the prepositional clusters, the ones adopted to categorize the SV-based are modified and presented in Tables 8.7–8.10.

Table 8.6   Frequency ranking of four subject verb clusters

Clusters	FRD	FRM
I think	3	3
you know	16	2
it is	5	42
it's	26	14
they are	24	816
they're	n/a	68

8.3.1 *I think*

As can be seen, *I think* occurred with the same frequency in DSS when pauses were or were not included (Appendix 6.4.4), indicating all of its instances were used as wholes by learners; accordingly, its pausing behavior is classified into five types, patterned as ‖ *I think* ‖ (type A), repeating *I* or *I think* (type B), *I think* ‖ (type C), ‖ *I think* (type D), and *I think* (type E) (Table 8.7), with detailed co-texts provided in Appendix 8.3.1.1. In type A, in lines 1–9, the instances of *I think* were placed at the beginning of a new turn and then followed by pauses; in lines 10–15, *I think* appears to have taken over the previous speaking turns, which were further followed by contribution from other group members in lines 16–19, and bounded by pauses on both sides in lines 20–29. One instance was further preceded by a conjunction (line 24) and seven were further followed pronouns (lines 2, 4, 5, 9, 23, 28 and 29). In the second type, either *I* (lines 1–17) or the entire cluster *I think* (lines 18–30) was repeated. Most instances of the three-word cluster *I I think* seem to have been used as individual units, since they were either used to start a new turn (lines 1–6) or surrounded by pauses on both sides (lines 7–9 and 17). Repeating *I think* as well as those instances that were either followed or preceded by pauses seems to have reinforced its holistic status (lines 18–30). Type C is concerned with the instances of *I think* whose turns were taken over by other speakers (lines 1–13) or those that were followed immediately by pauses (lines 14–34). The causes seem to be that either the speakers involved were hesitant in speaking (lines 1 and 13), the group members actively participated in discussion, indicated by the occurrence of multiple latching in the co-text (lines 2–6), or the preceding turn was already finished in that particular context (lines 5–12). Moreover, some instances were preceded by conjunctions, making up a three-word cluster *conj I think* (lines 14–23), several instances were used as lexical fillers (lines 24–28), and some were placed at the end of the preceding clauses (line 29–34). In type D, more than half of the instances were used at the beginning of a turn (lines 1–55), and the rest were preceded by pauses (lines 56–104). Three-word clusters such as *I think the* (lines 1–3, 24–33 and 56–65), *I think it's* (lines 4–6, 34–36 and 66–74), and *I think pron* (lines 7–13, 37–45 and 75–83) emerged.

Table 8.7 Pausing patterns of *I think* in DSS and MiniM

I think	FOD	FOM
Holistic use		
A: ‖ *I think* ‖	29	13
B: repeating	30	12
C: *I think* ‖	34	14
D: ‖ *I think*	104	69
E: *I think*	90	41

In the last type (type E), *I think* seems to have constituted two kinds of three-word clusters: one was about the instances used after conjunctions, forming *and I think* (lines 1–16), *because I think* (lines 17–21), *but I think* (lines 22–27), and *so I think* (lines 28–36), and the other was about *I think* collocating with pronouns or noun phrases, including *I think we* (lines 60–67), *I think you* (lines 68–71), *I think it's* (lines 40–48), and *I think the* (lines 51–58). The majority instances of these three-word clusters were used without pauses, as can be also seen in types C and D, but pauses also occurred in between the conjunctions and *I think* as well as *I think* and its following pronouns, examples of which can be found in pausing types A, B and D. As pointed out in the last paragraph, three causes may account for the occurrence of the pauses, but on the other hand, apart from the contextual influence, the different pausing patterns seem to reveal learners' developmental variation in the process of automatizing these clusters as single units. Moreover, when *I think* collocated with a conjunction and with a nominative pronoun, pauses seem to have occurred more frequently between the conjunction and *I think* than between *I think* and the pronoun.

The typical examples of the clusters of four or more words are *I think it is* and *I think the* (*NP*). As to the former, six instances of *I think it is* and thirty-six *I think it's* instances were retrieved from DSS. Among the *I think it's* instances, thirty-three of them were produced holistically (lines 4–5 and 26 in type B, lines 4–6, 34–36 and 66–74 in type D, lines 6–8, 24, 30–31 and 40–48 in type E), and three had internal pauses patterned as *I think* ‖ *it's* (lines 23 and 28 in type A, line 11 in type B). With regard to *I think it is*, five instances were used holistically (lines 75–76 in type D, lines 5 and 28–29 in type E), and one had a pause between *I think* and *it is* (line 21 in type C). As to the extended cluster *I think* followed by noun phrases beginning with *the*, thirty-six *I think the* instances were used holistically. As can be seen in types D and E, *I think the* was either followed by restarts or multiple pauses (lines 24–26 in type D and lines 51–52 in type E). There were three cases where *the* was repeated after *I think*, and then followed by a noun phrase (lines 56–57 in type D and line 9 in type E). Moreover, in six concordance lines, the speakers seem to have managed to produce the following fluent noun phrases after pausing, marked as *I think the* ‖ *NP* (line 22 in type B, lines 3, 27–28 and 58 in type D, lines 53 in type E). Some *I think* instances were coherently followed by the NP structure without pauses, and some *I think the NP* instances served as turn-openers or were preceded by pauses (lines 1–2, 29–33 and 59–65 in type D). Some were embedded in even larger units of fluent speech, as in lines 10, 20, 34 and 54–58 in type E. There were also, however, seven instances of *I think* that were followed first by pauses and then by fluent (line 7 in type A, lines 16 and 24 in type C) or hesitant NP structures (lines 21 and 27 in type A, lines 25 and 30 in type C). Based on the pausing at different locations, it can be seen that learners demonstrated different levels of holistic production and they did manifest individual differences in producing these three- and four-word clusters; moreover, pausing after *the* in *I think the NP* further supports that the beginning of a noun phrase is the critical location of online planning pressure.

All instances of *I think* in MiniM were also used holistically and all five pausing patterns found in DSS occurred in it (Table 8.7, with detailed co-texts provided in Appendix 8.3.1.2). Thirteen instances fell under type A. Five instances were used to start a new turn, with one followed by unintelligible speech (line 1), three by pauses (lines 2–4), and one interrupted by another group member (line 5). Not only preceded by pauses, but the remaining instances were also followed by contribution from group members (lines 6–8), pauses (lines 9–11), and reformulations (lines 12–13). Moreover, one instance was further preceded by a conjunction (line 12), and another two were further followed by pronouns (lines 3 and 13). Type B is about repeating *I think* or its components. Five *I think* instances were preceded by a repetition of *I* (lines 1–5), two by the partial start, *thi-* and *th-* (lines 6–7), another two by the repetition of *I I think* (lines 8–9), and three by *I think* (lines 10–12). In type C, six instances were followed by other speakers' turn (lines 1–6) and three by reformulations (lines 7–9), a three-word cluster *and I think* appeared (lines 9–10),

177

and in the rest four concordance lines, *I think* appears to have been used as a lexical filler (lines 11–14). In type D, thirty-three instances were used to start a new turn (lines 1–33), twenty-four preceded by pauses (lines 34, 36–48 and 50–59) and two by group members' contribution (lines 35 and 49). Moreover, ten of them may have served as lexical fillers (lines 60–69). A number of three-word clusters consisting of *I think* followed by pronouns appeared (lines 6–25 and 37–49). Moreover, three *I think* instances were preceded by conjunctions (lines 39 and 54–55); they seem to have formed the pattern of pausing *conj* ‖ *I think* with the instance in line 12 in type A. This is contrasted with the findings in lines 9-10 in type C, where no pause was placed in between them. In type E, forty-one *I think* instances were embedded in the co-texts, the majority of them made up three-word clusters *conj I think* (lines 10–11, 15–19, 21–23 and 30) and *I think pron* (lines 6–24), and there were cases where *I think* appears to have been used as a filler (lines 34–41).

With regard to the instances of *conj I think*, there was pausing in between conjunctions and *I think* (line 12 in type A, line 39 and 54–55 in type D), although most of them were uttered holistically, for instance, *and I think* in lines 9–10 in type C and lines 23 and 30 in type E, *but I think* in lines 10 and 18 in type E, *so I think* in lines 11 and 16–17 in type E, and *cuz I think* in lines 15, 19 and 22 in type E. Almost all instances of *I think pron* were uttered holistically, such as *I think I* (lines 6–9, 37–38, and 59–63 in type D, lines 6–13 in type E), *I think we* (lines 10–11, 39–40 and 68–69 in type D, lines 14–15 in type E), *I think you* (line 41 in type D, lines 16 and 41 in type E), *I think they* (line 43 in type D), *I think he* (line 12 in type D), *I think she* (line 65 in type D and line 21 in type E), *I think it* (lines 13, 43–47 and 64 in type D, lines 17 and 20 in type E), *I think it's* (lines 14–22 and 48 in type D, lines 18–19 in type E), and *I think that* (lines 24–25, 49 and 66 in type D, lines 22–24 in type E), except for one instance in line 3 in type A, which was patterned as *I think* ‖ *they*. On the other hand, the placement of adverbs and other elements in between *I think* and its following pronouns suggests that these two elements may not be always connected (line 36, 52–53 and 59 in type D, lines 30 and 41 in type E). The findings also indicate the clusters consisting of conjunctions and the subject pronouns may not necessarily be treated as intact units, and that pauses seem to be more likely to be placed in between conjunctions and *I think* than in between *I think* and its following pronouns.

Compared with the four-word cluster *I think it is* in DSS, no such use was found in MiniM, but there were fourteen instances of holistic production of *I think it's*. As can be seen, all of them were used holistically, with two instances directly followed by pauses (lines 2 in type B and 14 in type D) and twelve immediately followed by other speech chunks (lines 9 in type B, 15–22 and 48 in type D, and 18–19 in type E). This indicates that native speakers may have already contracted *it is* as one word — *it's*, and treated this cluster as wholes. With regard to *I think the NP*, nearly all of its instances were used without pauses (lines 4–5 and 38–39 in type E) except one particular case in line 40 in type E, where *the* was repeated and formed the pattern *I think the the NP*, which seems to confirm that the beginning of an NP-based cluster is the point of online planning. Although there is a possibility that native speakers may have paused after *I think the*, the concordance lines concerned show that they mostly treated *I think the NP* as a holistic unit.

8.3.2 *You know*

The results from the quantitative analysis in Chapter 6 reveal that all instances of *you know* were used holistically in DSS (Appendix 6.4.4). Same as *I think*, the pausing patterns of *you know* are categorized into five types (Table 8.8), with co-texts provided in Appendix 8.3.2.1. Marked as ‖ *you know* ‖, type A is not only concerned with the instances that were used to take speaking turns but also those followed by hesitant speech (lines 1–2), interrupted by group members (lines 3–7), or surrounded by pauses (lines 8–26). Three of the instances were also further preceded by conjunctions and formed the pattern of *conj* ‖ *you know* (lines 8–10), and a number of them were treated as stand-alone lexical fillers (lines 17–26). In type B, all instances involved the repetition of its first component, *you*. Except for the last two instances, the rest were further preceded by conjunctions, marked as *conj* ‖ *you* ‖ *you know* (lines 1–2), *conj you* ‖ *you know* (lines 3–4), *conj* ‖ *you you know* (lines 5–6), and *conj you you know* (lines 7–9). In this four-word cluster *conj you you know*, pauses appear to have occurred randomly in its first half, but the second half *you know* seems to have always been a holistic unit. Type C is marked as *you know* ‖, and all instances in this group were followed by pauses. Moreover, most instances in type C seem to have been used as a lexical filler (lines 1–12), and some constituted a three-word cluster *conj you know* (lines 13–15). In contrast to the location of the pauses in type C, the fourth type is marked as || *you know*, where the instances were either used to begin a new speech turn (lines 1–9) or were preceded by pauses (lines 10–35). However, on their right side, *you know* was followed by at least one word. Some instances were used in between grammatical constituents, serving as lexical fillers (lines 19–34). Some were preceded by conjunctions, but with pauses placed in between, making up the pattern *conj* || *you know* (lines 10–15). In contrast, in type E, eight instances of *you know* immediately collocated with conjunctions, so *conj you know* was produced without pauses (lines 1–8). Together with the findings from types B and C, it can be seen that *you know* itself appears more likely to be treated as an individual holistic unit. Furthermore, although some instances seem to have been embedded in longer fluent units such as *you know pron* (lines 10–14) and *do you know* (lines 33–36), most of them in type E in fact seem to have been used as lexical fillers (lines 10–36). Thus, *you know* appears to have been used as an independent holistic unit in most cases in learner speech.

Table 8.8 Pausing patterns of *you know* in DSS and MiniM

you know	FOD	FOM
Holistic use		
A: || *you know* ||	26	33
B: repeating	11	1
C: *you know* ||	15	18
D: || *you know*	35	53
E: *you know*	36	65

In MiniM, *you know* also had the same frequencies with pauses excluded or included and was produced without pauses. The pausing patterns also fall into five types but differ in numbers (Table 8.8). Thirty-three instances were grouped as type A, and they had clear boundaries on both sides. Two of the instances were used to initiate a new turn and then followed by pauses (lines 1–2). Ten of them were either preceded or followed by contribution from group members, but they also had pauses on the other side (lines 3–12). Moreover, eight of the instances were located in between two different clauses (lines 13–20), four were preceded by pauses and further by conjunctions such as *and, or, but* and *because*, patterned as *conj ‖ you know* (lines 21–24), and nine of them seem to have been used as lexical fillers (lines 25–33). In type B, only one instance had the repetition of *you*. Based on its co-text, the instance of *you you know* may have acted like a lexical filler. In type C, more than half of the instances were followed by boundary markers, some of which indicate that the turn was taken over (lines 3–4) or interrupted by another speaker (lines 5–8), and some suggest that the ongoing meaning unit was already complete (lines 1 and 9–11). In the remaining instances, *you know* was followed by its subordinate clause (lines 2 and 12–13) or used as fillers (lines 14–18). Three-word clusters such as *do you know, and you know, but you know* and *like you know* appeared in this type (lines 1–5, 14 and 16). All instances were preceded by pauses in type D, except for two instances, which were preceded by contribution from the group members (lines 20 and 51). Apart from its co-occurrence with pronouns including *I* (lines 1–7), *you* (lines 13–14 and 33), and *they* (lines 26 and 30) and constituting the cluster *you know pron*, it was also immediately followed by noun phrases or clauses. Nearly half of its use seems to have functioned as lexical fillers (lines 29–53). Moreover, some instances in type D were further preceded by conjunctions and formed the pattern *conj ‖ you know* (lines 2–4 and 17–22). This appears to be the same as the pattern occurring in lines 21–24 in type A. However, three-word clusters *and you know, but you know, cuz you know, if you know*, and *like you know* occurred repeatedly in type E. Based on the findings in types A and D, it can be seen that speakers can choose to use them as holistic units or to place pauses in between conjunctions and *you know*. Furthermore, although there were quite a number of recurrent *you know pron* structures in type E, pauses and other elements were previously found placed before pronouns, including *she* in line 3 in type A and line 23 in type D, *they* in line 24 in type D, *it's* in lines 11 in type A, and *I* in line 23 in type A and in line 43 in type E. Thus, it seems that *you know* and the following pronouns are not necessarily kept together as holistic units. Additionally, the recurrent *do you know* in type E seems to have confirmed its holistic status (lines 23–27), and nearly one-third of the instances in this type appear to have used *you know* as a lexical filler (lines 44–65).

8.3.3 *It is* and *it's*

All *it is* instances were produced holistically by learners (Appendix 6.4.5). Based on the pausing behavior, the investigation was initially categorized into types A to E, namely, ‖ *it is* ‖, repeating, *it is* ‖, ‖ *it is*, and *it is*. Considering that this cluster could be contracted as *it's*, type G is added to deal with the contracted form (Table 8.9). Detailed concordance lines for *it is* and *it's* instances are provided in Appendix 8.3.3.1. In type A, all instances were surrounded by pauses; some instances were used to start a new turn (line 1) or a new clause (lines 2–9), two were followed by reformulation (lines 10–11), and two were repairs (lines 12–13). Moreover, two instances were further preceded by conjunctions and formed the pattern *conj* ‖ *it is* (lines 2–3). Type B is concerned with the repetition of *it*, *it is*, or *it is* with their neighboring words. *It* was repeated in lines 1 to 5, three of which were preceded by conjunctions (lines 1–3) and two formed the pausing pattern *conj it* ‖ *it is* (lines 2–3). In lines 6–17, the entire cluster was repeated; pauses were placed after its first use, but then followed by relatively long fluent units. In lines 18–23, reformulations were followed after repeating *it is*. In lines 24–33, the repeated part included *it is* with its preceding conjunctions (lines 24–27) or the following words (lines 28–33). Repeating *it is* alone or with its neighboring words seems to have reinforced the holistic status of this cluster. Type C is about the instances that were followed by indecipherable speech (line 1), turn-taking (line 2), or pauses (lines 3–27). Moreover, after pausing, they were followed by reformulations (lines 3–13), noun phrases (lines 14–18), adjective phrases (lines 19–24), or verb phrases (lines 25–26). Additionally, the co-occurrence of conjunctions and *it is* reappeared, but this time they were holistically produced as *conj it is* (lines 8–9, 17 and 19–20).

In type D, except for the instances used for turn-taking (lines 12, 23–27 and 68-69), the rest were preceded by pauses. The majority of the *it is* instances were either followed by noun phrases (lines 1–24), adjective phrases (lines 25–52), or verb phrases (lines 53–64). Clusters of a longer length such as *it is a* (*NP*) (lines 2–12), *it is the NP* (lines 16–18) and *it is NP* (lines 19–24) emerged, but as shown by the instances in lines 13–15, *it is* and its following noun phrases were not necessarily produced as wholes. Except in line 28, there were some instances that consisted of *it is* and adjective phrases used without pauses, but the insertion of adverbs and negations between *it is* and its following adjective phrases in lines 44–52 also suggest that these two constituents can be separated. With regard to the instances of *it is* collocating its verb phrases, a four-word cluster *it is verb-ed that* appeared (lines 55–61); but based on the use of adverbs in lines 59–61, pauses could be located in between *it is* and *verb-ed that*. This seems to have also been supported by another two examples in lines 4–5 in type A, where pauses indeed occurred in between *it is* and *verb-ed that*. Some instances were further preceded by pauses, and the pattern *conj* ‖ *it is* reappeared in type D (lines 13, 28–35, 49 and 54–56). Thus, in clusters of this type, pauses could be placed in between these two components. In type E, the use of *it is* was mostly embedded in longer clusters such as *it is a (NP)* (lines 1–9), *conj it is a (NP)* (lines 10–19), *it is the (NP)* (lines 22–26), *conj it is the (NP)* (lines 27–32), *conj it is NP* (lines 33–35), *it is NP* (lines 36–47), *it is adj* (lines 48–59), *conj it is adj* (lines 60–72), *it is adv (‖) adj* (lines 73–87), *conj it is adv (‖) adj* (lines 88–100), *it is verb-ed* (lines 101–107), and *conj it is verb-ed* (lines 108–114), and it was found that not all of these clusters were produced holistically. What seems to have been certain, however, is that all instances of *it is* were treated as wholes, including in the last three lines where the cluster was grammatically incorrect (lines 120–122).

As to the 415 instances of *it's*, pausing is further categorized into types a to e (Table 8.9), with detailed co-texts provided under Type G in Appendix 8.3.3.1. Type a, marked as ‖ *it's* ‖, had twenty-eight instances. Eleven of them were used to start a new turn (lines 1–11) and seventeen were preceded by pauses (lines 12–27); on their right side, two of them were followed by other speakers' turn (lines 1–2), twelve by reformulations (lines 10–21), and the rest by pauses (lines 3–9 and 22–28). In type b, eighty-four instances had the repetition of *it*, *it's*, or *it's* along with the words occurring in its co-texts. In line 1, the preceding two instances of *it* were false starts. In lines 2–3, the first *it's* was preceded by a false start and then followed by pauses. When it was used for the second time, although still preceded by the same false start, its following elements were uttered fluently. In lines 4–18, *it's* was first used as a turn-taker, and it was then followed by ungrammatical speech and an attempt to repair the mistake (lines 4–5), or simply repeated in order to produce the remaining speech, which was not entirely successful in lines 6–7. In lines 19–30, the first attempt of *it's* was followed by pauses, so *it's* was used again to maintain the conversational flow, some of which were followed by meaningful noun or verb phrases (lines 23–30) but some were not (lines 19–22). Some of the repetitive use of *it's* seems to have aimed at reformulation (lines 31–39) or emphasis (lines 40–47). In lines 48–50, the first use of *it's* was followed by pauses and then by its double repetition. The repetition of *it's it's* was also found in lines 51–74. As can be seen, except in lines 51–52, the rest of this subgroup were followed by hesitant but nevertheless meaningful and complete adjective or noun phrases. In lines 75–76, the repeated use of *it's it's* was interrupted by a lexical filler, and in lines 77–84, the repeated elements included *it's* and the following elements. Type c is about pausing after *it's*. Some of the instances were further followed by noun phrases (lines 1–7) or adjective phrases (lines 8–12), some of them formed larger clusters such as *conj it's* (lines 2–5, 8–10, 22–24 and 27) or *I think it's* (lines 13–21), and some were followed by reformulations, grammatical errors, or interruptions (lines 17–27).

Table 8.9   Pausing patterns of *it is* and *it's* in DSS and MiniM

it is	FOD	FOM
Holistic use		
A: ‖ *it is* ‖	13	3
B: repeating	33	0
C: *it is* ‖	27	10
D: ‖ *it is*	69	7
E: *it is*	122	22
G: *it's*	415	475
a: ‖ *it's* ‖	28	10
b: repeating	84	75
c: *it's* ‖	27	26
d: ‖ *it's*	111	128
e: *it's*	165	236
F: *it* ‖ *is*	0	7

In type d, the *it's* instances were used to start a new speaking turn or preceded by pauses. Except for the first three instances that were followed by reformulations (lines 1–3), most of the rest formed the clusters *it's a* (‖) *NP* (lines 4–25), *it's the*

(*NP*) (lines 32–34), *it's NP* (lines 40–51), *it's adj* (lines 56–67), *it's verb-ed* (lines 84–88), and *it's PP* (lines 94–105), but on the other hand, the occurrence of adverbs or negation after *it's* in these clusters was also found (lines 26–31, 35–39, 52–55, 68–83, 89–91 and 106–107), showing that these clusters were not necessarily used as holistic units. In lines 108-111, *it's* was followed by clauses. The occurrence of an adverb in line 110 and negation in 111 in between *it's* and its following clauses indicates a possible placement of pauses. Furthermore, the extended clusters that were salient in type d also occurred frequently in type e. They co-occurred with their preceding conjunctions, such as in lines 3–4, 7–12, 23–26, 30, 34–35, 59–66. Grammatical errors were observed when *it's* collocated with other verbs (lines 146–150), which implies that some learners may have fossilized the use of *it's* as one unit, thus failing to change its form in different linguistic contexts.

In MiniM, forty-two *it is* instances were found holistically produced, whereas seven had pauses in between *it* and *is*. No repetition was found. Its holistic production is then categorized into four types (Table 8.9). As can be seen in Appendix 8.3.3.2, the first pausing pattern was applied to three *it is* instances: the first two were used to start a new turn and then immediately followed by pauses (lines 1–2); the third one was surrounded by pauses (line 3). With regard to the ten instances of *it is* that occurred in type C, seven of them were placed at the end of a turn and followed by another interlocutor's contribution (lines 3–9), one was followed by reformulation (line 1), and two were followed by clear indicators that the speech turns were finished (lines 2 and 10). In addition, two of them made up a three-word cluster *conj it is* (lines 1 and 3). All instances in type D were preceded by pauses on the left side, but on their right side, one instance was followed by a noun phrase (line 1), four by adjective phrases (lines 2–5), one by a verb phrase (line 6), and the last one was continued by a prepositional phrase (line 7). Although *it is* was embedded in longer fluent units in type E, *it* in fact belonged to the units preceding in lines 1–4, and in lines 5–17, *it is* seems to have served as a constituting component of a clause. Close co-occurrence of *it is* with a noun phrase, an adjective, and verb phrases was found (lines 18–21), and three of them were preceded by conjunctions, forming the three-word cluster *conj it is* (lines 19–21). Moreover, the last instance appears to have been a reformulation.

Type F is about the instances where pauses were placed in between *it* and *is*, but as can be seen, except for the last instance, these two elements seem to have been separately attached to their preceding or following elements. With its preceding words, *it* constituted an individual clause in lines 1–3, and *is* belonged to a new speaking turn in lines 1–2 and involved reformulation in lines 3–5. In line 6, *it* and *is* were not only separated by a pause but also by indecipherable speech. The last instance in line 7 formed the pattern of || *conj it* || *is verb-ed*. The occurrence of multiple pauses and relatively shorter fluent units in the co-text indicates that the speaker may have experienced difficulty in formulating the speech online, so the speaker might have paused on both sides of *if it* to buy time to plan the next words. This conversely suggests that the beginning of a clause is the major planning point.

Altogether 486 instances of *it's* were found in MiniM, 475 of which were contracted from *it is*, and eleven derived from *it has* (lines 1–11 in type F in Appendix 8.3.3.2). Respecting *it's*, as with what was found in DSS, the pausing patterns range from types a to e (Table 8.9), with detailed co-texts provided under Type G in Appendix 8.3.3.2. In type a, the instances were either used to start a new turn (lines 1–2) or preceded by pauses (lines 3–10), two of which were further preceded by conjunctions (lines 5–6), making up the pattern *conj* || *it's*. On the other side, they were followed by pauses and hesitations (lines 1 and 3), contribution from other group members (lines 2 and 4), or reformulations (lines 5–10). Type b is about repeating *it's* or *it's* and its neighboring words. Specifically, in lines 1–2, *it's* was firstly produced with a noun, making up a meaningful unit, but then followed by pauses and hesitations; when it was about to start a new meaning unit, it was interrupted. In lines 3–14, on the left side, half of the instances were used at the beginning of a new turn (lines 3–8), two were preceded by conjunctions (lines 9–10), and two by pauses (lines 11–12). On their right side, they were immediately followed by reformulations (lines 3–4), pauses (lines 5–6 and 11–14), or partial start of a lexical word (lines 7–10). When *it's* was used for the second time, except in lines 3–6, it was followed by fluent speech units. The repetitive use of some instances immediately followed the first-time use of *it's*, however, instances of *it's it's* were further followed by hesitations and interruptions (lines 15–16), reformulations (lines 19–20), or fluent and structurally complete phrases (lines 17-18 and 21–40). In lines 41–57, *it's* along with another element in its co-text was repeated, and in between the double use of *it's* together with its collocating words, most instances had internal pauses or hesitations (lines 41–51), although some did not (lines 52–55). A couple of them had lexical fillers placed in between (lines 56–57). Moreover, as in DSS, some of the repetitive use of *it's* seems to have been caused by the reformulation of the utterance (lines 58–69) or for the purpose of emphasizing (lines 70–75). In addition, some instances were immediately preceded by conjunctions, constituting the pattern of *conj it's* (lines 9, 20, 29, 31, 43, 66 and 74), and some were preceded first by pauses and further by conjunctions, making up the pattern *conj ‖ it's* (lines 15, 41 and 54).

Type c had twenty-six instances of *it's* that were followed by pauses (lines 1–4 and 16–26), contribution from group members (lines 5–8), false starts (lines 9–13), or indecipherable speech (lines 14-15). In the first four instances, *it's* seems to have been a false start. Moreover, holistic production of the two-word cluster *conj it's* was observed (lines 3–6, 8–9, 13-15 and 20–21). Pauses were found in between *it's* and its following prepositional phrases (lines 21–24), noun phrases (lines 13 and 25) and a verb phrase (line 26). In type d, the *it's* instances were either preceded by pauses (lines 1–4, 13–21, 26–28, 39–51, 57–73, 78–82, 86–91, 92–93, 96–99, 111–115 and 121–125), contribution of other speakers (lines 12, 29, 37–38, 109–110 and 116) or used to start a new turn (lines 5–11, 22–25, 30–36, 52–56, 74–77, 83–85, 92–95, 100–108, 117–120 and 126–128). Thirteen instances were preceded first by pauses and further by conjunctions (lines 4, 15, 27, 58, 66–67, 73, 78–79, 91, 97, 115 and 122), so the pattern of *conj ‖ it's* re-occurred in this group. Not only were two-word clusters such as *it's just* (lines 2–5, 18, 29–30, 53, 95 and 114–115) and *it's like* (lines 97–113) observed, but also clusters of more than two words, including *it's an NP* (lines 6–17), *it's the NP* (lines 23–28), *it's NP* (lines 31–48), *it's adj* (lines 55–63), *it's gonna (do)* (lines 84–89), and *it's PP* (lines 118–122). Adverbs and negations also occurred in between the components of the clusters such as *it's an NP* (lines 18–22), *it's the NP* (lines 29–30), *it's NP* (lines 49–54), *it's adj* (lines 64–81), and *it's PP* (lines 115–117 and 123), which suggests that these larger clusters may not be necessarily produced without pauses. This is further supported by the evidence observed in type e. Furthermore, that conjunctions were immediately placed before the patterns *it's a NP*, *it's the NP*, *it's NP*, *it's adj*, *it's gonna (verb)*, and *it's verb-ed* was also found in tupe e. Given the occurrence of the pattern *conj* ‖ *it's* in types a, b, and d, speakers seem to have individual variation regarding where they would pause in the extended clusters consisting of *conj it's* followed by other elements.

8.3.4 *They are* and *they're*

Except for three *they are* instances, the rest of them were produced without pauses in DSS (Appendix 8.3.4.1). Based on the taxonomy of pausing used for the other clusters discussed above, pausing regarding *they are* not only includes the five types that have been discussed, it also has types F and G, respectively marked as *they* ‖ *are* and *they're*, with the former referring to the clusters with internal pauses and the latter the contracted form (Table 8.10). In type A, two *they are* instances were found to be isolated from its co-texts. Type B is concerned with the repetitive use of *they*, *they are*, and *they are* with its neighboring words. As can be seen, *they* was repeated in lines 1–8 and formed the cluster *they they are*, some of which were followed by pauses (lines 1–2 and 6–8) but some had pauses in between *they* and *they are* (lines 4–7). In lines 9–16, *they are* was repeated and followed by either hesitant speech (lines 10–11), reformulations (lines 12–13), or fluent units (lines 9, 14–16). In lines 17–20, the chunks consisting of *they are* and its preceding or following word were repeated, two of which were followed by pauses (lines 17–18), but the other two were embedded in longer stretches of connected speech. The repetitive use of *they are* as such indicates that learners may have treated it as a holistic unit, but they tend to produce shorter fluent speech runs. In type C, *they are* was either followed by repairs (lines 1–7), interruption (line 8), or pauses (lines 9–10). A three-word cluster *conj they are* was observed (lines 6–9). However, the use of an adverb in between the conjunction and the cluster suggests that these two elements may not be always used as wholes (line 10). This pausing behavior seems similar to what occurred in the cluster *conj it is* discussed in the last section.

Table 8.10   Pausing patterns of *they are* and *they're* in DSS and MiniM

they are	FOD	FOM
Holistic use		
A: ‖ *they are* ‖	2	1
B: repeating	20	0

Continued

they are	FOD	FOM
C: *they are* ‖	10	4
D: ‖ *they are*	20	0
E: *they are*	40	2
G: *they're*	3	109
a: ‖ *they're* ‖	1	1
b: repeating	0	8
c: *they're* ‖	1	9
d: ‖ *they're*	0	29
e: *they're*	1	62
F: *they* ‖ *are*	3	0

In type D, all *they are* instances were preceded by pauses except when it was immediately used to take a turn (lines 6 and 18). Nearly half of the instances were followed by noun phrases (lines 2–9), but as in the findings from type C, the insertion of adverbs and negations in between the cluster and its following noun phrases indicates that these two elements may not have always co-occurred with one another (lines 4–9). Three instances were followed by adjective phrases (lines 10–12), two by prepositional phrases (lines 13–14), and seven by verb phrases (lines 15–20). Similar to what occurred in between *they are* and its following noun phrase, there were negations or adverbs placed between *they are* and the three types of phrases just mentioned, respectively indicated in lines 12, 14 and 18–20. The occurrence of pausing at this point confirms that learners tend to produce short formulaic sequences (Wray, 2002). On the other hand, it supports that the subject tends to be produced holistically with its following verbs when it has a simple structure. There is also the pattern *conj* ‖ *they are*, as a couple instances were first preceded by pauses and further by conjunctions (lines 14 and 17). In type E, nearly all instances were immediately followed by adjective phrases (lines 1–13), noun phrases (lines 14–28), prepositional phrase (lines 29–34), or verb phrases (lines 35–40). Some of such combinations had modifiers in between, as in lines 4–13, 21–28, 32–34 and 36–37, which again shows that the elements involved may not always be used as intact units. The three-word cluster *conj they are* recurred, as in lines 2–7, 20–28, 31–34 and 37–40, but in lines 9–10 there was also evidence suggesting that pauses can be placed in between the conjunction and *they are*.

Type F is about the three instances that had internal pauses. The occurrence of multiple pauses, repetitions, and short fluent units in the co-texts of lines 1–2 show that learners were probably trying to formulate the speech online. The second instance was further preceded by a pause and the conjunction *if*, which is marked as || *if* || *they* || *are*. In line 3, the speaker seems to have treated *they* with its preceding conjunction *if* as one unit, namely, *if they*, but he or she continued it with *are* and then the contracted form, *they're*, which suggest that *if they* as the beginning of the clause seems to indeed have been the location of planning pressure and that the learner seems to be in the processing automatizing *they are* as *they're*. The speaker appeared able to use this cluster holistically, so pausing in it may be simply the evidence of processing effort (Erman, 2007).

Type G is about the use of *they're*. Three instances were retrieved from DSS: one had pauses on both sides, one was preceded by a conjunction and followed by a pause, making up a two-word cluster *conj they're*, and the last one was just discussed in line 3 in type F, which seems to be the evidence that the learner may have been automatizing *they're* as a whole.

Seven *they are* and 109 *they're* instances were retrieved from MiniM (Appendix 8.3.4.2). As to the pausing patterns of *they are*, one has pauses on both sides, four are followed by pauses, and two are embedded in longer fluent units; regarding *they're*, the five common types of pausing are observed, although some of them are small in number, indicated as types a to e (Table 8.10). One instance of *they are* was surrounded by pauses, but before the occurrence of a pause on the left side, a conjunction was placed, making up the patterning *conj* || *they're*. On its right side, *they're* was followed by a pause and reformulated speech. Type b is about its repetitive use. In lines 1–2, when *they're* was used for the first time, it was followed by a pause; when it was repeated, it was followed by a long fluent unit. In lines 3-5, speakers seemed to have been hesitant in formulating the speech, as they not only placed a filler and a silent pause in between the uses of *they*, but also restructured the following expressions by changing the use of adjectives after *they're*. In lines 6–8, the speaker repeated *they're* and changed its following nouns. Changing the use of the elements surrounding *they're* but keeping it as it seems to have reinforced its holistic status. Type c is marked as *they're* ‖. It was either followed by pauses (lines 1–5), contribution from group members (lines 6–7), or reformulations (lines 8–9). After pausing, *they're* was further followed by adjective (lines 1–2), prepositional (line 3), and verb phrases (lines 4–5). On its left side, it collocated with conjunctions, making up a two-word cluster *conj they're* (lines 5–9). In type d, the cluster was either used to start a new turn (lines 1–7, 10 and 21–25) or preceded by interruption (line 1) or pauses (lines 8–9, 11–20 and 26–29). Some instances also had conjunctions before the occurrence of pauses, as in the instance found in type a, and they made up the pattern *conj* ‖ *they're*. On the other hand, *they're* was followed by noun phrases (lines 1–9), adjective phrases (lines 10–16), prepositional phrases (lines 17–21) and verb phrases (lines 22–29). The co-occurrence of *they're* and its following phrases also occurred frequently in type e, as did the intact production of the cluster *conj they're* previously found in type c. Both in types d and e, there were a number of lines where adverbs or negations were placed in between *they're* and different kinds of phrases (lines 5–9 and 14–21 in type d, lines 22–30, 32–34 and 54–58 in type e), so they may not necessarily be connectedly produced.

8.3.5 Summary and conclusion

Nearly all instances of these four subject verb clusters were produced without pauses by both learners and native speakers. As to *I think* and *you know*, all of their instances were produced as wholes and manifested five patterns of pausing, namely, having pauses placed on both sides, repeating part of the clusters or the entire clusters, pauses occurring right after the clusters, pauses preceding the clusters, or the clusters embedded in longer fluent units. When *I think* collocated with conjunctions on the left side and pronouns on the right side, it was found that pauses were more likely to occur in between the conjunctions and *I think*. Regarding the four-word cluster *I think it is*, most instances in learner speech were used holistically, with the most frequently used cluster being *I think it's*, followed by *I think it is*, and then *I think* ‖ *it's*. The pattern *I think* ‖ *it is* rarely occurred. In native speech, all instances were used holistically as *I think it's*. When *I think* was followed by noun phrases, learners presented different patterns, such as *I think the NP*, *I think the* ‖ *NP*, *I think the* ‖ *(NP)*, and *I think* ‖ *the NP*. The majority of instances were used as wholes, but in some instances, pauses occurred in between *I think the* and its following noun phrases, and in a few instances, pauses not only occurred after *I think* but also in its following noun phrases. Native speakers generally used *I think the NP* as a holistic unit. These different pausing patterns suggest that learners may not yet have completed the automatization processes and especially had difficulties in automatizing the NP-based clusters. The cluster *you know* was mostly used as a stand-alone holistic unit by both learners and native speakers, although it was also immediately preceded by conjunctions or followed by pronouns, and the pausing patterns related appear identical to those applied to *I think*.

With regard to *it is* and *they are*, three levels of the production were observed: most instances were used holistically, quite a number of them were contracted as one-word clusters, and several of them had internal pauses. Accordingly, in addition to the five patterns adopted by *I think* and *you know*, the contracted forms as well as the one containing internal pauses were examined. Native speakers were found to have used more contracted forms than learners, although the raw and refined frequencies in both corpora may be the other way around. Different levels of repetition of the two clusters are noticeable in DSS, but in MiniM the repetition involved the contracted forms only. This seems to be the additional evidence that the two clusters have been automated as single units in native speech. Moreover, both clusters and their contracted forms were produced coherently with conjunctions on their left side or the phrases on their right side, but pauses seem more likely to occur at the former location, which is similar to the pausing behavior found with *conj I think* and *conj you know* when they are also followed by other elements. No internal pause was observed in *it is* produced by learners, but several instances of this cluster and several *it's* were used inappropriately, which appears to be the evidence of fossilized use in learner speech. Several pauses were found in between *it* and *is* in native speech, but they may have functioned as boundary markers except in the last instance, which was probably due to online speech planning. This seems to be the cause of the occurrence of internal pauses in *they are* in learner speech as well. Along with the occurrence of pausing found after the conjunction, this also indicates that the beginning of a clause, conjunctions or conjunctions followed by the pronoun subject, may be the major location where speakers experience planning pressure.

8.4   *Verb to* clusters

Based on the quantitative results summarized in Chapter 6, the VP-based clusters account for a significant proportion in both corpora. Two subtypes occurred frequently, one consisting of verbs and particles, and the other made up of verb and noun phrases. Internal pauses have been investigated in Chapter 7 and the findings indicate that their placement regarding the clusters comprising verbs and the infinitive *to*, i.e., *verb to* clusters, appears especially controversial. When *verb to* clusters are followed by verbs, pauses may occur before, in, and after them, so their pausing patterns need elucidating. Based on the frequencies, the selected clusters are *want to*, *have to*, *going to*, and *I would like to*; their ranking in two- and four-word, pause-ignored cluster lists of DSS (Appendices 6.4 and 6.6) and MiniM (Appendices 6.9 and 6.11) is provided in Table 8.11, which also includes the ranking of their contracted equivalents in the wordlist indexes (Appendices 6.2–6.3) and three-word, pause-ignored cluster lists (Appendices 6.5 and 6.10). To avoid confusion, below if the verb following the *verb to* cluster discussed is a lexical verb, it would be represented by *do*; if it is auxiliary, it would be *be*.

Table 8.11   **Frequency ranking of four *verb to* clusters**

Clusters	FRD	FRM
want to	11	134
wanna	n/a	123
have to	35	26
going to	147	277
gonna	n/a	44
I would like to	418	285
I'd like to	657	739

8.4.1   *Want to* and *wanna*

No pause occurred in any *want to* instance in DSS (Appendix 8.4.1.1), elaborated below is therefore only its holistic production. Following the categorization applied to the previous PP- and SV-based clusters discussed in

Sections 8.2–8.3, the patterns that are examined include || *want to* ||, repeating, *want to* ||, || *want to*, and *want to* (Table 8.12). First, despite having pauses on both sides, the only one instance in type A was in effect part of a reformation of the preceding meaning unit *you don't want to change it*; it was, however, followed by a false start, a drawled filled pause, and then a verb. Second, seven instances of repetition were observed. In line 1, the instance was preceded by a partial start of *want* and followed by a verb with a wrong tense, indicating that this learner may have had difficulty producing *want to* as a whole, and may have been uncertain regarding what form was to be added after *to*. In lines 2–3, the speaker first used *want to get* as a holistic unit, then he or she seems to have attempted to repair this chunk but unsuccessfully, thus restarting the utterance by repeating *want to*, despite it being immediately followed by a topic shift. In lines 4–7, the instances were not only repeated but also immediately followed by verbs on its right side. These suggest that learners appear to have been in the process of using *want to do* as a holistic unit and that they may have used *want to* as a steppingstone to *want to do*.

Table 8.12 **Pausing patterns of *want to* and *wanna* in DSS and MiniM**

want to	FOD	FOM
Holistic use		
A: || *want to* ||	1	0
B: repeating	7	1
C: *want to* ||	25	0
D: || *want to*	7	0
E: *want to*	96	23
G: *wanna*	0	55
a: || *wanna* ||	0	0
b: repeating	0	4
c: *wanna* ||	0	6
d: || *wanna*	0	1
e: *wanna*	0	44
F: *want* || *to*	0	1

In type C, except for four instances, among which three were followed by reformulations (lines 1–3) and one by interruption (line 7), the rest made up the pattern *want to* || *do* (lines 4–6 and 8–25). The occurrence of pauses in between *want to* and verbs in these lines, along with the partial start of some verbs, seems to be evidence of learners' difficulty in retrieving these verbs from their mental lexicon. On the other hand, these instances collocated with the preceding pronouns, forming the patterns *pron want to* || *do*: *I want to* || *do* (lines 3–5), *you want to* || *do* (lines 8–13), *we want to* || *do* (lines 14–15), and *they want to* || *do* (lines 16–17). In type D, on the right side, all seven instances were produced coherently with verbs, constituting a pattern of *want to do*, and on the left side, they were preceded by pauses. Two of them were further preceded by pronouns, forming the pattern *pron* || *want to do* (lines 1–2). This is in contrast to part of the findings in type C that pronouns co-occurred with *want to*. By comparison, it can be seen that pauses appear to be more likely to occur after *want to* when it forms a four-word cluster with its preceding pronouns and following verbs, namely, *pron want to do*. In type E, ninety-six instances were immediately followed by verbs, patterned as *want to do*, the instances of which were also consistently combined with pronouns, forming four-word clusters such as *I want to do* (lines 1–14 and 17–27), *we want to do* (lines 29–35), *you want to do* (lines 36–57), *they want to do* (lines 62–69), and (*people*) *want to do* (lines 72–80), some of which can be specified as *I want to say* (lines 17–27) or extended to a five-word cluster such as *conj you want to do* (lines 44–57).

On the other hand, although fitting the pattern *want to do*, the use of *want* in lines 81-96 was not grammatically correct, because either its third person singular was missing, or the tense was misused. In addition, no contracted form, *wanna*, was found in DSS. Based on the observation from types D and E, and considering the occurrence of *want to* || *do* in types A and C as well as the repetitive use of *want to* in type B, it can be concluded that first, learners may have treated *want to* as a holistic unit; second, they seem to have mostly treated *want to do* as a whole, but they may have difficulty in retrieving the verbs that followed, thus presenting the pausing pattern *want to* || *do*.

In MiniM, all instances were produced without pauses, except for one (Table 8.12). Regarding its holistic use, except for one particular case that involved repeating *to*, none of the rest was next to pausing, turn-taking or interruption (Appendix 8.4.1.2). When *to* was repeated, it was preceded by a pronoun and followed by a verb phrase, forming a cluster *I want to to do*. Repeating *to* seems to have helped the speaker to gain time for the planning of the subsequent verb phrase, but it also indicates that he or she may have had difficulty retrieving the relevant verb. In the other co-texts, *want to* was embedded in three-, four-, or five-word clusters such as *want to be* (lines 1–3), *want to do* (lines 4–16 and 18–23), *I want to (do)* (lines 4–7), *they want to do* (lines 13–14), and *do pron want to do* (lines 20–23). Some adverbs or negating elements were found in between pronouns and *want to do* in lines 8-12 and 15-17, suggesting that these two elements did not always closely co-occur. Based on the observation that one instance was followed by a reformulation (line 17) and another by a lexical filler (line 20), there seems to be a possibility that pauses may occur after *want to*. In the only case where an internal pause occurred (type F), it can be seen that pausing before *to* but keeping it and its following verb phrase as a holistic unit may be a strategy of speech production adopted by native speakers. As pointed out in Subsection 7.4.3, the occurrence of this internal pause seems to have been affected by speakers' individual pausing preference.

Fifty-five *wanna* instances were retrieved in MiniM and are categorized as type G (Table 8.12). As with *it's* and *they're* discussed Section 8.3, using the contracted form suggests that this cluster has been well accepted as a formulaic sequence and reduced into one word because of its common use in everyday language (Erman & Warren, 2000; Foster, 2001). Four patterns of pausing are observed, ranging from b to e (Table 8.12). In type b, first, two *wanna* instances together with its preceding pronoun *I* were repeated and immediately followed by the verb *be*, marked as *I wanna || I wanna be* (lines 1–2). Second, the instance of *I wanna* was followed by a false start and further by a three-word reformulation, the wider structure of which is indicated as *I wanna || I wanna do* (lines 3–4). These repetitive uses indicate that the cluster *I wanna* seems to be more formulaic than the ones made up of this cluster collocating with its following verbs. In type c, one instance was followed by interruption (line 1), two by reformulation (lines 2–3), and three first by pauses and then by verbs, forming the pattern *pron (don't) wanna || do* (line 4–6). Type d had one instance of *wanna* preceded by back-channeling. In type e, forty-three *wanna* instances co-occurred both with the pronoun preceding and the verbs following. The typical clusters were further specified as *I wanna do* (lines 5–23), *I don't wanna do* (lines 30–33), and *do (pron) wanna do* (lines 39–43). Between the combinations of pronouns and *wanna*, however, there were insertions of adverbs or negations, which is contrary to the right side of this cluster, where the instances of *wanna* were immediately followed by *be* or *do*. If integrated with the findings from types b and c, it can be seen that pauses would be more likely to occur after *wanna* when it collocates with preceding pronouns and following verbs. This is similar to the finding reported in DSS.

8.4.2 *Have to*

The quantitative results suggest that all *have to* instances in DSS were used as holistic units except for one. Four patterns of its holistic use are recognized (Table 8.13), with concordance lines provided in Appendix 8.4.2.1. In type A, the four instances were preceded by pauses; two of them later met with interruptions (lines 1–2) and the other two were followed by pauses (lines 3–4). In line 3, the cluster was further followed by a verb noun structure, *educate the children*. In a way, it shows that the learner had shorter formulaic language. In line 4, *have to* was followed by a drawl in a verb and two more pauses. No repetition of *have* or *have to* was found in type B. In type C, three instances were followed by contribution from another speakers (lines 1–3), another three by reformulations (lines 5–6), and sixteen were followed by pauses and continued with their following verbs, making up the pausing pattern *have to ‖ do* (lines 7–22). Some of them were extended as *we have to ‖ do* (lines 7–13) or *you have to ‖ do* (lines 16–22). The majority of the pauses at this point seem to have separated the units such as *we have to* or *you have to* from their following elements (lines 6–9 and 14–20). Some of them might have been caused by the difficulty in formulating the ongoing speech, indicated by the occurrence of multiple pauses in the co-texts (lines 5, 10–13 and 21–22). By comparison, three out of four instances in type D formed the pattern *pron ‖ have to do*. All four instances of *have to* were immediately followed by verbs on the right side in this type, although they were preceded by pauses (lines 1–3) or unintelligible speech (line 4). In the last type, most instances made up the structure, *have to do*, with the majority further specified as *I have to do* (lines 1–5), *we have to do* (lines 6–19), *you have to do* (lines

24–30), *don't have to do* (lines 22–23, 31 and 38–39), or other (*people*) *have to do* structures (lines 32–37). In lines 40–45, the instances of *have to* were uttered without pauses with their preceding elements, but either the third singular of *have* was misplaced or its following components did not use correct part of speech. Similar to part of the findings regarding *want to*, this indicates that the cluster *pron have to* seems to have been more automatized than *have to* collocating with its following elements.

Table 8.13   Pausing patterns of have to in DSS and MiniM

have to	FOD	FOM
Holistic use		
A: ‖ *have to* ‖	4	0
B: repeating	0	6
C: *have to* ‖	22	1
D: ‖ *have to*	4	0
E: *have to*	45	58
F: *have* ‖ *to*	1	0

Only one instance had an internal pause (type F), the extended chunk of which can be represented as *pron don't have ‖ to do*. The fluent units separated by this pause were relatively short and its preceding co-text involved a repetition of the pronoun. As discussed in Subsection 7.3.5, the cause of its occurrence may have been due to difficulty in speech formulation. However, this pattern of pausing is in contrast to the findings observed in type E, where the entire cluster *pron don't have to do* was uttered without any disruption in lines 22–23, 31 and 38, the structure *don't have to do* was holistic in line 39, and in lines 42–43 *pron don't have to* was used without pauses. Thus, in terms of *have to do*, its holistic production seems to have occurred most frequently and *have to ‖ do* occasionally; *have ‖ to do* was least frequently used.

In MiniM, the calculated frequencies suggest that this cluster was always used as a whole (Appendix 6.4.6). Following the pausing patterns used for the other clusters that have been discussed, three patterns are summarized: six instances involved repetition, one had a pause following *have to*, and the rest were embedded in three- or four-word clusters (Table 8.13). Detailed co-texts are provided in Appendix 8.4.2.2. In terms of repetitive use, the instances of *have to* were used as a constituent component of a four-word cluster, *do I have to*. In lines 1–2, *have to* first appeared as part of *do I have to*, and then it was repeated; in lines 3–4, the repeated part was the entire four-word cluster. The repetition in lines 5–6 was *I have to*, which seems to have been a reformulation in these lines, but its holistic status was later supported in lines 1–3 in type E. Type C had one instance only, where a pause was placed in between the cluster *have to* and its following verb. By contrast, quite a number of *have to* instances were immediately followed by verbs in type E. As can be seen, lines 1–25, 28–33, 36–38 and 41–51 had the holistic cluster *have to do*, and lines 27, 34–35, 39–40 and 52–54 had the holistic *have to be* structure. More specified and longer clusters such as *pron have to do* (lines 1–18) and *do pron have to do* (lines 43–49) were also observed. The *have to* instances in lines 55–58 were used differently from the others in this type: they were first followed by lexical fillers and then by verb phrases, the last of which also involved a partial start of a verb and a repetition of a filler. These indicate a possible pausing pattern of *have to* ‖ *do*, and it is similar to the finding of the *want to* instances in type E. Consequently, *have to do* in MiniM was most frequently treated as one unit; there were several cases where pauses occurred after *have to*, but no pausing was found in between *have* and *to do*.

8.4.3 *Going to* and *gonna*

The holistic production of *going to* falls into four types; neither any internal pauses nor contracted forms were found in DSS (Table 8.14, Appendix 8.4.3.1). In type A, preceded by a pause and further by *we are*, *going to* was followed by a pause and a verb phrase, showing the speaker may have treated it as one unit and produced short fluent units. In type B, partial repetition of the word *go-* occurred before the cluster *going to do* was produced, indicating that the speaker might have been unable to use the cluster *I am going to do* as one unit, although he or she managed the holistic production of *going to do*. In type C, pauses were placed after *going to*. Three instances were embedded in the structure *pron are going to* (lines 1–3) and four instances were followed by pauses and verbs, making up the pattern *going to* ‖ *do* (lines 1–4). The occurrence of multiple pauses around the verbs indicates that the speakers may have retrieved the verbs with effort. The fourth type of pausing was not found in DSS, but there was a similar case in type B, resulting from the partial repetitive use of the word *going*. In type E, most instances constituted a larger cluster, *be* (*am*, *are*, *was*, and *is*) *going to do*, which were free from any internal disruption (lines 1–20). This is in contrast to the pattern *going to* || *do* observed from type C. Furthermore, *going to* was also used together with noun phrases and made up the cluster *going to* (*some place*) (lines 22–24). Thus, when it was followed by verbs, in the majority of the concordance lines *going to do* was used holistically, but the pattern of *going to* || *do* was also found in a small number of the instances. Moreover, no instance of *going* || *to do* occurred in DSS.

Table 8.14   Pausing patterns of *going to* and *gonna* in DSS and MiniM

going to	FOD	FOM
Holistic use		
A: || *going to* ||	1	0
B: repeating	1	0
C: *going to* ||	5	0
D: || *going to*	0	1
E: *going to*	25	13
G: *gonna*	0	184
a: || *gonna* ||	0	1
b: repeating	0	11
c: *gonna* ||	0	15
d: || *gonna*	0	0
e: *gonna*	0	157
F: *going* || *to*	0	1

In MiniM, this cluster includes *going to* and *gonna*. With regard to *going to*, fourteen instances were used as wholes, and one had an internal pause (Table 8.14, Appendix 8.4.3.2). As can be seen, only one instance had an interruption from another participant before its occurrence in type D; otherwise, the cluster *and they're going to hell* would have been produced without pauses. The rest of the instances were embedded in the co-texts and made up longer fluent units in type E, including *be* (*is*/*am*) *going to do* (lines 1–5), *be* (*is*) *going to be* (lines 7–8), or *be* (*is*, *am*, *was*, and *are*) *going to* (*some place*) (lines 9–13). As to the internal pause, the trigger for its occurrence seems to be clarifying the question addressed to the group members, as discussed in Subsection 7.4.3.

As to the contracted form *gonna*, 184 instances were retrieved in MiniM. As can be seen from Table 8.14, four pausing patterns are summarized and marked respectively as ‖ *gonna* ‖, repeating, *gonna* ‖, and *gonna*. In type a, the instance was preceded by a pause on the left side, whereas on its right side, it was followed by a false start and then an attempt to continue the utterance with a noun phrase by repeating *the*. This suggests that the speaker may have experienced online planning pressure. In the first two lines in type b, the repeated elements were a combination of *gonna* and the verb *have*, and a long pause was placed before the second use of *gonna have*, which seems to have indicated the holistic status of this combination. In lines 3-6, two clusters were repeated: one is *it's gonna be* and the other *I was gonna be*. As in lines 1–2, pauses occurred between the repetition of these two extended clusters, indicating that the speakers may have treated the combinations as intact units. In lines 7–8, the second use of *gonna* in *which one's gonna* was a repaired chunk of the preceding segment, *which is gonna be*. In lines 9–11, *gonna* respectively occurred in clusters (*someone*) *is gonna* ‖, *he's gonna be*, and *he's gonna have*. The occurrence of multiple pauses in the co-texts of these lines indicates that the speakers probably had pressure in formulating speech, but they managed to produce holistically *gonna* with its preceding elements. In type c, *gonna* was either followed by contribution from other speakers (lines 1–3), repairs (lines 4–8), or pauses and verb phrases (lines 9–15). No pause was found before *gonna*. Findings based on types a to d suggest that pauses are more likely to occur in between *gonna* and its following verbs, although as displayed in type e, a large number of *gonna* instances collocated seamlessly with their following verbs. It thus can be concluded that in MiniM the majority of *gonna do* and *going to do* were produced without pauses, a small number of them had pauses placed before *do*, and a pause before *to do* rarely occurred.

8.4.4 *I would like to* and *I'd like to*

The pausing of *I would like to* falls into four groups, and no repeating or no internal pause was found in DSS (Table 8.15). The detailed co-texts are provided in

Appendix 8.4.4.1. Regarding the instance that was surrounded by pauses, *I would like to* was a repaired fragment for the preceding chunk *I will* and followed by a verb phrase. In type C, a pause was found between *I would like to* and its following verb phrase. The instances in types A and C show that pauses were placed after the cluster. In types D and E, all instances were immediately followed by verb phrases, suggesting that in these concordance lines *I would like to do* appears to have been used as a holistic unit. Since the two words *I* and *would* tend to be contracted as *I'd*, and the four-word cluster may have been shortened as *I'd like to*, its pausing patterns were considered under type G. Nine *I'd like to* instances were found, all of which were not only free from internal pauses but also coherently followed by verbs, making *I'd like to do* a holistic unit. Thus, it can be seen the clusters *I would like to do* and *I'd like to do* were basically used as wholes, with pauses occasionally placed before *do*.

Table 8.15   Pausing patterns of *I would like to* and *I'd like to* in DSS and MiniM

I would like to	FOD	FOM
Holistic use		
A: ‖ *I would like to* ‖	1	0
B: repeating	0	1
C: *I would like to* ‖	1	0
D: ‖ *I would like to*	4	1
E: *I would like to*	3	2
G: *I'd like to*	9	6
a: ‖ *I'd like to* ‖	0	0
b: repeating	0	0
c: *I'd like to* ‖	0	0
d: ‖ *I'd like to*	4	2
e: *I'd like to*	5	2
f: *I'd* (‖) *like to*	0	(2)

Four *I would like to* instances were found free from internal pauses in MiniM (Table 8.15), the detailed co-texts of which are provided in Appendix 8.4.4.2. When repeating took place in type B, the first *I would like* may have been a partial start, and was then followed by the entire cluster, *I would like to*, which was again followed by a pause and a verb. This on the one hand confirms the holistic status of *I would like to*, but on the other side suggests that pauses might have been placed after *I would like*. Moreover, the repetition and the short fluent units in the co-text seem to have been marks of cognitive effort. Three instances made up a holistic cluster *I would like to do* (lines 1 in type D and 1–2 in type E). In addition, together with their following verbs, four instances of its contracted form *I'd like to* coherently made up the cluster *I'd like to do* (lines 1-4 in type G). Although quite small in number, these uses nevertheless support its holistic status. There were also two more cases where lexical fillers were placed in between *I'd* and *like to do* (lines 5–6), indicating that the cluster *I'd like to do* might have been segmented into two smaller components like *I'd* and *like to do* if needed. Therefore, in native speech, from the most to the least frequent, the pausing patterns were respectively *I'd like to do*, *I would like to do*, *I'd || like to do*, and *I would like to || do*.

8.4.5   Summary and conclusion

Based on the analyses, it can be seen that all *want to*, *going to*, and *I would like to* instances were produced holistically in DSS, and in MiniM all *have to* instances were used as wholes. All of the five pausing patterns occurred to the four clusters investigated in DSS, but in MiniM, the patterns of pauses being placed immediately on both sides of the clusters (type A) and right before *verb to* (type D) rarely occurred, which evidently shows that learners tend to produce shorter fluent units than native speakers, who generally connected *verb to* with the preceding subject. Different levels of repetition were found in the instances of *want to* and *going to* in DSS, where learners seem to have used repetition as a time-gaining device so that they could plan the verb for the structure *want to do* and *going to do* afterwards. No repetition of *have to* or *I would like to* was found in learner speech. In MiniM, repetition did occur to each of the clusters discussed but basically involved its neighboring elements, most of which are the preceding subject pronouns, which again validates the close relation between the subject and the verb in native speech. In response to the issue regarding which pausing pattern occurs more frequently when the *verb to* clusters are followed by verbs, it was found that the predominant majority of *verb to do* instances were produced holistically, some of them presented the pattern of *verb to* || *do*, and the pattern *verb* || *to do* only occurred in a couple instances. Learners seem to have attempted to produce *verb to do*. The probable reason why pauses occurred after *verb to* seems to be that the verbs after *verb to* are difficult to retrieve. Most instances of *want to*, *have to*, and *going to* were found closely linked to their preceding pronouns, and many of them seem to have constituted a four-word cluster, *pron verb to do*. Pauses appear more likely to occur between *verb to* clusters and their following verbs than between the clusters and the subject pronouns that preceded, which reinforces that the SV-based clusters tend to be treated as wholes. In addition, a number of *want to* and *going to* instances were contracted as one-word units in native speech, which seemingly confirms their holistic status, but such use was not found in DSS.

Interestingly, more internal pauses were found in the instances of the selected *verb to* clusters in native speech than in learner speech. In DSS, only one *have to* instance had an internal pause, while in MiniM, one instance of *want to*, one instance of *going to*, and two instances of *I'd like to* had internal pauses. The causes for their occurrence in these instances have been detailed in Subsections 7.3.5 and 7.4.3, but to recapitulate, the placement of the internal pause in DSS seems to be affected by online speech planning; in MiniM, it may be related to planning pressure too, but also probably due to the conversational strategy or the speaker's pausing preferences.

8.5   Noun phrase clusters

The findings of Chapters 6 and 7 and Section 8.2 in this chapter show that in both DSS and MiniM pauses occurred in the clusters consisting of noun phrases especially when they are interconnected with the PP- or VP-based clusters. What has been known so far is largely confined to pausing regarding either the instances that had internal pauses or those that are the PP- or VP-based, which involve relatively complex grammatical structures. It remains unanswered how pauses behave in or around high frequency simple noun phrase clusters. To explore this, the pausing patterns of *the fact*, *the time*, *the question*, and *the people* are investigated below, for which the primary consideration is that in spontaneous spoken English noun phrases generally have a simple grammatical structure (Biber et al., 1999; Carter and McCarthy, 2006). Moreover, these four clusters occurred with relatively high frequencies in DSS and MiniM. Provided in Table 8.16 is the frequency ranking extracted from their respective pause-ignored cluster lists (Appendices 6.4 and 6.9).

Table 8.16   Frequency ranking of four noun phrase clusters

Clusters	FRD	FRM
the fact	761	358
the time	662	241
the question	765	405
the people	149	360

8.5.1 *The fact*

Nine *the fact* instances were holistically used and their pausing falls into three types, indicated in Table 8.17; concordance lines are provided in Appendix 8.5. No types A, C, or internal pause was found in DSS. Two instances involved repetition in type B. When *the fact* was uttered for the first time, it served as the object noun phrase for its preceding verb phrase and followed by a filled and a silent pause; the repeated instance seems to have been a repaired chunk for the preceding unit, because it involved a change of the verb before *the fact* from *mention* to *face*, and followed by *that* without pauses. This shows *the fact* was reproduced as part of a four-word cluster, *face the fact that*. In type D, one instance was preceded by indecipherable speech but directly followed by *that*, making up a three-word cluster *the fact that*. This cluster recurred in type E in lines 1–5, with three instances followed by pauses (lines 1–3) and two by their appositive clauses (lines 4–5). On their left side, one of them was preceded by a prepositional phrase (line 1), one by *admit* (line 2), and three by *face* (lines 3–5). Thus, the cluster *the fact* mostly makes up the three-word cluster, *the fact that*, and the four-word cluster, *face the fact that*.

Table 8.17   Pausing patterns of *the fact* in DSS and MiniM

the fact	FOD	FOM
Holistic use		
A: ‖ *the fact* ‖	0	0
B: repeating	2	2

Continued

the fact	FOD	FOM
C: *the fact* ‖	0	0
D: ‖ *the fact*	1	1
E: *the fact*	6	10

As in DSS, all instances were used without internal pauses in MiniM (Table 8.17), and detailed co-texts can be seen in Appendix 8.5. No instance of type A or C was found. Except for the two instances that involved repetition (type B) and the last one in type E followed by the verb *is*, the rest seem to have constituted the three-word cluster *the fact that* (line 1 in type D and lines 1–9 in type E). Moreover, one instance of *the fact that* was preceded by a pause (line 1 in type D), three were followed by pauses (lines 1, 5 and 9), and the rest were embedded in even longer fluent units such as *just the fact that*. As to its repetitive use, *the fact* was bounded by pauses on both sides when it was produced the first time, but its second use indicates that this cluster was used to start a clause, supporting that the beginning of a clause tends to be where the speaker plans what words to follow (Biber et al., 1999).

8.5.2 *The time*

Regarding *the time*, except for two instances, the rest were produced without pauses in DSS (Appendix 8.5). The pausing patterns range from C to F; no instance occurred in type A or B (Table 8.18). In type C, five *the time* instances were followed by contribution from other group members (lines 1–3) or pauses (lines 4–5). Together with the preceding co-texts, one instance constituted a PP-based cluster, *for a period of the time* (line 1) and the other four seem to have made up an extended cluster comprising an SV-based cluster followed by *the time* (lines 2–5). In type D, two instances were preceded by pauses, one of which seems to have been a repair for its preceding unit (line 1), and the other was further preceded by a verb (line 2). On their right side, both of them were immediately followed by attributive clauses. In type E, *the time* was directly preceded by a preposition (line 1) or a verb (line 2). Type F is where two internal pauses occurred, both of which were preceded by verb phrases, making up the pattern *verb the ‖ time*, and on their right side, both of them were followed by repairing or repeating some of the elements in the co-texts. The occurrence of multiple pauses as well as the repetition in the co-texts suggests that pressure on online speech planning may have been what caused the occurrence of the internal pause in these two instances.

Table 8.18 Pausing patterns of *the time* in DSS and MiniM

the time	FOD	FOM
Holistic use		
A: ‖ *the time* ‖	0	0
B: repeating	0	0
C: *the time* ‖	5	7
D: ‖ *the time*	2	0
E: *the time*	2	10
F: *the* ‖ *time*	2	0

In MiniM, all instances of *the time* were used holistically, and they fall into either type C or E, mostly produced as part of another extended NP-based cluster with the words in their preceding co-texts; no instance was found representing type A, B or D pattern of pausing (Table 8.18). As can be seen in Appendix 8.5, in type C, with their preceding modifiers, six of them made up longer noun phrase clusters such as *most of the time* (lines 1–4) and *all the time* (lines 5–6). In type E, except *by the time* (lines 8–9), other instances were preceded by quantifiers such as *all*, *half*, and *percent of*. Moreover, except for the instances in lines 5 and 9, others were followed either by conjunctions (lines 1–2) or pronouns (lines 3–4 and 6–7), which seem to have been used to start a new clause. In line 10, *the time* was used as a modifier for its following noun.

8.5.3 *The question*

The pausing patterns regarding *the question* range from type B to F in DSS, one instance of which had an internal pause whereas the rest were produced holistically (Table 8.19, Appendix 8.5). No instance was found regarding the first pausing pattern. In type B, *the* was repeated, with the preceding unit of which being *the meaning of the*, and the wider co-text was *the meaning of the the question*. This indicates *the* as the beginning of an NP-based cluster may be the point of planning pressure and that the speaker may have treated the partial repetition as a time-buyer to plan the noun head. The same phenomenon was observed above in Subsection 8.2.1, the co-text of which was *of the the the the diet* in line 7 (Appendix 8.2.1.1). In type C, two instances of *the question* were followed by interruption (lines 1–2) and two by pauses (lines 3–4). On their left side, all of them were immediately preceded by verb phrases. Moreover, the preceding co-text in line 4 involved a repetition of *analyze the*, indicating that the speaker may have been again in the process of retrieving the noun head, *question*. In type D, both instances were preceded by pauses, one of which was followed by a preposition and the other a verb. In type E, one was embedded in the three-word cluster *answer the question* (line 1) and the other collocated with *most of*, serving as the subject of the clause in the context. In type F, the occurrence of the pause in between *the* and *question* appears to have been caused by a false start. As can be seen, the speaker used the chunk *question one* in the preceding context, so he or she may have been intended to use *question two* to parallel the previous expression.

Table 8.19   Pausing patterns of *the question* in DSS and MiniM

the question	FOD	FOM
Holistic use		
A: ‖ *the question* ‖	0	0
B: repeating	1	1
C: *the question* ‖	4	5
D: ‖ *the question*	2	0
E: *the question*	2	6
F: *the* ‖ *question*	1	0

All *the question* instances were used as wholes in MiniM, and no instance occurred in type A or D (Table 8.19). Detailed concordance lines are also provided in Appendix 8.5. First, similar to type B in DSS, one instance involved partial repetition of the cluster. Starting the utterance with *with the*, the speaker paused, and then he or she continued with the rest of the information, producing *with the ‖ the question*. This is identical to the pausing pattern of *the meaning of the ‖ the question* in DSS. The structure of this type on the one hand supports the close relation between the preposition *with* and *the*, but on the other hand it indicates that the native speaker may have also used the partial repetition to buy time to plan the noun that followed. Moreover, the three-word *prep the NP* cluster may not have been always produced as a holistic unit, which was also observed in learner speech, suggesting that nouns may require large amounts of planning in both learner and native speech. The rest of the instances were embedded in longer fluent units: in type C, the first three instances were immediately preceded by verbs (lines 1–3) and the last two were preceded by modifiers, constituting extended NP-based clusters (lines 4–5); in type E, four of them were part of the extended NP-based clusters (lines 1–4) and two were preceded by the SV-based clusters (lines 5–6).

8.5.4 *The people*

All patterns of pausing are detected in *the people* instances (Table 8.20); details are provided in Appendix 8.5. In type A, two instances were isolated from their co-texts, with one resulting from immediate turn-taking, and the other reflecting that learners produced shorter fluent units, as the co-text was || *the number of* || *the people* || *who lost his job is over* ||. Occurring at the beginning of a speaking turn, both instances in type B were preceded by partial repetition of *the*, but then continued with the holistic production of the cluster itself, with one closely followed by a verb phrase (line 1) and the other by an attributive clause introduced by *who*, making up a three-word cluster *the people who* (line 2). The partial repetition, however, indicates that learners were hesitating in retrieving this cluster. In type C, two instances were followed by interruption (lines 1–2) and the rest were followed by pauses (lines 3–5); on the left side, they were preceded by conjunctions or prepositions, thus serving either as the subject of a clause or the object of the preceding preposition. Five instances in type D were preceded by pauses, three of which were further preceded by conjunctions (lines 3–5). On their right side, they were followed by prepositional phrases (lines 1–2) or by an attributive clause, making up once more the cluster *the people who* (lines 3–5). In type E, seven of them seem to have functioned as the subject in the clause (lines 1–7) and six of them as objects (lines 8–13); the three-word cluster *the people who* recurred (lines 2 and 13).

Five instances of *the people* had internal pauses (type F). The occurrence of multiple pauses, repetitions, and repairs in lines 1-3 suggest that speakers might have had the pressure on formulating the speech online. The pattern *for the* || *people* in lines 2–3 seems to further support that *the* is the point of speech planning. In lines 4–5, the pattern *the* || *people who* occurred when the cluster is followed by an attributive clause. Moreover, the co-text in line 4 shows that learners did produce shorter fluent speech runs; other pauses and hesitations in line 5 suggest that learners probably experienced difficulty in retrieving the noun that followed, as the co-text is *the <0.33> people who is <0.25> <um> mas- ma- majority*. Moreover, the pattern of *the* || *people who* is different from what was found in types A, B, D, and E, where the pause either occurred after *the people*, patterned as *the people* || *who* (line 2 in type A), or *the people who* was used holistically (line 2 in type B, lines 3–5 in type D, lines 2 and 13 in type E). Thus, this three-word cluster manifested different levels of holistic production.

Table 8.20 Pausing patterns of *the people* in DSS and MiniM

the people	FOD	FOM
Holistic use		
A: || *the people* ||	2	1
B: repeating	2	0
C: *the people* ||	5	0
D: || *the people*	5	2
E: *the people*	13	9
F: *the* || *people*	5	1

Not all instances of *the people* were used as intact units in MiniM either; the patterns of pausing fall into four groups (Table 8.20). Details can be found in Appendix 8.5. No instance occurred in type B or C. In type A, one instance was used to start a turn but was immediately followed by a pause and a prepositional expression of directions. In type D, two instances were preceded by pauses, one of them further preceded by a noun phrase, and the other seems to have been a reformulation of the preceding pronoun *they*. Moreover, the second instance was immediately followed by an attributive clause. In type E, all *the people* instances were embedded in longer fluent units, two of which functioned as the subject of the clause (lines 1–2), four were coherently followed by attributive clauses (lines 3–6), and the other three served as the object after prepositions or verbs (lines 7–9). In type F, a pause occurred in *the people* when it was preceded by a verb and followed by an attributive clause, the pausing of which can be marked as *verb* ‖ *the* ‖ *people who*. As discussed in Section 7.4.3, the cause for the occurrence of this internal pause is probably due to the pressure of online speech planning, as the speaker seems to be elaborating an example.

8.5.5 Summary and conclusion

Based on the analyses above, most instances of the NP-based clusters were used holistically by learners, but a few of them were interrupted by pauses, including two instances of *the time*, one instance of *the question*, and five instances of *the people*. By contrast, except one instance of *the people*, all were produced as wholes by native speakers. In both DSS and MiniM, except for *the people*, the pattern of pauses occurring on both sides of the cluster did not occur in the other three clusters; most instances were embedded in longer fluent units, either collocating with their preceding verbs or prepositions, or the elements that followed. No instance of *the time* was repeated, or no partial repetition was found in the instances of *the fact* in either of the corpora, indicating that noun phrases with a simple structure tend to be treated as wholes. As to *the question*, one instance in DSS and one in MiniM were found to have repeated *the*, both of which were preceded by prepositions. This supports that *the* as the beginning of a full noun phrase seems to be a common point of online planning pressure and that both the learner and the native speaker may have had pressure while formulating the noun head. No repetition regarding *the people* was found in MiniM. In DSS *the* was repeated in two instances when they were used to start a clause, which were further followed by long fluent units. This indeed suggests that the beginning of a clause can be the location where the learners have planning pressure.

To align with the findings observed from Chapter 7 and Section 8.2, as can be seen, the pausing patterns of the NP-based clusters may indeed be affected by the PP- or VP-based clusters in the co-texts. This also reinforces that the beginning of a noun phrase, namely the location of *the*, is one major point where speakers conduct speech planning, and accordingly, pausing after *the* can help them to relieve planning pressure. Additionally, when an NP-based cluster is modified by an attributive clause and constitutes an extended cluster with the words that introduce the clause such as *the people who*, most instances seem to have been used as wholes, but there are also instances that were produced with pauses, the occurrence of which may be due to the challenges of online speech formulation in both corpora.

8.6   Conjunction pronoun clusters

Conjunction pronoun clusters here refer to the combinations of the conjunction and the subject pronoun used in their subsequent clause (Carter & McCarthy, 2006). The conjunction-based clusters overall seem quite likely disrupted by pauses based on the quantitative results from Chapter 6, and according to the qualitative analysis in Chapter 7, internal pauses did occur frequently in the investigated conjunction-based instances. However, conjunctions are generally believed to be built into the clauses that follow (Pawley & Syder, 2000), and pauses are typically placed before them in speaking (Chung, 2012). To further understand how pauses behave in and around the clusters of this grammatical category, and to narrow the scope, four high frequency conjunction pronoun clusters, *if you*, *if they*, *when you*, and *when they*, are investigated in the following subsections. Considering subject pronouns and their following verbs may be contracted, *if you're*, *if they're*, and *when you're* are included in the analysis; *when they're* is excluded because only one instance was retrieved from MiniM. Their frequency ranking in the pause-ignored, two-word cluster lists extracted from DSS and MiniM (Appendices 6.4 and 6.9) is provided in Table 8.21.

Table 8.21   Frequency ranking of four conjunction pronoun clusters

Clusters	FRD	FRM
if you	30	33
if you're	n/a	928
if they	115	434
if they're	n/a	489
when you	302	121

Continued

Clusters	FRD	FRM
when you're	n/a	610
when they	476	531

8.6.1 *If you*

The frequencies of *if you* in DSS were 79 with or without pauses considered; all instances were produced holistically (Appendix 8.6), and the pausing patterns range from types A to E (Table 8.22). In type A, despite the fact that pauses were scattered around in their co-texts, *if* and *you* stayed together (lines 1–5). Two instances were further followed by verb phrases, forming the pattern *if you* || *verb* (lines 2–3), and the others were either followed by new speaking turns (lines 1 and 5) or reformulated speech (line 4). Type B is about repeating *if* (lines 1–2), *you* (lines 3–5), the entire cluster (lines 6–10), and the cluster along with a word in its co-text (lines 11–12). The partial repetition in lines 1–2 indicates that conjunctions are the probable points of planning pressure for learners, whereas in lines 3–5, it reveals that planning the verbs that followed might be the cause of the repetition. In lines 6–7, the word *if* appeared twice before the first use of *if you*; repeating *if* and *if you* seems to have enabled them to produce the subsequent long fluent unit. The indications seem to be the same as what was observed from the partial repetition in lines 1–5. In lines 8–10, the repetition was immediately followed by a repair of the tense, indicating that the speaker may have had pressure on the correct of use of the verb form. In lines 11–12, a three-word cluster, *if you don't*, was repeated, reinforcing that the learners may have had the pressure to plan the following verbs. In type C, on the right side, *if you* was followed by interruption (line 1), reformulation (line 2), or a pause and a verb phrase, making up the pattern *if you* || *verb* (line 3); on the left side, it was preceded by another conjunction (lines 1–2) or another clause (line 3). These indicate *if you* as the beginning of a clause is one major point where learners may have planning pressure. Except for the two instances that were used to start a turn (lines 17–18), other *if you* instances in type D were preceded by pauses, and together with the elements that followed on the right side, they made up three- or four-word clusters such as *if you are* (lines 1–2), *if you have* (lines 3–5), *if you eat* (lines 6–8),

213

if you want to (lines 13–17), and *if you don't verb* (lines 20–22). The co-occurrence of *if you* with other verbs in type E confirms that the clusters occurring in type D may have been used as wholes, namely *if you are* (lines 1–5), *if you have* (lines 6–10), *if you eat* (lines 11–12), *if you want to* (lines 15–20), and *if you don't verb* (lines 32–35).

Table 8.22   Pausing patterns of *if you* in DSS and MiniM

if you	FOD	FOM
Holistic use		
A: ‖ *if you* ‖	5	0
B: repeating	12	3
C: *if you* ‖	3	3
D: ‖ *if you*	23	22
E: *if you*	36	34
F: *if* ‖ *you*	0	3

In MiniM, three *if you* instances had internal pauses, the rest were used holistically (Appendix 8.6) and are categorized into typers B to E (Table 8.22). Three instances involved repetition (type B). In line 1, *if* was repeated; it was immediately followed by a verb phrase, *you have*, and then a false start *s-* in the co-text. In lines 2–3, the repeated element was *if you're a*. As can be seen from the co-text, when the speaker complemented the structure as *if you're a criminal*, the participants were laughing, indicating that the repetition occurred probably for the rhetoric effect. In type C, one instance was followed by a false start, *d-*, and then a verb phrase, patterned as *if you* ‖ *verb* (line 1), one by a false start, *jus-*, and a reformulation beginning with a noun phrase (line 2), and one by an interruption (line 3). Similar to line 1 in type B, the occurrence of the false starts in lines 1–2 reveals that native speakers may have experienced pressure when planning the whole of the subsequent clause including the verb. In type D, all *if you* instances were preceded by pauses except for those in lines 2 and 16–18, which were placed at the beginning of a new speaking turn. On their right side, they made up clusters including *if you're* (lines 1–2), *if you have* (lines 14–15), *if you want* (lines 16-17), *if you don't* (lines 18–20), and other *if you verb* structures (lines 3–13). If the contracted cluster *if you're* in lines 1–2 were compared with the other two instances of *if you are* in lines 1–2 in type D in DSS, it can be seen again that native speakers tend to contract high frequency subject verb patterns as one word. All instances of *if you* in type E were embedded in the fluent units of three words or more except for those in the last two lines, where not only the three-word clusters which occurred in type D recurred, namely *if you have* in lines 4–6 and *if you don't* in lines 1–3, but a wide range of verbs made up other *if you verb* structures (lines 8–29). In line 33, *if you're* was followed by an interruption, and in line 34, *if you're* was followed by negation. The recurrence of *if you're* indicates that native speakers tend to contract *you are*.

The instances that had internal pauses were categorized as type F, two of which were followed by verb phrases and thus marked as *if ‖ you verb* (lines 1–2), and the last one was further followed by topic-shifting (line 3). The cause of the occurrence of the pauses before *you verb* in the first two instances seems to further support that native speakers may have preferred to produce the SV-based clusters as wholes. As to the last pause between *if* and *you*, it probably resulted from the planning pressure, indicated by the occurrence of multiple pauses as well as a shift of topic in its immediate context.

8.6.2 *If they*

The pausing patterns applied to the cluster *if they* range from types A to F in DSS (Table 8.23), and concordance lines are provided in Appendix 8.6. Four instances manifested the first pausing pattern, with both sides bounded by pauses; on their right side, one was further followed by a shift of topic (line 1), and three by verb phrases, making up the pattern *if they ‖ verb* (lines 2–4). Type B is about the repetitive use of *if* (lines 1–4), *if they* (lines 5–8), and *if they* with the words in the immediate co-text (lines 9–10). When *if* was repeated, two of them coherently co-occurred (lines 1–2), and the other two had pauses in between, forming the pattern *if ‖ if they* (lines 3–4). Produced by the same speaker in line 4, *if they* was repeated in lines 5–6, pauses occurred in between its first and second time use. These indicate that for learners either the conjunction or the conjunction pronoun cluster may have been the point of pressure while formulating the speech. In lines 7–8, repetitive uses occurred next to each other without disruption from pauses in between, but they were immediately followed by a change of the ongoing topic. Lines 9–10 are where a four-word cluster *if they reduce the* was repeated. It may be related to the partial repetition in line 2, because they were produced by the same speaker. Based on the repetitions in these three lines, the speaker might have had difficulty in retrieving the verb and the noun, *reduce* and *tax*. In type C, two *if they* instances were followed by pauses. One was further followed by a reformulation (line 1), and the other by a verb phrase, forming the pattern *if they* || *verb* (line 2). Conversely in type D, nine instances were preceded by pauses, but they collocated with the words on the right side, making up three-word clusters such as *if they say* (lines 1–3), *if they are* (lines 4–5), and other *if they verb* structures (lines 6–7). Moreover, there appeared the use of negation and a modal verb in between *if they* and the following verbs (lines 8–9). In type E, not only the clusters *if they say* (line 2) and *if they are* (line 8) recurred, but other *if they verb* structures also occurred, with some specified as *if they want to* (lines 3–4), or *if they have* (lines 5–7). In addition, four *if they* instances were followed by negation or adverbs (lines 8–11). In type F, not only *if they* was interrupted by an internal pause, but also bounded by pauses on both sides. Further preceded by a noun phrase, it was followed by a verb and a lexical filler. The occurrence of multiple pauses in its co-text indicates the learner's pressure on speech formulation, which is probably the same cause for the occurrence of this internal pause.

All instances of *if they* in MiniM were used holistically except for two, and accordingly, their patterns of pausing fall into four types, namely, B, D, E, and F (Table 8.23), with the concordance lines provided in Appendix 8.6. As can be seen, in type B, when *if they* was used for the first time, it seems to have been a repaired chunk for the preceding unit *if it's*. The repeated use immediately followed along with its following verbs, *if they're*, and the speaker successfully completed the rest of the speech. The repetition itself suggests *if they're* may have been treated as a whole. In type D, five instances were preceded by pauses (lines 1–5) and one by indecipherable speech (line 6). On their right side, all six instances were followed by verbs. Three of them made up the two-word cluster *if they're* (lines 1–3), if aligned with *if they are* that occurred in DSS; it can be seen that in native speech contractions have been common in use. In another three lines, negation or adverbs were placed in between the subject pronoun and their following verb phrases (lines 4–6). Type

E has four instances of the contracted cluster *if they're* (lines 1–4); negation and adverbs were also observed between *if they* and the verbs followed (lines 8–11). With regard to the two instances that had internal pauses, one appears to be a result of cross-turn calculation (line 1), and the other seems to support that in native speech the conjunction may be a crucial location for speech planning and that the SV-based cluster is preferably produced as a whole (line 2).

Table 8.23   Pausing patterns of *if they* in DSS and MiniM

if they	FOD	FOM
Holistic use		
A: ‖ *if they* ‖	4	0
B: repeating	10	2
C: *if they* ‖	2	0
D: ‖ *if they*	9	6
E: *if they*	11	11
F: *if* ‖ *they*	1	2

8.6.3   *When you*

All instances of *when you* were used holistically in DSS (Appendix 8.6), and their pausing patterns are categorized into four types (Table 8.24). In type A, preceded by a pause on its left side, it was followed by a false start and a reformulation on its right side; this shows *when you* was produced as a whole. The immediate repetition of the whole cluster also suggests it may have been used as an intact unit by the speaker indicated in lines 1–2 in type B. In lines 3–4, *when* was first repeated, followed by a three-word cluster *when you use*, but again *use* was uttered and then followed by the repetition of *when you use*. In line 5, the pausing pattern is *when* ‖ *when you*. Apart from the fact that one component of the cluster was repeated, the placement of multiple pauses in between the repetitions indicates that the location of *when* might have been where the planning pressure was being built up (Biber et al. 1999). On the other hand, all instances in types D and E were directly followed by verb phrases, making up the cluster *when you verb*, except one being *when you are* (line 8 in type E).

Table 8.24   Pausing patterns of *when you* in DSS and MiniM

when you	FOD	FOM
Holistic use		
A: ‖ *when you* ‖	1	0
B: repeating	5	2
C: *when you* ‖	0	1
D: ‖ *when you*	5	11
E: *when you*	8	20
F: *when* ‖ *you*	0	2

In MiniM, two instances had an internal pause (Appendix 8.6), and the pausing patterns are categorized into five types, ranging from B to F (Table 8.24). In type B, before its repetitive use, *when you* was used to start a new speaking turn, and after its repetition, it was immediately followed by other elements. The repetition might have been a pressure-relieving strategy, facilitating the planning of the following content. In type C, *when you* was first followed by a false start and then by a verb phrase; given *s-* was immediately followed by *think*, this false start seems to have been a slip of tongue. In type D, nine instances were preceded by pauses (lines 1–6 and 9–11) and two were used to start a new turn (lines 7–8). On their right side, along with their following verb phrases, the majority constituted the cluster *when you verb*, and three of them were shortened as the two-word, *when you're* (lines 9–11). In type E, not only many instances of *when you verb* were holistically used (lines 1–12), five instances of *when you're* seem to have reinforced its holistic use in native speech (lines 16–20). This once again provides evidence that common two-word SV-based clusters tend to be contracted as one word in native speech (Erman & Warren, 2000). Type F had two instances of *when you*: the occurrence of the internal pause in the first instance was due to cross-turn calculation, but in the second, *when* was followed by *you know*. As discussed in Section 8.3.2, *you know* has been well treated as an independent holistic unit in both corpora. Accordingly, pausing here seems to reinforce that in native speech the conjunction may be the common point of planning pressure and that SV-based clusters are generally produced as wholes.

8.6.4 *When they*

As can be seen, one *when they* instance had an internal pause (type F) and the rest were used without pauses (Appendix 8.6), indicated from types B to E (Table 8.25). In lines 1–2 in type B, repeated was either *when* or *they*, but both were immediately followed by verbs, *spend* and *are*. These suggest on the on hand, learners may have individual differences in automatizing this cluster, and on the other hand, both the conjunction and the subject at the beginning of a clause could be the points of online planning pressure (Biber et al., 1999). In lines 3–4, the repeated units are *when they are*. In type C, one instance was first followed by a pause and then by a verb phrase, making up the pattern *when they* || *verb*, but in types D and E, *when they* and its following verb phrases were produced without pauses, two of which are *when they are*. In type F, apart from containing an internal pause, the cluster was also followed by a pause and the repetition of *they*. The occurrence of this internal pause as well as other hesitations in the co-text is probably related to the great build-up of planning pressure, given that the beginning of a clause is where the learner is especially likely to have this issue.

Table 8.25 Pausing patterns of *when they* in DSS and MiniM

when they	FOD	FOM
Holistic use		
A: || *when they* ||	0	0
B: repeating	4	0
C: *when they* ||	1	0
D: || *when they*	4	4
E: *when they*	4	6
F: *when* || *they*	1	0

All instances of *when they* were free from internal pauses in MiniM (Appendix 8.6), and their pausing falls into two types, D and E (Table 8.25). Four of them were preceded by pauses (type D) and six of them were embedded in the clusters of a longer length (type E). Although small in number, it can be seen that the clusters *when they were* (lines 1–2 in type D and lines 1–2 in type E) and *when they verb* (lines 3–4 in type D and lines 3–6 in type E) were produced without pauses.

8.6.5　Summary and conclusion

All pausing patterns used to describe other grammatical structures occurred in the conjunction pronoun clusters in DSS. In MiniM, no instance was found for type A, and type C only applied to three instances of *if you* and one *when you*; the overwhelming majority were embedded in the clusters comprising conjunctions and the SV-based clusters. Several types of repetition, including partial repetition of either conjunctions or pronouns, repeating the entire conjunction pronoun cluster or along with their following verbs were found with the four clusters in DSS, suggesting that the conjunction, the subject, the conjunction subject cluster, or the combination of these two elements with the verb that followed may have constituted the planning pressure points, so the learners may have unusual challenges in planning the whole of the subsequent clause, with the verb that included. Conversely, the repeated elements in MiniM were either the entire conjunction pronoun cluster or the cluster with its neighboring words, indicating that the conjunction and the subject pronoun together or the extended unit comprising the conjunction and the SV-based clusters may be the points of planning pressure. These pausing patterns evidently confirm that the fluent units in the learner speech are much shorter than those in the native speech and that in native speech the subject and the verb seem to have a closer connection than the subject with its preceding conjunction.

To resolve the controversies pointed out at the very beginning of Section 8.6, based on the pausing patterns observed, first, almost all conjunctions were built into their following clause, since almost all the instances investigated were produced without pauses, and second, pauses tend to be placed before the conjunction especially when they occurred at the beginning of a clause. Most conjunction pronoun instances were fluently produced with the verbs that followed, but this occurred more frequently in MiniM than in DSS, as learners were found to have paused after the conjunction pronoun cluster in order to plan the verb that followed. By contrast, native speakers occasionally paused after the conjunction but produced holistic SV-based clusters instead. They also contracted some subject verb patterns as one word, as in the clusters of *if you're*, *if they're*, and *when you're*; no such contractions were found in DSS. However, more internal pauses were found in the four conjunction pronoun clusters in MiniM than in DSS, and the cause seems to be that native speakers tend to take the conjunction as the planning point for the clause.

8.7   Chapter summary

To fully test the Holistic Hypothesis, this chapter has systematically analyzed twenty high frequency formulaic sequences and their patterns of pausing in both corpora. Building on Chapters 6 and 7, four formulaic sequences were selected from each grammatical category under investigation, that is, prepositional clusters, subject verb clusters, *verb to* clusters, noun phrase clusters with a simple structure, and conjunction pronoun clusters. These clusters were inspected based on whether they were produced with or without pauses, with their holistic production probed based on whether there were pauses on both ends of the clusters, whether the clusters involved repetitions, whether there were pauses on the left and the right side, and whether they were embedded in some extended units comprising three or more words. When the clusters have the contracted forms, they were investigated separately. The overall results are summarized in Chapter 9.

Chapter 9

Summary and Conclusion

With the aim of testing the validity of the Holistic Hypothesis, i.e., whether formulaic sequences are produced without pauses, in adult learner speech and in native speech, two corpora of academic spoken English were compiled and an in-depth, mixed-methods, contrastive investigation of pausing and the production of formulaic sequences was conducted. This chapter summarizes the overall findings of the investigation, discusses their relevance, and consider pedagogical implications. Concluding remarks include limitations of the study and recommendations for future research.

9.1 Summary of findings

Three questions were addressed to test the Holistic Hypothesis. The first one sought to ascertain whether formulaic sequences were indeed produced as wholes in adult learners' and native speakers' academic spoken English and in which clusters pauses might occur. Quantitative analysis in Chapter 6 first showed that 469 two-word, 151 three-word, and 13 four-word clusters that were extracted from both DSS and MiniM met the required frequency and dispersion criteria. Among the 469 two-word clusters, approximately two-thirds of them had instances interrupted by pauses in learner speech, but in native speech, nearly two-thirds were entirely produced as wholes. With regard to the 151 three-word clusters, more than half of them had some instances with pauses in learner speech; the vast majority of the clusters were completely produced as wholes in native speech. As to the four-word clusters, although quite small in number, the majority were produced without pauses by both groups of speakers. After the production of the two-word and three-word formulaic sequences in learner speech was cross-checked with those in native speech, about one-third of these clusters were found completely produced as holistic units by both groups, another one-third used as wholes by native speakers only, and the remaining one-third mostly produced with pauses in both DSS and MiniM except for a small number of them, which were produced without pauses by learners only. Furthermore, pauses were found in the clusters of different grammatical structures. In both corpora, the SV-based clusters were extensively produced without pauses, and the conjunction-based clusters and those consisting of *that*, repetitions, and other elements appeared most likely to be interrupted by pauses. The substantial majority of the SV-, PP-, and NP-based as well as more than two-thirds of the VP-based clusters were found produced holistically in MiniM, which are in contrast to more or less half of the clusters of these types used as wholes in DSS. Additionally, twice as many conjunction-based clusters were produced as holistic units in MiniM as in DSS, but the total numbers in both corpora were limited.

Based on the findings from the first question, the second question was aimed to establish what the patterns and the causes of internal pausing were in learner and native speaker formulaic sequences, and whether there were any individual or group differences in them. Five categories of internal pausing were investigated in both corpora. The first category was concerned with the clusters that had one internal pause. The second included those that not only had one internal pause but also were bounded by another pause on either side of the cluster, those had two or more internal pauses, and those the immediate contexts of which were peppered with pauses. In the third category, internal pauses co-occurred with repetitions, and in the fourth, either repairs or restarts. The last category presented within-individual differences in pausing, where speakers produced the same clusters with different pausing behavior in different co-texts or contexts. The common causes of why internal pauses occurred are as follows. First, some internal pauses may have been used to separate two grammatical constituents. For instance, the pauses found in certain PP-based clusters such as *to the* and *with the* may have been used to separate the preceding VP-based clusters, *talk to* and *deal with*, from their following NP-based clusters, *the government officials* and *the harassment of defenders*. Second, some internal pauses seem to be marks of online planning pressure and related to the effort exerted on the retrieval of the linguistic elements such as the noun or the verb that comprise certain clusters, as indicated by the co-occurrence of multiple pauses, repetitions, indecipherable speech, drawls, repairs, or restarts in their immediate contexts. When the occurrence of internal pauses was accompanied by repetitions or reformulations of the clusters involved, it indicates that the speakers may indeed have planning pressure and experienced difficulty in formulating the speech with these clusters. The placement of internal pausing may also have been affected by topic-shifting, individual preferred pausing patterns, or conversational strategies such as holding speech floor or pausing for the purpose of emphasis. The main differences between the learners' and the native speakers' internal pausing are manifested in three aspects. First, more of the internal pauses found in learner speech seem to be caused by the difficulty in online planning. Second, internal pauses appear to have played a wider range of interactional functions in native speech than in learner speech. There are cases where native speakers may have employed pauses as rhetoric devices, to slow down the speed of production or to clarify the meaning conveyed, and there are also instances where they paused probably because of thinking in process or the limitations of working memory capacity; such manipulations are not obvious in DSS. When the occurrence of internal pauses involved multiple types of pauses, repairs, and restarts, learners appear to have presented different processes of automatizing the use of formulaic language, or may not have had the awareness or the automaticity of speaking it as a holistic unit, but native speakers seem to be aiming for the accuracy in manipulating the topic-related expressions.

Although the second question vigorously investigated a substantial number of clusters with internal pausing, the issues that needed further testifying included where pauses would most likely occur when the PP- had followed the VP- or had been followed by the NP-based clusters, when the clusters comprising the lexical verb and the infinitive *to* had been followed by another verb, and when the SV-based clusters had followed the conjunctions. Moreover, it needed confirming whether pausing in the SV- and NP-based clusters may have been related to their syntactic complexity. On the other hand, the predominant majority instances of the clusters that had internal pausing were actually produced without pauses, and approximately one-third of the clusters extracted from DSS and two-thirds from MiniM were entirely used as wholes. Thus, apart from addressing the issues just listed, the third question was also intended to probe the details of pausing and the production of the five groups of high frequency formulaic sequences retrieved from both corpora, namely four PP- and four SV-based, four *verb to*, four simply-structured NP-based, and four conjunction pronoun clusters. The analysis of each cluster was performed first based on whether it was produced without or with pauses; its holistic production was then carefully examined regarding whether it had pauses on both sides, whether it involved repetitions, whether it had pauses on the right and the left side, or whether it was embedded in the extended clusters of three or more words. Some of the clusters may have been contracted, which were then separately inspected in the analysis.

The four *prep the* clusters investigated were *of the*, *to the*, *in the*, and *on the*. With regard to *of the* in DSS, apart from pausing on both ends, different levels of repetition were found, including repeating *of*, *the*, *of the*, and *of the* with its neighboring words, but in MiniM, the number of the instances of these two types was much smaller, and the repeated part generally contained the entire cluster. The predominant majority *of the* instances made up the extended noun phrase cluster, *(the) NP of the NP*, in which learners placed pauses more frequently and variously than native speakers. These not only show that learners produced shorter fluent speech units than native speakers did, but also reflect learners' developmental variation in the automatization process. Moreover, it was found in both corpora that pauses occurred more frequently in the second noun phrase than in the first, indicating that the first part, namely, *(the) NP of*, is more likely to be produced as a holistic unit. This also seems to be the reason why pauses occurred in *of the* in MiniM, but in DSS, the occurrence of internal pausing seems to be related to the planning for the noun phrases. Natives speakars were also found having online pressure for planning the nouns for the second half of the structure. As to the other three *prep the* clusters, some instances had pauses on both ends and involved different levels of repetition, but the majority were generally followed by noun phrases, making up the cluster *prep the NP*. Some of them seem to have constituted even lengthy units with their preceding verbs or other elements. In response to the issue regarding where pauses tend to occur especially when the PP- are interconnected with the following NP- or the preceding VP-based clusters, it was observed that the instances of *prep the NP* and its extended clusters were largely produced without pauses in both corpora. Pauses are more likely to occur after *prep the* in DSS, including when preceded by verbs, probably because the beginning of a noun phrase is indeed the primary point of online planning pressure for learners. In MiniM, pauses tend to be placed before *prep the NP*. Even when the PP- were preceded by the VP-based clusters, pauses may have been placed after the lexical verbs, saving the second part of the verb phrases, namely the prepositions, as the beginning of the PP-based clusters, which were then altogether produced as wholes with the noun phrase that followed. As to the pauses placed in between the preposition and *the*, they might have been taken as the boundary markers or affected by the pressure on planning the noun head in both corpora.

The four subject verb clusters investigated were *I think*, *you know*, *it is* (*it's*), and *they are* (*they're*). In both corpora all instances of *I think* and *you know* were produced as holistic units, but *I think* involved different levels of repetition and *you know* only partial repetition. Both clusters were treated more than just as an independent unit. The majority instances were embedded in longer fluent units. A large number of them made up three-word clusters with the conjunctions preceded or the pronouns followed, and pauses seem to have occurred more frequently after the conjunctions in both DSS and MiniM. Moreover, when *I think* was followed by *it is* or noun phrases, making up the clusters of three or more words, they were generally produced as wholes in native speech, but in learner speech with pauses at different places, showing different levels of holistic use. As to *it is* and *they are*, they were not only produced holistically, but also extensively contracted as one word, namely *it's* and *they're*. The contracted forms appeared significantly more frequent in MiniM. Repetition of *it is* and *they are* involved several levels in DSS, but in

MiniM only the contracted forms. When the two clusters and their contracted forms were embedded in the extended clusters preceded by conjunctions or followed by different phrases, there was individual variation regarding where pauses were placed, but pauses did occur more frequently after conjunctions, which is similar to what was found with *I think* and *you know*. No instance of *it is* had any internal pause in DSS, but some were used ungrammatically. Pauses found in the instances of *it is* in MiniM seem to be mainly used to mark the boundary, but one pause occurred after *if it* and was followed by the whole of the subsequent clause. This pausing behavior was also observed in one *they are* instance in DSS, which was likewise preceded by a conjunction and continued with the rest of the clause. Noticeably, the co-texts of both clusters had pauses and repetitions. These again validate that the beginning of a clause is the critical point where both the learner and the native speaker may be confronted with online planning pressure, and thus, pauses may occur after the conjunction or after the conjunction subject combination.

The investigated *verb to* clusters included *want to* (*wanna*), *have to*, *going to* (*gonna*), and *I would like to* (*I'd like to*). Except one instance, all were used holistically in DSS; several internal pauses were observed in MiniM, but still almost all of them were used as wholes. Learners clearly produced shorter fluent speech runs than native speakers, as the patterns of pausing on both ends of the clusters and pausing before *verb to* were not found in MiniM. Repeats may have been used as a time-buying strategy in DSS, because different repetitions were found in the instances of *want to* and *going to*, where after repeating, the learners seem to have managed to plan the subsequent verbs. In MiniM, the repetition always involved their preceding subject pronouns, and the subject and the verb thus appear to be habitually used as holistic units. When *verb to* clusters were followed by other lexical verbs, in both corpora most *verb to do* instances were produced as wholes, and some pauses may have occurred after *verb to*, but rarely before *to do*. When pauses occurred after *verb to*, in DSS the causes seem to be same as why repetitions as well as the internal pause occurred, that is, learners may have pressure on the planning for the verb that followed. In MiniM, the occurrence of pauses in *verb to* seems to be affected by conversational strategies or individuals' pausing preferences. When *verb to* clusters made up the extended units such as *pron verb to do* collocating with the pronouns preceded as well as their following verb phrases, pauses seem to be more likely occur in between *verb to* and the verb followed. This verifies that SV-based clusters tend to be produced as holistic units. Furthermore, the contracted forms *wanna* and *gonna* were only found in MiniM.

The four noun phrase clusters investigated were *the fact, the time, the question,* and *the people*. Not only were nearly all instances used as wholes, but they were generally embedded in the extended PP- or VP-based clusters. Repetitions rarely occurred, except for a couple of instances where *the* was repeated, which indicates that noun phrases with a simple structure are generally used as single units and that their beginning elements could be where speakers have the pressure on speech planning. Repeating *the* or pausing after *the* thus can be used as a strategy to ease the pressure and to plan the following noun head. This also confirms the finding of why pauses may have occurred in the NP-based clusters when they co-occur with the PP- or VP-based clusters. In addition, when the clusters were followed by the words introducing an attributive clause, both groups seem to have produced holistically most instances of the extended clusters, with the introducing words included. The cause of internal pausing seems to be mainly related to online planning pressure in both learner and native speech.

Among the high frequency clusters that consist of conjunctions and pronouns, *if you, if they, when you,* and *when they* were analyzed. All patterns of pausing occurred to those comprising other grammatical structures were found in this group in DSS, whereas in MiniM, having pauses on both ends and pausing after the conjunction pronoun clusters rarely occurred. Different levels of repetition were observed in DSS, whereas in MiniM the repeats involved the entire conjunction pronoun cluster or the cluster including its following verb. Accordingly, the major point of online planning pressure in the learner speech appears various: it could be the conjunction, the subject pronoun, the conjunction pronoun cluster, or the conjunction pronoun cluster along with its following verb. In native speech the pressure point may be the conjunction pronoun cluster or the extended conjunction-pronoun-verb cluster. These differences not only suggest learners may have more pressure on planning the whole clause including the verb, but also show that they did produce shorter fluent units than native speakers. Moreover, pauses were found occurring frequently before the conjunction when it is used to introduce a clause, with most instances of the combined conjunction-pronoun-verb clusters produced as wholes in both DSS and MiniM. They were also found after the conjunction and pronoun cluster in the learner speech, and after the conjunction in the native speech, the possible explanations being that learners may have difficulty in planning the verbs, but in native speech the SV-based clusters are commonly treated as holistic units. The latter is also supported by the extensive use of contracted SV-based clusters in MiniM.

In summary, the Holistic Hypothesis finds more solid and empirical support in native speech than in adult learner speech, as considerably more instances of the formulaic sequences of the six grammatical categories extracted from MiniM were produced without pauses than those from DSS. Internal pauses occurred in all types of the clusters. In both corpora, clusters consisting of the subject and the verb were found widely used as wholes, and those comprising conjunctions and other elements tend to be disrupted by pauses. The patterns of internal pausing found in DSS also occurred in MiniM, but causes were not entirely the same. In terms of the common causes, some pauses may have been employed to separate syntactic units from one another, some to cope with online planning pressure, formulating the next noun or verb, and topic-shifting, some to hold the speech floor, and some may be due to individual pausing preferences. The main differences lie in that learners appear to have more occurrences of internal pauses affected by the difficulty in planning the next NP- or VP-based clusters, but in MiniM, they seem to be mainly related to conversational strategies or evidence of cognitive effort.

Regarding pausing and the five categories of high frequency clusters investigated, the vast majority instances of the two-word clusters were produced as wholes and quite often so with their preceding or following elements. As to the three- or four-word clusters comprised of the two-word, most instances were produced holistically by native speakers, and the predominant majority of them were also used as wholes by the learners, who may, however, have had online planning pressure or not have fully automatized the clusters, manifesting individual variations in holistic production. Moreover, pausing in relation to the PP-based clusters may have been affected by their close NP-based in the co-texts. Generally, pauses tended to occur in their subsequent noun phrases, although there seems a tight link between *of* and its preceding nouns, and there is also some close relationship between the other three prepositions and the NP-based clusters that immediately follow. Pausing in the NP-based clusters especially after articles or other determiners when they were preceded by PP- or VP-based clusters was commonly observed in both corpora, the cause for which is probably that the beginning of a noun phrase is likely to be where the speakers plan hardest the noun head and other words that follow. On the other hand, nearly all instances of the high frequency NP-based clusters with simple grammatical structures were used as wholes, with several occurrences of internal pausing seemingly affected by their preceding PP- or VP-based clusters. Thus, whether or not pauses may occur in the NP-based clusters seems to do with their preceding co-texts and the syntactic complexity of the noun phrases. SV-based clusters were mainly produced as single units, with substantial evidence found in the contracted forms of the SV-based clusters themselves, the holistically produced extended clusters that comprised the *verb to* clusters with their preceding pronouns, and those consisting of the conjunction, the pronoun subject, and the verb. The *verb to* clusters followed by verbs also tend to be produced as wholes. It was found pausing after or in *verb to* in DSS may have been affected by the pressure on planning the next verb, but in MiniM it may have been employed as a conversational strategy. As to the conjunction pronoun clusters, pauses tended to occur before conjunctions, but they were also noticeably found after conjunctions and after the conjunction and pronoun clusters in both corpora, which is probably due to that both the conjunctions and the conjunction and pronoun clusters can be the points of planning pressure. When the subject involved has a simple structure, there is another possibility that the conjunction, the subject, and the verb that follows are combined together as a point of online planning pressure. Learners seem to have more planning pressure points at the beginning of a clause, because they may have more challenges when formulating the whole clause. Lastly, native speakers tended to contract some of the high frequency two-word SV-based clusters and *verb to* clusters as one word; few contractions were observed in learner speech.

9.2   Relevance and implications

This study testifies that formulaic sequences are generally produced as holistic units and that phonological coherence in terms of the absence of pausing is one of their primary and defining features. Some instances are found with internal pauses, but they do not necessarily challenge the Holistic Hypothesis. The reasons are as follows. First, based on the investigation of the patterns and causes of their occurrence, some of them are indeed found to be unavoidable in spontaneous speech. The results show that native speakers and the learners may universally have online pressure when planning the verb and especially the noun for the formulaic sequences that follow, although the number of pausing caused by this is significantly smaller in native speech than in learner speech. This resonates with the findings of some language processing studies, that is, content words such as nouns and verbs require more effort than function words in speech production, and that nouns, which usually represent new or unexpected information, require even more planning than complex verbs (Bell et al., 2009; Seifart et al., 2018). Second, some internal pauses occurred for certain topic-related cognitive reasons, which is in line with the finding that task types and online planning may affect performance fluency (Foster & Skehan, 1996; Ellis, 2009); some occurrences may be due to speakers' personalized speaking styles, particularly with reference to the rhythm, pace, or pausing, or because of the influence from the patterns of pausing in their native language, their physiological conditions, or working memory limitations (Chambers, 1997; Pawley & Syder, 2000; Mizera, 2006; Segalowitz, 2010). Most importantly, individual speakers may exercise their agency in pausing (Larsen-Freeman & Cameron, 2008a; Segalowitz, 2010). As shown, some occurrences seem to have been deliberated in terms of the location, the length, and the purposes of holding the speech floor, emphasizing, or achieving certain rhetoric effects. Speakers may also have different perceptions of speech fluency (Chambers, 1997; Koponen & Riggenbach, 2000; McCarthy, 2005) and of what is formulaicity (Wray, 2008; Schmitt, 2010). These may also affect the occurrence of pauses in formulaic sequences.

As the main supporting evidence of the Holistic Hypothesis, clusters of two or more words that are used as wholes are unanimously considered as the salient features of speech fluency (Towell et al., 1996; Guillot, 1999; Segalowitz, 2010). Long stretches of fluent units can be safely generalized based on the pausing patterns in question in MiniM, as only a few instances of the two-word clusters had pauses on both ends, and repetitions generally involved the entire clusters. Moreover, significantly more contracted clusters are found in MiniM; if the cluster has an equivalent contraction, it is generally the contracted form that is repeated when the repetition occurs. In DSS, learners did produce the majority instances of the two-word-based, three- and four-word formulaic sequences as wholes, but the occurrence of internal pauses also reveals their individual variations in automatizing the clusters of different lengths as wholes, noticeably manifested in terms of comparatively short fluent runs and different levels of repetitions. These are the actual fluency indicators that reflect the underlying processes of learners' planning and formulating the speech (Towell et al., 1996; Koponen & Riggenbach, 2000; Lennon, 2000; Segalowitz, 2010). As can be seen, more two-word instances found in DSS are bounded by pauses on both sides, repetition of some clusters has several types, such as repeating either of the component elements of the clusters or the entire clusters, and more pauses are found in the instances of the specific three- or four-word clusters such as *the people who* and *I think it is* as well as the abstracted ones with structural variability such as *prep the NP* and *verb to do* in DSS than in MiniM. Pausing frequently after the clusters *prep the* or *verb to* in DSS not only reinforces that for learners nouns and verbs especially create increased planning load in speech production (Seifart et al., 2018), but also is an indicator that they may have structured the speech on a word-by-word basis, thus affecting perceived fluency (Lennon, 2000; Hilton, 2008; Skehan, 2009; Gan, 2013; Mirzaei & Heidari, 2013).

In DSS, pausing at various locations in and around the clusters of more than two words and the observed different types of repetitions show that individual learners may have different points of planning pressure (Biber et al., 1999) and produce the clusters with various levels of automaticity (Myles & Cordier, 2017). Improving speech fluency from a dynamic systems perspective, it is fundamental to help learners become aware of formulaicity and build knowledge about it, and accelerate or complete the automatization of formulaic language in academic speech, so that they can increase the lengths of holistically produced clusters and reduce the occurrence of repetitions. To achieve these, four strategies are proposed. First, it is crucial to have learners engage in repetitive but meaningful communicative activities focusing on automatizing contextualized NP- or VP-based formulaic sequences (Segalowitz, 2010). The reasons are that learners seem to have special challenges in planning the noun and the verb for the extended clusters with relatively complex structures, but for them, as well as for native speakers, repetitions can be used to reduce the pressure on the subsequent speech planning and to increase the length of fluent units (Biber et al., 1999; Ejzenberg, 2000). Second, as learners may not be aware of the importance of keeping the wholeness when producing the formulaic sequences of longer lengths, it should be effective to consciously raise their awareness of holistic production than to have them conduct implicit or incidental learning. Explicit teaching of contractions like *wanna* and *gonna* as holistic units can also be implemented. On the other hand, English language teaching in China has been widely criticized for having learners memorize lists of single words out of context (Hu, 2003, 2005; Yang, 2006; Pan, 2011; McPherron, 2017), which probably explains why learners lack holistic awareness or are not well prepared for real time conversation (McCarthy & Carter, 2002). Thus, focusing on teaching formulaic language rather than individual words could help to improve the situation (Hyland, 2012; Myles & Cordier, 2017). Moreover, explicitly teaching common patterns of pausing should be conducive to the increased length of fluent runs and other production skills, although it was believed that learners' pausing would develop naturally as a result of their progress towards overall language proficiency (Watanabe & Rose, 2013). Lastly, along with authentic teaching materials and tasks in class, learners can be provided with repeated exposure to authentic language input by having them watch subtitled TV programs. This is crucial for the learners in China whose opportunities of using the English language outside the classroom can be rather limited (Frumuselu et al., 2015; Peters et al., 2016).

9.3   Limitations and future directions

Due to the difficulty in collecting and computerizing the data, the size of the corpora used for this study is modest. It is challenging enough for individual researchers to build a longitudinal learner corpus of academic spoken English, let alone one with detailed annotations of pausing and other linguistic features (Granger, 2002; Hasko, 2013). However, according to a complex dynamic systems perspective, more longitudinal learner spoken corpora are needed to describe and to understand the processes of language development and production (Larsen-Freeman & Cameron, 2008b; Hasko, 2013; Gilquin & Granger, 2015). As advanced audio and video recording devices are facilitating data collection, an increasing number of sophisticated applications are automating the transcription and the annotation of the data, it may be soon possible to compile longitudinal mega corpora of learner speech.

As to the future developments of this study, five aspects seem worth exploring. First, as learners are presenting individual variations, showing different levels of holistic use when producing formulaic sequences of longer lengths or with flexible structures, an integrative longitudinal design that combines individual and group levels of analysis can be conducted to track the acquisition process. Second, since learners' fluent speech runs are in general shorter than native speakers', it would be interesting to examine more closely different lengths of fluent units in learner speech and then establish what types of formulaic sequences are mostly commonly embedded in them. Third, pausing in the clusters that occur with mid or low frequencies may provide additional information about the Holistic Hypothesis, as this study focused on the formulaic sequences with internal pauses and those recurring with high frequencies. Moreover, exploring cross-lingual transfer or interference in pausing could be pedagogically informative, because learners' pausing patterns in the target language are arguably influenced by the pausing in their native languages (Chambers, 1997; Riazantseva, 2001; Segalowitz, 2010; De Jong et al., 2015). Finally, studying interpersonal functions of the SV-based clusters such as *you know* and *I think* which occurred frequently in both corpora can further the understanding of pragmatic aspects of speech fluency, considering that learners may have used formulaic sequences in a wrong register or inappropriately to perform a particular function (Pawley & Syder, 1983; Lennon, 2000).

References

Adolphs, S. *Introducing Electronic Text Analysis: A Practical Guide for Language and Literary Studies*. London: Routledge, 2006.

Adolphs, S. & Knight, D. Building a spoken corpus: What are the basics?. In O'Keeffe, A. & McCarthy, M. (eds.). *The Routledge Handbook of Corpus Linguistics*. London: Routledge, 2010: 38-52.

Aijmer, K. *Conversational Routines in English: Convention and Creativity*. London: Routledge, 1996.

Aijmer, K. Introduction: Corpora and language teaching. In Aijmer, K. (ed.). *Corpora and Language Teaching*. Amsterdam: John Benjamins, 2009: 1-10.

Alali, F. & Schmitt, N. Teaching formulaic sequences: The same as or different from teaching single words?. *TESOL Journal*, 2012, 3(2): 153-180.

Altenberg, B. On the phraseology of spoken English: The evidence of recurrent word combinations. In Cowie, A. (ed.). *Phraseology: Theory, Analysis and Applications*. Oxford: Oxford University Press, 1998: 101-122.

Altenberg, B. Preface. In Meunier, F., De Cock, S., Gilquin, G. & Paquot, M. (eds.). *A Taste for Corpora: In Honour of Sylviane Granger*. Amsterdam: John Benjamins, 2011: xiii-xv.

Ashby, M. Prosody and idioms in English. *Journal of Pragmatics*, 2006, 38(10): 1580-1597.

Bannard, C. & Lieven, E. Formulaic language in L1 acquisition. *Annual Review of Applied Linguistics*, 2012, 32: 3-16.

Barlow, M. Computer-based analyses of learner language. In Ellis, R. & Barkhuizen, G. (eds.). *Analysing Learner Language*. Oxford: Oxford University Press, 2005: 335-357.

Bavelas, J. Nonverbal aspects of fluency. In Riggenbach, H. (ed.). *Perspectives on Fluency*. Ann Arbor: The University of Michigan Press, 2000: 91-101.

Beckner, C., Ellis, N. & Blythe, R. et al. Language is a complex adaptive system: Position paper. *Language Learning*, 2009, 59(S1): 1-26.

Bell, A., Brenier, J. & Gregory, M. et al. Predictability effects on durations of content and function words in conversational English. *Journal of Memory and Language*, 2009, 60(1): 92-111.

Biber, D. *University Language: A Corpus-based Study of Spoken and Written Registers*. Amsterdam: John Benjamins, 2006.

Biber, D. A corpus-driven approach to formulaic language in English: Multi-word patterns in speech and writing. *International Journal of Corpus Linguistics*, 2009, 14(3): 275-311.

Biber, D. & Barbieri, F. Lexical bundles in university spoken and written registers. *English for Specific Purposes,* 2007, 26(3): 263-286.

Biber, D., Conrad, S. & Cortes, V. *If you look at...*: Lexical bundles in university teaching and textbooks. *Applied Linguistics*, 2004, 25(3): 371-405.

Biber, D., Johansson, S. & Leech, G. et al. *Longman Grammar of Spoken and Written English*. London: Longman, 1999.

Bolton, K. & Graddol, D. English in China today. *English Today*, 2012, 28(3): 3-9.

Bosker, H., Pinget, A. & Quené, H. et al. What makes speech sound fluent? The contributions of pauses, speed and repairs. *Language Testing*, 2013, 30(2): 159-175.

Brand, C. & Götz, S. Fluency versus accuracy in advanced spoken learner language: A multi-method approach. *International Journal of Corpus Linguistics*, 2011, 16(2): 255-275.

Brown, J. Promoting fluency in EFL classrooms. Proceedings of the 2nd Annual JALT Pan-SIG Conference. Kyoto, Japan, May 10-11, 2003.

Brown, P. & Muller, T. Introduction. In Muller, T., Adamson, J., Brown, P. & Herder, S. (eds.). *Exploring EFL Fluency in Asia*. London: Palgrave Macmillan, 2014: 1-7.

Brumfit, C. Accuracy and fluency: The basic polarity. In Riggenbach, H. (ed.). *Perspectives on Fluency*. Ann Arbor: The University of Michigan Press, 2000: 61-73.

Bybee, J. Phonological evidence for exemplar storage of multiword sequences. *Studies in Second Language Acquisition*, 2002, 24(2): 215-221.

Bybee, J. Sequentiality as the basis of constituent structure. In Givón, T. & Malle, B. (eds.). *The Evolution of Language out of Pre-language*. Amsterdam: John Benjamins, 2002: 109-134.

Bybee, J. From usage to grammar: The mind's response to repetition. *Language*, 2006, 82(4): 711-733.

Bygate, M. Effects of task repetition: Appraising the developing language of learners. In Willis, J. & Willis, D. (eds.). *Challenge and Change in Language Teaching*. Oxford: Macmillan Education, 1996: 136-146.

Bygate, M. Theoretical perspectives on speaking. *Annual Review of Applied Linguistics*, 1998, 18: 20-42.

Bygate, M. Structuring learning within the flux of communication: A role for constructive repetition in oral language pedagogy. In Foley, J. (ed.). *New Dimensions in the Teaching of Oral Communication*. Singapore: Southeast Asian Ministers of Education Organization (SEAMEO) Regional Language Centre (RELC), 2005: 70-90.

Bygate, M. Teaching and testing speaking. In Long, M. & Doughty, C. (eds.). *The Handbook of Language Teaching*. Oxford: Wiley-Blackwell, 2009: 412-440.

Callies, M. & Paquot, M. Learner corpus research: An interdisciplinary field on the move. *International Journal of Learner Corpus Research*, 2015, 1(1): 1-6.

Carter, R. *Vocabulary: Applied Linguistic Perspectives*. London: Routledge, 2012.

Carter, R. & McCarthy, M. Grammar and the spoken language. *Applied Linguistics*, 1995, 16(2): 141-158.

Carter, R. & McCarthy, M. *Cambridge Grammar of English: A Comprehensive Guide*. Cambridge: Cambridge University Press, 2006.

Čermák, F. Spoken corpora design: Their constitutive parameters. *International Journal of Corpus Linguistics*, 2009, 14(1): 113-123.

Chafe, W. Some reasons for hesitating. In Dechert, H. & Raupach, M. (eds.). *Temporal Variables in Speech*. Berlin: De Gruyter Mouton, 1980: 169-180.

Chambers, F. What do we mean by fluency?. *System*, 1997, 25(4): 535-544.

Chen, X. The role of formulaic sequence in speech fluency development in ESL. 2009 International Conference on Computational Intelligence and Software Engineering. Wuhan, China, Dec. 11-13, 2009.

Chen, Y. & Baker, P. Investigating criterial discourse features across second language development: Lexical bundles in rated learner essays, CEFR B1, B2 and C1. *Applied Linguistics*, 2014, 37(6): 849-880.

Chung, K. Ten core themes in pronunciation teaching. Proceedings of the Phonetics Teaching and Learning Conference (PTLC). University College London, July 27-30, 2005.

Chung, K. 抑扬顿挫：英语的语调和断句 . *Hello! E.T.*, 2012, 74: 12-14.

Conklin, K. & Schmitt, N. Formulaic sequences: Are they processed more quickly than nonformulaic language by native and nonnative speakers?. *Applied Linguistics*, 2008, 29(1): 72-89.

Conklin, K. & Schmitt, N. The processing of formulaic language. *Annual Review of Applied Linguistics*, 2012, 32: 45-61.

Corrigan, R., Moravcsik, E., Ouali, H. & Wheatley, K. Introduction. Approaches to the study of formulae. In Corrigan, R., Moravcsik, E., Ouali, H. & Wheatley, K. (eds.). *Formulaic Language, Volume 1: Distribution and Historical Change*. Amsterdam: John Benjamins, 2009: XI-XXIV.

Cortes, V. *The purpose of this study is to*: Connecting lexical bundles and moves in research article introductions. *Journal of English for Academic Purposes*, 2013, 12(1): 33-43.

Coulmas, F. On the sociolinguistic relevance of routine formulae. *Journal of Pragmatics*, 1979, 3(3-4): 239-266.

Cowie, A. Introduction. In Cowie, A. (ed.). *Phraseology: Theory, Analysis, and Applications*. Oxford: Oxford University Press, 1998: 1-20.

Coxhead, A. What can corpora tell us about English for academic purposes?. In

O'Keeffe, A. & McCarthy, M. (eds.). *The Routledge Handbook of Corpus Linguistics*. London: Routledge, 2010: 458-470.

Cucchiarini, C., Strik, H. & Boves, L. Quantitative assessment of second language learners' fluency by means of automatic speech recognition technology. *Journal of the Acoustical Society of America*, 2000, 107(2): 989-999.

Cutting, J. *Analysing the Language of Discourse Communities*. Oxford: Elsevier, 2000.

Dahlmann, I. Towards a multi-word unit inventory of spoken discourse. Nottingham: The University of Nottingham (Doctoral Dissertation), 2009.

Dahlmann, I. & Adolphs, S. Pauses as an indicator of psycholinguistically valid multi-word expressions (MWEs)?. Proceedings of the Workshop on a Broader Perspective on Multiword Expressions. Prague, Czech Republic, June 28, 2007.

Dahlmann, I. & Adolphs, S. Spoken corpus analysis: Multimodal approaches to language description. In Baker, P. (ed.). *Contemporary Corpus Linguistics*. London: Continuum, 2009: 125-139.

De Cock, S. A recurrent word combination approach to the study of formulae in the speech of native and non-native speakers of English. *International Journal of Corpus Linguistics*, 1998, 3(1): 59-80.

De Cock, S. Repetitive phrasal chunkiness and advanced EFL speech and writing. In Mair, C. & Hundt, M. (eds.). *Corpus Linguistics and Linguistic Theory: Papers from ICAME 20 1999*. Amsterdam: Rodopi, 2000: 51-68.

De Cock, S. Preferred sequences of words in NS and NNS speech. *Belgian Journal of English Language and Literatures*, 2004, 2: 225-246.

De Jong, N. Predicting pauses in L1 and L2 speech: The effects of utterance boundaries and word frequency. *International Review of Applied Linguistics in Language Teaching*, 2016, 54(2): 113-132.

De Jong, N., Steinel, M. & Florijn, A. et al. Linguistic skills and speaking fluency in a second language. *Applied Psycholinguistics*, 2013, 34(5): 893-916.

De Jong, N., Groenhout, R. & Schoonen, R. et al. Second language fluency: Speaking style or proficiency? Correcting measures of second language fluency for first language behaviour. *Applied Psycholinguistics*, 2015, 36(2): 223-243.

De Knop, S. & Meunier, F. The 'learner corpus research, cognitive linguistics and second language acquisition' nexus: A SWOT analysis. *Corpus Linguistics and Linguistic Theory*, 2015, 11(1): 1-18.

Derwing, T., Munro, M. & Thomson, R. A longitudinal study of ESL learners' fluency and comprehensibility development. *Applied Linguistics*, 2007, 29(3): 359-380.

Derwing, T., Munro, M. & Thomson, R. et al. The relationship between L1 fluency and L2 fluency development. *Studies in Second Language Acquisition*, 2009, 31(4): 533-557.

Derwing, T., Rossiter, M. & Munro, M. et al. Second language fluency: Judgments on different tasks. *Language Learning*, 2004, 54(4): 655-679.

Derwing, T., Thomson, R. & Munro, M. English pronunciation and fluency development in Mandarin and Slavic speakers. *System*, 2006, 34(2): 183-193.

Deschamps, A. The syntactical distribution of pauses in English spoken as a second language by French students. In Dechert, H. & Raupach, M. (eds.). *Temporal Variables in Speech*. Berlin: De Gruyter Mouton, 1980: 255-262.

Dewaele, J. Individual differences in L2 fluency: The effect of neurobiological correlates. In Cook, V. (ed.). *Portraits of the L2 User*. Clevedon: Multilingual Matters, 2002: 219-250.

Dörnyei, Z. *Research Methods in Applied Linguistics: Quantitative, Qualitative, and Mixed Methodologies*. Oxford: Oxford University Press, 2007.

Dörnyei, Z. Individual differences: Interplay of learner characteristics and learning environment. *Language Learning*, 2009, 59(S1): 230-248.

Dörnyei, Z. & Thurrell, S. Teaching conversational skills intensively: Course content and rationale. *ELT Journal*, 1994, 48(1): 40-49.

Doutrich, D. Cultural fluency, marginality, and the sense of self. In Riggenbach, H. (ed.). *Perspectives on Fluency*. Ann Arbor: The University of Michigan Press, 2000: 141-159.

Durrant, P. & Mathews-Aydınlı, J. A function-first approach to identifying formulaic language in academic writing. *English for Specific Purposes*, 2011, 30(1): 58-72.

Durrant, P. & Siyanova-Chanturia, A. Learner corpora and psycholinguistics. In Granger, S., Gilquin, G. & Meunier, F. (eds.). *The Cambridge Handbook of*

Learner Corpus Research. Cambridge: Cambridge University Press, 2015: 57-78.

Ejzenberg, R. Understanding nonnative oral fluency: The role of task structure and discourse variability. New York: State University of New York (EdD Thesis), 1992.

Ejzenberg, R. The juggling act of oral fluency: A psycho-sociolinguistic metaphor. In Riggenbach, H. (ed.). *Perspectives on Fluency*. Ann Arbor: The University of Michigan Press, 2000: 287-314.

Ellis, N. Sequencing in SLA: Phonological memory, chunking, and points of order. *Studies in Second Language Acquisition*, 1996, 18(1): 91-126.

Ellis, N. At the interface: Dynamic interactions of explicit and implicit language knowledge. *Studies in Second Language Acquisition*, 2005, 27(2): 305-352.

Ellis, N. Phraseology: The periphery and the heart of language. In Meunier, F. & Granger, S. (eds.). *Phraseology in Foreign Language Learning and Teaching*. Amsterdam: John Benjamins, 2008: 1-13.

Ellis, N. Formulaic language and second language acquisition: Zipf and the phrasal teddy bear. *Annual Review of Applied Linguistics*, 2012, 32: 17-44.

Ellis, N., Simpson-Vlach, R. & Maynard, C. Formulaic language in native and second language speakers: Psycholinguistics, corpus linguistics, and TESOL. *TESOL Quarterly*, 2008, 42(3): 375-396.

Ellis, R. *Task-based Language Learning and Teaching*. Oxford: Oxford University Press, 2003.

Ellis, R. The differential effects of three types of task planning on the fluency, complexity, and accuracy in L2 oral production. *Applied Linguistics*, 2009, 30(4): 474-509.

Ellis, R. & Barkhuizen, G. *Analysing Learner Language*. Oxford: Oxford University Press, 2005.

Erman, B. Cognitive processes as evidence of the idiom principle. *International Journal of Corpus Linguistics*, 2007, 12(1): 25-53.

Erman, B. Formulaic language from a learner perspective: What the learner needs to know. In Corrigan, R., Moravcsik, E., Ouali, H. & Wheatley, K. (eds.). *Formulaic Language, Volume 2: Acquisition, Loss, Psychological Reality, and*

Functional Explanations. Amsterdam: John Benjamins, 2009: 323-346.

Erman, B. & Warren, B. The idiom principle and the open choice principle. *Text & Talk*, 2000, 20(1): 29-62.

Evison, J. What are the basics of analysing a corpus?. In O'Keeffe, A. & McCarthy, M. (eds.). *The Routledge Handbook of Corpus Linguistics*. London: Routledge, 2010: 122-135.

Fillmore, C. On fluency. In Riggenbach, H. (ed.). *Perspectives on Fluency*. Ann Arbor: The University of Michigan Press, 2000: 43-60.

Flowerdew, L. Applying corpus linguistics to pedagogy: A critical evaluation. *International Journal of Corpus Linguistics*, 2009, 14(3): 393-417.

Flowerdew, L. Learner corpus research in EAP: Some key issues and future pathways. *English Language and Linguistics*, 2014, 20(2): 43-60.

Foster, P. Doing the task better: How planning time influences students' performance. In Willis, J. & Willis, D. (eds.). *Challenge and Change in Language Teaching*. Oxford: Macmillan Education, 1996: 126-135.

Foster, P. Rules and routines: A consideration of their role in the task-based language production of native and non-native speakers. In Bygate, M., Skehan, P. & Swain, M. (eds.). *Researching Pedagogic Tasks: Second Language Learning, Teaching, and Testing*. London: Longman, 2001: 75-93.

Foster, P. Fluency. In Chapelle, C. (ed.). *The Encyclopedia of Applied Linguistics*. Oxford: Wiley-Blackwell, 2013: 1-7.

Foster, P. & Skehan, P. The influence of planning and task type on second language performance. *Studies in Second Language Acquisition*, 1996, 18(3): 299-323.

Freeborn, D. *A Course Book in English Grammar: Standard English and the Dialects*. 2nd ed. London: Macmillan, 1995.

Freed, B. What makes us think that students who study abroad become fluent?. In Freed, B. (ed.). *Second Language Acquisition in a Study Abroad Context*. Amsterdam: John Benjamins, 1995: 123-148.

Freed, B. Is fluency, like beauty, in the eyes (and ears) of the beholder?. In Riggenbach, H. (ed.). *Perspectives on Fluency*. Ann Arbor: The University of Michigan Press, 2000: 243-265.

Friedman, D. How to collect and analyse qualitative data. In Mackey, A. & Gass, S.

(eds.). *Research Methods in Second Language Acquisition: A Practical Guide*. Oxford: Wiley-Blackwell, 2012: 180-200.

Frumuselu, A., Maeyer, S., Donche, V. & Plana, M. Television series inside the EFL classroom: Bridging the gap between teaching and learning informal language through subtitles. *Linguistics and Education*, 2015, 32(B): 107-117.

Fung, L. & Carter, R. Discourse markers and spoken English: Native and learner use in pedagogic settings. *Applied Linguistics*, 2007, 28(3): 410-439.

Gan, Z. Understanding English speaking difficulties: An investigation of two Chinese populations. *Journal of Multilingual and Multicultural Development*, 2013, 34(3): 231-248.

Gao, Y. & Fan, Y. Pauses in narrative oral English as compared between Chinese and American college students: A corpus-based study. *Journal of PLA University of Foreign Languages*, 2011, 34(4): 71-75.

Gatbonton, E. & Segalowitz, N. Creative automatization: Principles for promoting fluency within a communicative framework. *TESOL Quarterly*, 1988, 22(3): 473-492.

Gatbonton, E. & Segalowitz, N. Rethinking communicative language teaching: A focus on access to fluency. *The Canadian Modern Language Review*, 2005, 61(3): 325-353.

Gilbert, J. *Clear Speech: Pronunciation and Listening Comprehension in North American English: Student's Book*. 3rd ed. Cambridge: Cambridge University Press, 2005.

Gilquin, G. & De Cock, S. Errors and disfluencies in spoken corpora: Setting the scene. *International Journal of Corpus Linguistics*, 2011, 16(2): 141-172.

Gilquin, G. & Granger, S. Learner language. In Biber, D. & Reppen, R. (eds.). *The Cambridge Handbook of English Corpus Linguistics*. Cambridge: Cambridge University Press, 2015: 418-435.

Goh, C. & Burns, A. *Teaching Speaking: A Holistic Approach*. Cambridge: Cambridge University Press, 2012.

Goldberg, A. *Constructions at Work: The Nature of Generalization in Language*. Oxford: Oxford University Press, 2006.

Götz, S. *Fluency in Native and Nonnative English Speech*. Amsterdam: John

Benjamins, 2013.

Götz, S. & Schilk, M. Formulaic sequences in spoken ENL, ESL and EFL: Focus on British English, Indian English and learner English of advanced German learners. In Mukherjee, J. & Hundt, M. (eds.). *Exploring Second-Language Varieties of English and Learner Englishes: Bridging a Paradigm Gap*. Amsterdam: John Benjamins, 2011: 79-100.

Graddol, D. & Mesthrie, R. Editorial. *English Today*, 2012, 28(3): 2.

Granger, S. Prefabricated patterns in advanced EFL writing: Collocations and formulae. In Cowie, A. (ed.). *Phraseology: Theory, Analysis, and Applications*. Oxford: Oxford University Press, 1998: 145-160.

Granger, S. A bird's-eye view of learner corpus research. In Granger, S., Hung, J. & Petch-Tyson, S. (eds.). *Computer Learner Corpora, Second Language Acquisition and Foreign Language Teaching*. Amsterdam: John Benjamins, 2002: 3-33.

Granger, S. The contribution of learner corpora to second language acquisition and foreign language teaching: A critical evaluation. In Aijmer, K. (ed.). *Corpora and Language Teaching*. Amsterdam: John Benjamins, 2009: 13-32.

Granger, S. How to use foreign and second language learner corpora. In Mackey, A. & Gass, S. (eds.). *Research Methods in Second Language Acquisition: A Practical Guide*. Oxford: Wiley-Blackwell, 2012: 7-29.

Granger, S. Contrastive interlanguage analysis: A reappraisal. *International Journal of Learner Corpus Research*, 2015, 1(1): 7-24.

Grant, L. *Well Said: Pronunciation for Clear Communication*. 2nd ed. Boston: Heinle & Heinle, 2001.

Gray, B. & Biber, D. Lexical frames in academic prose and conversation. *International Journal of Corpus Linguistics*, 2013, 18(1): 109-136.

Gray, D. *Doing Research in the Real World*. 3rd ed. London: SAGE, 2014.

Greaves, C. *ConcGram 1.0: A Phraseological Search Engine*. Amsterdam: John Benjamins, 2009.

Gries, S. Phraseology and linguistic theory: A brief survey. In Granger, S. & Meunier, F. (eds.). *Phraseology: An Interdisciplinary Perspective*. Amsterdam: John Benjamins, 2008: 3-25.

Gries, S. Corpus linguistics and theoretical linguistics: A love-hate relationship? Not necessarily. *International Journal of Corpus Linguistics*, 2010,15(3): 327-343.

Gries, S. Methodological and interdisciplinary stance in corpus linguistics. In Viana, V., Zyngier, S. & Barnbrook, G. (eds.). *Perspectives on Corpus Linguistics*. Amsterdam: John Benjamins, 2011: 81-98.

Gries, S. Corpus linguistics, theoretical linguistics, and cognitive/psycholinguistics: Towards more and more fruitful exchanges. In Mukherjee, J. & Huber, M. (eds.). *Corpus Linguistics and Variation in English: Theory and Description*. Amsterdam: Rodopi, 2012: 41-63.

Gries, S. Some current quantitative problems in corpus linguistics and a sketch of some solutions. *Language and Linguistics*, 2015, 16(1): 93-117.

Gries, S. & Ellis, N. Statistic measures for usage-based linguistics. *Language Learning*, 2015, 65(S1): 228-255.

Griffiths, R. Pausological research in an L2 context: A rationale, and review of selected studies. *Applied Linguistics*, 1991, 12(4): 345-364.

Guillot, M. *Fluency and Its Teaching*. Clevedon: Multilingual Matters, 1999.

Hasko, V. Capturing the dynamics of second language development via learner corpus research: A very long engagement. *The Modern Language Journal*, 2013, 97(S1): 1-10.

Hasselgård, H. & Johansson, S. Learner corpora and contrastive interlanguage analysis. In Meunier, F., De Cock, S., Gilquin, G. & Paquot, M. (eds.). *A Taste for Corpora: In Honour of Sylviane Granger*. Amsterdam: John Benjamins, 2011: 33-72.

Hasselgren, A. Learner corpora and language testing: Smallwords as markers of learner fluency. In Granger, S., Hung, J. & Petch-Tyson, S. (eds.). *Computer Learner Corpora, Second Language Acquisition and Foreign Language Teaching*. Amsterdam: John Benjamins, 2002: 143-173.

Hellwig, B., Van Uytvanck, D. & Hulsbosch, M. 2002–2009. *EUDICO Linguistic Annotator (ELAN)*. Max Planck Institut für Psycholinguistik. (Nov. 7, 2013)[Feb. 23, 2014]. http://www.lat-mpi.eu/tools/elan.

Hickey, T. Identifying formulas in first language acquisition. *Journal of Child Language*, 1993, 20(1): 27-41.

Hilton, H. The link between vocabulary knowledge and spoken L2 fluency. *The Language Learning Journal*, 2008, 36(2): 153-166.

Hilton, H. Annotation and analyses of temporal aspects of spoken fluency. *CALICO Journal*, 2009, 26(3): 644-661.

House, J. Developing pragmatic fluency in English as a foreign language: Routines and metapragmatic awareness. *Studies in Second Language Acquisition*, 1996, 18(2): 225-252.

Housen, A. & Kuiken, F. Complexity, accuracy, and fluency in second language acquisition. *Applied Linguistics*, 2009, 30(4): 461-473.

Howarth, P. Phraseology and second language proficiency. *Applied Linguistics*, 1998, 19(1): 24-44.

Hu, G. Potential cultural resistance to pedagogical imports: The case of communicative language teaching in China. *Language, Culture and Curriculum*, 2002, 15(2): 93-105.

Hu, G. English language teaching in China: Regional differences and contributing factors. *Journal of Multilingual and Multicultural Development*, 2003, 24(4): 290-318.

Hu, G. English language education in China: Policies, progress, and problems. *Language Policy*, 2005, 4: 5-24.

Hughes, R. *Teaching and Researching Speaking*. London: Longman, 2002.

Hughes, R. Researching speaking. In Paltridge, B. & Phakiti, A. (eds.). *Continuum Companion to Research Methods in Applied Linguistics*. London: Continuum, 2010: 145-159.

Hulstijn, J. Psycholinguistic perspectives on language and its acquisition. In Cummins, J. & Davison, C. (eds.). *International Handbook of English Language Teaching*. New York: Springer, 2007: 783-795.

Hunston, S. *Corpora in Applied Linguistics*. Cambridge: Cambridge University Press, 2002.

Hunston, S. How can a corpus be used to explore patterns?. In O'Keeffe, A. & McCarthy, M. (eds.). *The Routledge Handbook of Corpus Linguistics*. London: Routledge, 2010: 152-166.

Huth, A., De Heer, W., Griffiths, T., Theunissen, F. & Gallant, J. Natural speech reveals the semantic maps that tile human cerebral cortex. *Nature*, 2016, 532: 453-458.

Hüttner, J. Fluent speakers – fluent interactions: On the creation of (co)-fluency in English as a lingua franca. In Mauranen, A. & Ranta, E. (eds.). *English as a Lingua Franca: Studies and Findings*. Newcastle upon Tyne: Cambridge Scholars Publishing, 2009: 274-297.

Hyland, K. As can be seen: Lexical bundles and disciplinary variation. *English for Specific Purposes*, 2008, 27(1): 4-21.

Hyland, K. Bundles in academic discourse. *Annual Review of Applied Linguistics*, 2012, 32: 150-169.

Hyland, K. & Hamp-Lyons, L. EAP: Issues and directions. *Journal of English for Academic Purposes*, 2002, 1(1): 1-12.

Jeong, H., Sugiura, M., Suzuki, W., Sassa, Y., Hashizume, H. & Kawashima, R. Neural correlates of second-language communication and the effect of language anxiety. *Neuropsychologia*, 2016, 84: e2-e12.

Jiang, N. & Nekrasova, T. The processing of formulaic sequences by second language speakers. *The Modern Language Journal*, 2007, 91(3): 433-445.

Johnson, R., Onwuegbuzie, A. & Turner, L. Toward a definition of mixed methods research. *Journal of Mixed Methods Research*, 2007, 1(2): 112-133.

Kachru, B. Standards, codification and sociolinguistic realism: The English language in the outer circle. In Quirk, R. & Widdowson, H. (eds.). *English in the World: Teaching and Learning the Language and Literatures*. Cambridge: Cambridge University Press, 1985: 11-30.

Kirk, S. & Carter, R. Fluency and spoken English. In Jaén, M., Valverde, F. & Pérez, M. (eds.). *Exploring New Paths in Language Pedagogy: Lexis and Corpus-based Language Teaching*. Sheffield: Equinox, 2010: 25-39.

Knight, D. A multi-modal corpus approach to the analysis of backchanneling behaviour. Nottingham: University of Nottingham (Doctoral Dissertation), 2009.

Koester, A. *Investigating Workplace Discourse*. London: Routledge, 2006.

Koester, A. Building small specialised corpora. In O'Keeffe, A. & McCarthy, M. (eds.). *The Routledge Handbook of Corpus Linguistics*. London: Routledge,

2010: 66-79.

Koponen, M. & Riggenbach, H. Overview: Varying perspectives on fluency. In Riggenbach, H. (ed.). *Perspectives on Fluency*. Ann Arbor: The University of Michigan Press, 2000: 5-24.

Kormos, J. *Speech Production and Second Language Acquisition*. Mahwah, NJ: Lawrence Erlbaum Associates, 2006.

Kormos, J. & Dénes, M. Exploring measures and perceptions of fluency in the speech of second language learners. *System*, 2004, 32(2): 145-164.

Larsen-Freeman, D. The emergence of complexity, fluency, and accuracy in the oral and written production of five Chinese learners of English. *Applied Linguistics*, 2006, 27(4): 590-619.

Larsen-Freeman, D. Adjusting expectations: The study of complexity, accuracy, and fluency in second language acquisition. *Applied Linguistics*, 2009, 30(4): 579-589.

Larsen-Freeman, D. Complex, dynamic systems: A new transdisciplinary theme for applied linguistics?. *Language Teaching*, 2012, 45(2): 202-214.

Larsen-Freeman, D. & Cameron, L. *Complex Systems and Applied Linguistics*. Oxford: Oxford University Press, 2008a.

Larsen-Freeman, D. & Cameron, L. Research methodology on language development from a complex systems perspective. *The Modern Language Journal*, 2008b, 92(2): 200-213.

Leech, G. Grammars of spoken English: New outcomes of corpus-oriented research. *Language Learning*, 2000, 50(4): 675-724.

Leech, G. Frequency, corpora and language learning. In Meunier, F., De Cock, S., Gilquin, G. & Paquot, M. (eds.). *A Taste for Corpora: In Honour of Sylviane Granger*. Amsterdam: John Benjamins, 2011: 7-31.

Lennon, P. Investigating fluency in EFL: A quantitative approach. *Language Learning*, 1990, 40(3): 387-417.

Lennon, P. The lexical element in spoken second language fluency. In Riggenbach, H. (ed.). *Perspectives on Fluency*. Ann Arbor: The University of Michigan Press, 2000: 25-42.

Levis J. & Wichmann, A. English intonation – form and meaning. In Reed, M.

& Levis, J. (eds.). *The Handbook of English Pronunciation*. Oxford: Wiley-Blackwell, 2015: 139-155.

Levrai, P. From push to pull: Evolving EAP support in an offshore university. *International Student Experience Journal*, 2013, 1(1): 4-9.

Li, D. Learning English for academic purposes: Why Chinese EFL learners find EAP so difficult to master. *Revista Canaria de Estudios Ingleses*, 2009, 59: 33-48.

Lin, P. The phonology of formulaic sequences: A review. In Wood, D. (ed.). *Perspectives on Formulaic Language: Acquisition and Communication*. London: Continuum, 2010: 174-193.

Lin, P. Sound evidence: The missing piece of the jigsaw in formulaic language research. *Applied Linguistics*, 2012, 33(3): 342-347.

Lin, P. & Adolphs, S. Sound evidence: Phraseological units in spoken corpora. In Barfield, A. & Gyllstad, H. (eds.). *Researching Collocations in Another Language: Multiple Interpretations*. Basingstoke: Palgrave Macmillan, 2009: 34-48.

Lu, X. What can corpus software reveal about language development?. In O'Keeffe, A. & McCarthy, M. (eds.). *The Routledge Handbook of Corpus Linguistics*. London: Routledge, 2010: 184-193.

Mackey A. & Gass, S. Introduction. In Mackey, A. & Gass, S. (eds.). *Research Methods in Second Language Acquisition: A Practical Guide*. Oxford: Wiley-Blackwell, 2012: 1-4.

Marshall, R. Speech fluency and aphasia. In Riggenbach, H. (ed.). *Perspectives on Fluency*. Ann Arbor: The University of Michigan Press, 2000: 74-88.

Martinez, R. & Schmitt, N. A phrasal expressions list. *Applied Linguistics*, 2012, 33(3): 299-320.

Mauranen, A. Learners and users—Who do we want corpus data from?. In Meunier, F., De Cock, S. & Gilquin, G. et al. (eds.). *A Taste for Corpora: In Honour of Sylviane Granger*. Amsterdam: John Benjamins, 2011: 155-171.

McCarthy, M. Fluency and confluence: What fluent speakers do. *The Language Teacher*, 2005, 29(6): 26-28.

McCarthy, M. Rethinking spoken fluency. *Estudios de Lingüística Inglesa Aplicada*, 2009, 9: 11-29.

McCarthy, M. Spoken fluency revisited. *English Profile Journal*, 2010, 1(1): 1-15.

McCarthy, M. & O'Keeffe, A. Historical perspective: What are corpora and how have they evolved?. In O'Keeffe, A. & McCarthy, M. (eds.). *The Routledge Handbook of Corpus Linguistics*. London: Routledge, 2010: 3-13.

McCarthy, M. & Carter, R. This that and the other: Multi-word clusters in spoken English as visible patterns of interaction. *Teanga (The Journal of the Irish Association for Applied Linguistics)*, 2002, 21: 30-52.

McEnery, T. & Hardie, A. *Corpus Linguistics: Method, Theory and Practice*. Cambridge: Cambridge University Press, 2012.

McEnery, T., Xiao, R. & Tono, Y. *Corpus-based Language Studies: An Advanced Resource Book*. London: Routledge, 2006.

McPherron, P. *Internationalizing Teaching, Localizing Learning: An Examination of English Language Teaching Reforms and English Use in China*. London: Palgrave Macmillan, 2017.

Mehnert, U. The effects of different lengths of time for planning on second language performance. *Studies in Second Language Acquisition*, 1998, 20(1): 83-108.

Meunier, F. Learner corpora and English language teaching: Checkup time. *International Journal of English Studies*, 2010, 21(1): 209-220.

Mirzaei, A. & Heidari, N. Researching (non)fluent L2 speakers' oral communication deficiencies: A psycholinguistic perspective. *Journal of Teaching Language Skills*, 2013, 32(1): 45-70.

Mizera, G. Working memory and L2 oral fluency. Pittsburgh: University of Pittsburgh (Doctoral Dissertation), 2006.

Moon, R. Frequencies and forms of phrasal lexemes in English. In Cowie, A. (ed.) *Phraseology: Theory, Analysis and Applications*. Oxford: Oxford University Press, 1998: 79-100.

Morales-López, E. Fluency levels and the organization of conversation in nonnative Spanish speakers' speech. In Riggenbach, H. (ed.). *Perspectives on Fluency*. Ann Arbor: The University of Michigan Press, 2000: 266-286.

Myles, F. Investigating learner language development with electronic longitudinal corpora: Theoretical and methodological issues. In Ortega, L. & Byrnes, H. (eds.). *The Longitudinal Study of Advanced L2 Capacities*. New York:

Routledge, 2008: 58-72.

Myles, F. & Cordier, C. Formulaic sequence (FS) cannot be an umbrella term in SLA: Focusing on psycholinguistic FSs and their identification. *Studies in Second Language Acquisition*, 2017, 39(1): 3-28.

Myles, F., Hooper, J. & Mitchell, R. Rote or rule? Exploring the role of formulaic language in classroom foreign language learning. *Language Learning*, 1998, 48(3): 323-363.

Nation, P. Improving speaking fluency. *System*, 1989, 17(3): 377-384.

Nation, P. Fluency and learning. *The English Teacher*, 1991, 20: 1-8.

Nattinger, J. & DeCarrico, J. *Lexical Phrases and Language Teaching*. Oxford: Oxford University Press, 1992.

O'Keeffe, A., McCarthy, M. & Carter, R. *From Corpus to Classroom: Language Use and Language Teaching*. Cambridge: Cambridge University Press, 2007.

Oliver, P. *Writing Your Thesis*. 3rd ed. London: SAGE, 2014.

Oppenheim, N. The importance of recurrent sequences for nonnative speaker fluency and cognition. In Riggenbach, H. (ed.). *Perspectives on Fluency*. Ann Arbor: The University of Michigan Press, 2000: 220-240.

Pan, L. English language ideologies in the Chinese foreign language education policies: A world-system perspective. *Language Policy*, 2011, 10: 245-263.

Pan, L. *English as a Global Language in China: Deconstructing the Ideological Discourses of English in Language Education*. New York: Springer, 2015.

Pawley, A. Developments in the study of formulaic language since 1970: A personal view. In Skandera, P. (ed.). *Phraseology and Culture in English*. Berlin: De Gruyter Mouton, 2007: 3-45.

Pawley, A. & Syder, F. Two puzzles for linguistic theory: Nativelike selection and nativelike fluency. In Richards, J. & Schmidt, R. (eds.). *Language and Communication*. London: Longman, 1983: 191-226.

Pawley, A. & Syder, F. The one-clause-at-a-time hypothesis. In Riggenbach, H. (ed.). *Perspectives on Fluency*. Ann Arbor: The University of Michigan Press, 2000: 163-199.

Peters, A. *The Units of Language Acquisition*. Cambridge: Cambridge University Press, 1983.

Peters, A. Connecting the dots to unpack the language. In Corrigan, R., Moravcsik, E., Ouali, H. & Wheatley, K. (eds.). *Formulaic Language, Volume 2: Acquisition, Loss, Psychological Reality, and Functional Explanations*. Amsterdam: John Benjamins, 2009: 387-404.

Peters, E., Heynen, E. & Puimège, E. Learning vocabulary through audiovisual input: The differential effect of L1 subtitles and captions. *System*, 2016, 63: 134-148.

Raupach, M. Formulae in second language speech production. In Dechert, H., Möhle, D. & Raupach, M. (eds.). *Second Language Productions*. Tübingen: Gunter Narr, 1984: 114-137.

Riazantseva, A. Second language proficiency and pausing: A study of Russian speakers of English. *Studies in Second Language Acquisition*, 2001, 23(4): 497-526.

Richards, K., Ross, S. & Seedhouse, P. *Research Methods for Applied Language Studies: An Advanced Resource Book for Students*. London: Routledge, 2012.

Riggenbach, H. Toward an understanding of fluency: A microanalysis of nonnative speaker conversations. *Discourse Processes*, 1991, 14(4): 423-441.

Römer, U. The inseparability of lexis and grammar: Corpus linguistic perspectives. *Annual Review of Cognitive Linguistics*, 2009, 7(4): 140-162.

Rossiter, M. Perceptions of L2 fluency by native and non-native speakers of English. *The Canadian Modern Language Review*, 2009, 65(3): 395-412.

Rossiter, M., Derwing, T., Manimtim, L. & Thomson, R. Oral fluency: The neglected component in the communicative language classroom. *The Canadian Modern Language Review*, 2010, 66(4): 583-606.

Rublik, N. An investigation into the role of culture and the development of oral fluency: A case study involving Chinese learners of English. Ontario: The University of Western Ontario (Doctoral Dissertation), 2006.

Sacks, H., Schegloff, E. & Jefferson, G. A simplest systematics for the organization of turn taking for conversation. *Language*, 1974, 50(4): 696-735.

Sajavaara, K. Second language speech production: Factors affecting fluency. In Dechert, H. & Raupach, M. (eds.). *Psycholinguistic Models of Production*. Norwood, NJ: Ablex, 1987: 45-65.

Schmidt, R. Interaction, acculturation, and the acquisition of communicative competence: A case study of an adult. In Wolfson, N. & Judd, E. (eds.). *Sociolinguistics and Language Acquisition.* Rowley, MA: Newbury House, 1983: 137-174.

Schmidt, R. Psychological mechanisms underlying second language fluency. *Studies in Second Language Acquisition*, 1992, 14(4): 357-385.

Schmidt, R. Foreword. In Riggenbach, H. (ed.). *Perspectives on Fluency.* Ann Arbor: The University of Michigan Press, 2000: v-viii.

Schmitt, N. *Researching Vocabulary: A Vocabulary Research Manual.* London: Palgrave Macmillan, 2010.

Schmitt, N. Formulaic language and collocation. In Chapelle, C. (ed.). *The Encyclopedia of Applied Linguistics.* Oxford: Wiley-Blackwell, 2013: 1-10.

Schmitt, N. Norbert Schmitt's essential bookshelf: Formulaic language. *Language Teaching*, 2023, 56(3): 420-431.

Schmitt, N. & Carter, R. Formulaic sequences in action: An introduction. In Schmitt, N. (ed.). *Formulaic Sequences: Acquisition, Processing and Use.* Amsterdam: John Benjamins, 2004: 1-22.

Schmitt, N., Grandage, S. & Adolphs, S. Are corpus-derived recurrent clusters psycholinguistically valid?. In Schmitt, N. (ed.). *Formulaic Sequences: Acquisition, Processing and Use.* Amsterdam: John Benjamins, 2004: 127-152.

Schmitt, N. & Underwood, G. Exploring the processing of formulaic sequences through a self-paced reading task. In Schmitt, N. (ed.). *Formulaic Sequences: Acquisition, Processing and Use.* Amsterdam: John Benjamins, 2004: 173-190.

Scott, M. *WordSmith Tools Version 6.0.* Oxford: Oxford University Press, 2015.

Segalowitz, N. Automaticity and attentional skill in fluent performance. In Riggenbach, H. (ed.). *Perspectives on Fluency.* Ann Arbor: The University of Michigan Press, 2000: 200-219.

Segalowitz, N. *Cognitive Bases of Second Language Fluency.* New York: Routledge, 2010.

Segalowitz, N. & Freed, B. Context, contact, and cognition in oral fluency acquisition: Learning Spanish in at home and study abroad contexts. *Studies in Second Language Acquisition*, 2004, 26(2): 173-199.

Segalowitz, N., Gatbonton, E. & Trofimovich, P. Links between ethnolinguistic affiliation, self-related motivation and second language fluency: Are they mediated by psycholinguistic variables?. In Dörnyei, Z. & Ushioda, E. (eds.). *Motivation, Language Identity and the L2 Self.* Clevedon: Multilingual Matters, 2009: 172-192.

Seifart, F., Strunk, J., Danielsen, S., Hartmann, I., Pakendorf, B., Wichmann, S., Witzlack-Makarevich, A., De Jong, N. & Bickel, B. Nouns slow down speech across structurally and culturally diverse languages. *PNAS (Proceedings of the National Academy of Sciences of the United States of America)*, 2018, 115(22): 5720-5725.

Shu, D. & Chen, S. The way to success in TEFL in China: A study of the UNNC academic English model. *Journal of Foreign Language Teaching and Research*, 2010, 42(6): 478-479.

Simpson, R. Stylistic features of academic speech: The role of formulaic expressions. In Upton, T. & Connor, U. (eds.). *Discourse in the Professions: Perspectives from Corpus Linguistics.* Amsterdam: John Benjamins, 2004: 37-64.

Simpson, R., Briggs, S. & Ovens, J. et al. *The Michigan Corpus of Academic Spoken English.* Ann Arbor: The Regents of the University of Michigan, 2002.

Simpson, R., Lee, D. & Leicher, S. *MICASE Manual: The Michigan Corpus of Academic Spoken English Version 1.1.* Ann Arbor: The Regents of the University of Michigan, 2003.

Simpson-Vlach, R. & Ellis, N. An academic formulas list: New methods in phraseology research. *Applied Linguistics*, 2010, 31(4): 487-512.

Sinclair, J. *Corpus, Concordance, Collocation.* Oxford: Oxford University Press, 1991.

Sinclair, J. *EAGLES: Preliminary Recommendations on Corpus Typology.* (May 1996)[Nov. 6, 2018]. http://www.ilc.cnr.it/EAGLES96/corpustyp/corpustyp.html.

Sinclair, J. *Trust the Text: Language, Corpus and Discourse.* London: Routledge, 2004.

Sinclair, J. The phrase, the whole phrase, and nothing but the phrase. In Granger, S. & Meunier, F. (eds.). *Phraseology: An Interdisciplinary Perspective.* Amsterdam:

John Benjamins, 2008: 407-410.

Siyanova-Chanturia, A. On the 'holistic' nature of formulaic language. *Corpus Linguistics and Linguistic Theory*, 2015, 11(2): 285-301.

Siyanova-Chanturia, A., Conklin, K. & Schmitt, N. Adding more fuel to the fire: An eye-tracking study of idiom processing by native and non-native speakers. *Second Language Research*, 2011a, 27(2): 251-272.

Siyanova-Chanturia, A., Conklin, K. & Van Heuven, W. Seeing a phrase 'time and again' matters: The role of phrasal frequency in the processing of multiword sequences. *Journal of Experimental Psychology: Language, Memory, and Cognition*, 2011b, 37(3): 776-784.

Skehan, P. A framework for the implementation of task-based instruction. *Applied Linguistics*, 1996, 17(1): 38-62.

Skehan, P. *A Cognitive Approach to Language Learning*. Oxford: Oxford University Press, 1998.

Skehan, P. Task-based instruction. *Language Teaching*, 2003, 36(1): 1-14.

Skehan, P. Modelling second language performance: Integrating complexity, accuracy, fluency, and lexis. *Applied Linguistics*, 2009, 30(4): 510-532.

Skehan, P. & Foster, P. The influence of task structure and processing conditions on narrative Retellings. *Language Learning*, 1999, 49(1): 93-120.

Skehan, P. & Foster, P. Strategic and on-line planning: The influence of surprise information and task time on second language performance. In Ellis, R. (ed.). *Planning and Task Performance in a Second Language*. Amsterdam: John Benjamins, 2005: 193-216.

Stivers, T., Enfield, N. & Brown, P. et al. Universals and cultural variation in turn-taking in conversation. *PNAS (Proceedings of the National Academy of Sciences of the United States of America)*, 2009, 106(26): 10587-10592.

Strik, H., Hulsbosch, M. & Cucchiarini, C. Analyzing and identifying multiword expressions in spoken language. *Language Resources and Evaluation*, 2010, 44: 41-58.

Stubbs, M. Two quantitative methods of studying phraseology in English. *International Journal of Corpus Linguistics*, 2002, 7(2): 215-244.

Swales, J. *Genre Analysis: English in Academic and Research Settings*. Cambridge:

Cambridge University Press, 1990.

Tavakoli, P. Pausing patterns: Differences between L2 learners and native speakers. *ELT Journal*, 2011, 65(1): 71-79.

Tavakoli, P. & Skehan, P. Strategic planning, task structure, and performance testing. In Ellis, R. (ed.). *Planning and Task Performance in a Second Language*. Amsterdam: John Benjamins, 2005: 239-273.

Thompson, P. Spoken language corpora. In Wynne, M. (ed.). *Developing Linguistic Corpora: A Guide to Good Practice*. (2004)[Nov. 6, 2018]. https://bond-lab. github.io/Corpus-Linguistics/dlc/chapter5.htm.

Thornbury, S. What can a corpus tell us about discourse?. In O'Keeffe, A. & McCarthy, M. (eds.). *The Routledge Handbook of Corpus Linguistics*. London: Routledge, 2010: 270-287.

Tognini Bonelli, E. *Corpus Linguistics at Work*. Amsterdam: John Benjamins, 2001.

Tognini Bonelli, E. Theoretical overview of the evolution of corpus linguistics. In O'Keeffe, A. & McCarthy, M. (eds.). *The Routledge Handbook of Corpus Linguistics*. London: Routledge, 2010: 14-27.

Towell, R. & Dewaele, J. The role of psycholinguistic factors in the development of fluency amongst advanced learners of French. In Dewaele, J. (ed.). *Focus on French as a Foreign Language: Multidisciplinary Approaches*. Clevedon: Multilingual Matters, 2005: 210-239.

Towell, R., Hawkins, R. & Bazergui, N. The development of fluency in advanced learners of French. *Applied Linguistics*, 1996, 17(1): 84-119.

Tribble, C. Improvising corpora for ELT: Quick-and-dirty ways of developing corpora for language teaching. In Lewandowska-Tomaszczyk, B. & Melia, P. (eds.). *Proceedings of the First International Conference on Practical Applications in Language Corpora*. Lodz: Lodz University Press, 1997: 106-117.

Underhill, A. *Sound Foundations: Learning and Teaching Pronunciation*. Oxford: Macmillan Education, 1994.

Underwood, G., Schmitt, N. & Galpin, A. The eyes have it: An eye-movement study into the processing of formulaic sequences. In Schmitt, N. (ed.). *Formulaic Sequences: Acquisition, Processing and Use*. Amsterdam: John Benjamins,

2004: 153-172.

Ushigusa, S. The relationships between oral fluency, multiword units, and proficiency scores. West Lafayette, IN: Purdue University (Doctoral Dissertation), 2008.

Walsh, S. What features of spoken and written corpora can be exploited in creating language teaching materials and syllabuses?. In O'Keeffe, A. & McCarthy, M. (eds.). *The Routledge Handbook of Corpus Linguistics.* London: Routledge, 2010: 333-344.

Watanabe, M. & Rose, R. Pausology and hesitation phenomena in SLA. In Robinson, P. (ed.). *The Routledge Encyclopedia of Second Language Acquisition.* New York: Routledge, 2013: 480-483.

Weinert, R. The role of formulaic language in second language acquisition: A review. *Applied Linguistics*, 1995, 16(2): 180-205.

Wen, Q. & Wang, J. *Spoken and Written English Corpus of Chinese Learners.* 2nd ed. Beijing: Foreign Language Teaching and Research Press, 2008.

Wennerstrom, A. The role of intonation in second language fluency. In Riggenbach, H. (ed.). *Perspectives on Fluency.* Ann Arbor: The University of Michigan Press, 2000: 102-127.

Widdowson, H. Knowledge of language and ability for use. *Applied Linguistics*, 1989, 10(2): 128-137.

Wong-Fillmore, L. Individual differences in second language acquisition. In Fillmore, C., Kempler, D. & Wang, W. (eds.). *Individual Differences in Language Ability and Language Behavior.* New York: Academic Press, 1979: 203-228.

Wood, D. In search of fluency: What is it and how can we teach It?. *The Canadian Modern Language Review*, 2001, 57(4): 573-589.

Wood, D. An empirical investigation into the facilitating role of automatized lexical phrases in second language fluency development. *Journal of Language and Learning*, 2004, 2(1): 27-50.

Wood, D. Uses and functions of formulaic sequences in second language speech: An exploration of the foundations of fluency. *The Canadian Modern Language Review*, 2006, 63(1): 13-33.

Wood, D. Mandarin Chinese speakers in a study abroad context: Does acquisition of formulaic sequences facilitate fluent speech in English?. *The East Asian Learner*, 2007, 3(2): 43-62.

Wood, D. Preparing ESP learners for workplace placement. *ELT Journal*, 2009, 63(4): 323-331.

Wood, D. *Formulaic Language and Second Language Speech Fluency: Background, Evidence and Classroom Applications*. London: Continuum, 2010.

Wood, D. *Fundamentals of Formulaic Language: An Introduction*. London: Bloomsbury, 2015.

Wray, A. *Formulaic Language and the Lexicon*. Cambridge: Cambridge University Press, 2002.

Wray, A. 'Here's one I prepared earlier': Formulaic language learning on television. In Schmitt, N. (ed.). *Formulaic Sequences: Acquisition, Processing and Use*. Amsterdam: John Benjamins, 2004: 249-268.

Wray, A. *Formulaic Language: Pushing the Boundaries*. Oxford: Oxford University Press, 2008.

Wray, A. Identifying formulaic language: Persistent challenges and new opportunities. In Corrigan, R., Moravcsik, E., Ouali, H. & Wheatley, K. (eds.). *Formulaic Language, Volume 1: Distribution and Historical Change*. Amsterdam: John Benjamins, 2009: 27-51.

Wray, A. & Bloomer, A. *Projects in Linguistics: A Practical Guide to Researching Language*. London: Hodder Arnold, 2006.

Wray, A. & Perkins, M. The functions of formulaic language: An integrated model. *Language & Communication*, 2000, 20: 1-28.

Wu, C. On the mid-clause pausing patterns in speaking English as a foreign language. *Journal of Zhanjiang Normal University*, 2012, 33(5): 162-165.

Xiao, R. Theory-driven corpus research: Using corpora to inform aspect theory. In Lüdeling, A. & Kytö, M. (eds.). *Corpus Linguistics: An International Handbook, Volume 2*. Berlin: Walter de Gruyter, 2009: 987-1008.

Yang, H. & Wei, N. *College Learners Spoken English Corpus*. Shanghai: Shanghai Foreign Language Education Press, 2005.

Yang, J. Learners and users of English in China. *English Today*, 2006, 22(2): 3-10.

Yule, G. *The Study of Language*. 4th ed. Cambridge: Cambridge University Press,

2010.

Zellner, B. Pauses and the temporal structure of speech. In Keller, E. (ed.). *Fundamentals of Speech Synthesis and Speech Recognition*. Chichester: John Wiley, 1994: 41-62.

Acknowledgments

I owe various debts of gratitude to many people for their support in the completion of this study. First and foremost, I would like to express my deepest gratitude to my supervisors, Prof. Margaret Gillon Dowens, Dr. John McKenny, Prof. Ronald Carter, and Prof. Peter Stockwell. I thank Meg for taking me under her wing after John left, and for her close reading of and extensive feedback on the drafts. I have been fortunate to benefit from her rigorous academic coaching and life savvy. She shows me incredible patience and provides me with timely intellectual, practical, and moral support. Without Meg, it would be impossible to finish the study. I thank John for his inspiration, encouragement, and support at the stages of formulating the research proposal, data collecting and transcribing. I thank Ron for his prompt and useful feedback. Not only did he show me encouragement and support after the first and the second annual review, he pinpointed the problems I had with academic writing and offered detailed advice on the progress. I am deeply amazed at how he knew so clearly how much time I needed to write up each chapter of the then thesis, the original mould of this book. He also offered me detailed reading lists on speech fluency and research methods that I had missed. The interest I take in speech fluency I owe to the great teacher that Ron is. Lastly, I thank Prof. Stockwell for taking me in after Ron's retirement.

I would also like to express my sincere gratitude to the people who offered help at the stages of data collection and transcription. First, thanks must go to the management and staff at the Center for English Language Education for allowing me to collect data there. In particular, I thank Peter Waters, James Arthurs, Susannah Davis, Julianne Williams, Barry Jones, Boon-Hiah Gwee, and Timothy Wallis for their kindness and help, and thank my participants for allowing me to collect their spoken English. Sincere thanks must go to Sunny Qi, the IT technician, who helped me with the use of the recording equipment. Without her help, my data collection would have been a much more painful experience. My appreciation also goes to Prof. Louise Mullany for her introducing to me Dr Dawn Knight, who offered suggestions on the choice of recording devices. I would also like to thank Dr Stefanie Wulff for explaining to me how pauses in MICASE were timed.

I am hugely grateful to the teachers and the researchers who helped me at other stages of writing down this study. Prof. Geoff Hall, my first and second internal annual reviewer, checked part of the literature review and the methodology, suggested that I should explore the studies of pauses in wider contexts, and kept an eye on books for me. Thanks to Geoff, I got to know that I should aim for at least two hours a day and eighteen hours a week working on the study so that I can finish it within the time frame. Thanks must go to Dr Yuhua Chen for helping me clear doubts on some issues in corpus linguistics, and, together with Dr Matthew Beedham, providing constructive advice on the improvement of the study based on my third annual review. I am also grateful to Dr Simon Harrison for lending me his time to discuss cognitive linguistic matters. I cannot possibly thank Prof. Alison Wray enough for showing me directions when I was hesitating where to head with the analysis, and for taking an interest in my then thesis even when it was a proposal, which made me believe my study has actual value when I was about to give up. Special thanks must go to Prof. Mike Scott for helping me with various statistical problems and replying to my email even on holidays.

Thanks are also due to my friends and e-pals in this long ride. I thank my fellow PhD students, Steven Kirk, Grace Hongmei Wang, Dai Lin, and Dawei Wei, for their help and kindness. It is Steve to whom I owe a huge debt of gratitude. He showed me with great patience how to work with Elan by email and shared with me a number of papers and photocopied book chapters I was not able to access. Grace has always been a very good friend, helping me in various ways, and is the one who introduced to me WeChat, through which I get to know peers who share similar anxieties and concerns. Thanks also go to Wilson Dawang Huang, Hong Lyu, Jiajia Xu, and other colleagues from Ningcorp, for the vibrant discussions on many aspects of corpus linguistics. Finally, thanks to the academics on the Formulaic Language Research Network (FLaRN) and Corpus4u who participated in the discussion of the issues I posted over there.

Most of all, I thank my family for their support and giving me space over the years, and particularly to my son for tolerating my horrible culinary skills and giving me joys during periods of stress.